Set Your Sights

Also by Teresa Houghteling

**The "Unhealed" Believer:
What to Do When You've Done It All**

Website: https://fullyknownministries.com/shop
(Available in English, Telugu, Mandarin Chinese, and German.)

Amazon: https://rb.gy/8zgzs
(Available in English only.)

365 DAY
DEVOTIONAL

set
your
sights

CHANGE
YOUR
FOCUS

RECEIVE
YOUR
HEALING

TERESA HOUGHTELING

To you tired ones…

Table of Contents

Introduction

Let's start with a question: Why do some people receive healing while others don't?

My body was riddled with autoimmune diseases and debilitating spinal issues, and I repeatedly asked that exact question for 13 years ... until the answer came. I realized I was giving my body, its symptoms, and the opinions of doctors all of my attention. That approach was leading to death rather than life. It was leading to more sickness and pain rather than health. If I wanted to live, my focus and approach had to change.

So, I set my sights on God's Word. I yielded to the truth that it was (and is) the only Source with the power to heal my ailing body. After six months of changing my focus, the healing that was mine all along manifested in my body on March 13, 2014.

Maybe you've asked the same question during your healing journey. Maybe it seems like every time you take a shot at healing, you miss. Maybe you believe that no matter how hard you try, how much you believe, and how much you speak God's Word, you can't hit the target.

I'm here to tell you that the shift in your favor is here. It's yours for the taking. The days, weeks, months, and years of frustration as it relates to you receiving your blood-bought healing can, officially, be a distant memory. With a bit of practice, your sights will become laser-focused, and the healing bullseye will clearly come into view.

I will show you precisely how to practice receiving through these daily devotions. One step at a time, I'll walk with you and guide your journey as you set your sights on God's promises. Before you know it, you will have mastered zeroing in on the target and rest in receiving your results.

After striving for years to be healed (with no improvement in my body to show for it), I resigned myself to accepting that I would be sick for the rest of my life. Because of that exhausting experience, my heart is bent toward those who are tired and have given up. I wrote this devotional to encourage and strengthen you tired ones. I wrote it to embolden you to keep believing while changing your focus and approach to receiving.

God heals. The Word works. Every day, set your sights on the only target that matters and can bring healing to your body … God's Word.

JANUARY

January 1

The Target:

But if the Spirit of Him who raised Jesus from the dead dwells in you, He who raised Christ from the dead will also give life to your mortal bodies through His Spirit who dwells in you.

Romans 8:11

Set Your Sights:

Let's hit the ground running. God promises healing to every believer, and this verse reveals how He does it. God said He would repair, restore, and rebuild your physical body through the Spirit who lives in you, the same Spirit who put breath into Jesus's lifeless body. So if the Spirit lives in you—which He does in every born-again believer (Acts 2:38)—so does the source of all healing.

The Spirit can get to work when the Word is your focus, when you allow His promises to drown out the other words that are constantly competing for your attention. And when the Spirit is working, there is no damage too significant, no report too bad, no diagnosis too terrible that He can't crush in the one whose sights are set on Him.

Hit Your Mark:

Imagine the Holy Spirit doing His work in the part of your life that needs healing. Imagine Him relaxing muscles and restoring cells. Imagine Him healing nagging emotional scars. Imagine Him bringing your back into alignment. Imagine Him obliterating the cancer trespassing in your body. Fix Him in your mind today and watch Him do what only He can do with perfection: heal you.

January 2

The Target:

God is not a man, that He should lie, nor a son of man, that He should repent. Has He said, and will He not do? Or has He spoken, and will He not make it good?

Numbers 23:19

Set Your Sights:

This verse assures you God cannot lie when He makes a promise. Not that He won't lie, but He can't because whatever He says becomes the truth. If He says it, it is so. His promises to you are unwavering, unchanging truths.

A promise doesn't hold the same weight as in times past when a man's word was as good as a signed contract. Your experience with promises and man has most likely brought disappointment, but here's the difference: God is not a man. He is God.

As this truth touches your heart, you will see His promises as more than ink on a page, more than mere words penned by men of old that have little or no relevance to you today. Instead, you'll see them for what they are: promises to you for the here and now directly from the heart of your God.

Hit the Mark:

When you read His Word today, read with this thought in mind: *The Bible is a book of promises written for me, and because I know my God cannot lie, I will put my complete trust and confidence in those promises. If I read a promise, I know it's true. If I read it, it is mine.*

January 3

The Target:

Now the body is not for sexual immorality but for the Lord, and the Lord for the body.

1 Corinthians 6:13

Set Your Sights:

We will set aside a part of this verse for today's devotion. Rest assured, even without it, the verse holds the very same meaning. Taking out the reference to sexual immorality, this is the truth that remains:

"Now the body is … for the Lord, and the Lord for the body."

The "body" refers to your physical body. God doesn't mince words: your body is for Him. The chapter continues to say He purchased your body at a price, and it belongs to Him, so your body is for Him and belongs to Him. Because of this, your body and its health are of great importance to God, and He proved that through shedding the precious blood of His Son, Jesus Christ, whose stripes paid for your healing.

Hit the Mark:

It's essential to have the right mindset about your body, which is too often viewed as the enemy. It is a good thing, not your enemy. It is from God, for God, and it is good. See your body as He sees it and purpose to speak words of blessing over it. Bless it. Don't curse it. Speak words of life and health over and into it today.

January 4

The Target:

He sent His word and healed them, and delivered them from their destructions.

Psalm 107:20

Set Your Sights:

His Word was sent to heal "them." Who are they? They were rebellious fools on the brink of death whose sins had caused their troubles (vv. 17–19). In desperation, they were crying out to God to save them. And He did.

Question: If He sent His Word to heal them, those lost in their sins and without a savior, how much more is His Word sent to heal you, His child?

God speaks through His Word, which He gave to reveal Himself and His abundant blessings. Your healing, one of His many blessings, is in His Word. You can be sure of that because you will find Him there. This healing will not only heal you but also make you whole, cure what the doctors say is incurable, and mend the irreparably broken things. That is His promise.

Hit Your Mark:

As you read today, ask God to show you what verse will heal you. He may surprise you by highlighting one that's not even about healing. That's okay! Your healing journey doesn't have to make sense to you. God knows what He's doing. Trust Him and hold onto His Word. Then don't ever let it go, even after you get what you're believing for.

January 5

The Target:

A joyful heart is good medicine, but a crushed spirit dries up the bones.

Proverbs 17:22 (ESV)

Set Your Sights:

God wouldn't have said it if He didn't mean it. Joy in the heart is good medicine for the body. Nothing brings out joy like a good belly laugh, which we all need every now and then, especially when things are heading in the wrong direction or taking longer than expected.

What elicits an unrestrainable laugh from you? Silly dog videos? A bad joke such as:

Question: What did the horse say after it fell down?
Answer: Help! I've fallen, and I can't giddy-up!

It's not easy to laugh when your flesh doesn't feel like it, but you do have a source of joy to tap into (Gal. 5:22). So even though you may not like it, and even though on the surface you may have no reason to laugh, do it anyway. There's no better medicine, and nothing declares to the enemy, "I will overcome!" like laughing in his face.

Hit the Mark:

Seek out the things that give you joy today and decide that you will have at least one good laugh … out loud … until it hurts. It is good medicine that will help heal your heart and body. Take it. It's just what your heavenly doctor ordered.

January 6

The Target:

Or do you not know that your body is the temple of the Holy Spirit who is in you, whom you have from God, and you are not your own? For you were bought at a price; therefore glorify God in your body and in your spirit, which are God's.

1 Corinthians 6:19–20

Set Your Sights:

You read that too fast. Reread it.

Your physical body is the dwelling place of the Holy Spirit, the Holy of Holies. Not only did God give you your body, but He purchased it and is the rightful owner of it. Your body does not belong to you. That profound truth warrants serious consideration with the potential to revolutionize how you view and treat your body.

Put it in perspective. If your boss loaned you a car, how would you treat it? You would fill it up with the proper fuel, you wouldn't drive it recklessly, and you'd keep it running smoothly until you no longer needed it. Same case with your body. On loan from God, it is the vehicle He's given you to navigate this earth, and it is your responsibility to take care of it.

Hit the Mark:

Ask yourself: Am I treating my body like God owns it? No condemnation is intended, but honest answers are required because only honesty can bring change. Let's turn your car around if you haven't treated it right. Start by identifying one thing—no matter how small—you can do today to better care for God's body, then employ this key to success: Start doing it. Today.

The Target:

If you diligently heed the voice of the Lord your God and do what is right in His sight, give ear to His commandments and keep all His statutes, I will put none of the diseases on you which I have brought on the Egyptians. For I am the Lord who heals you.

Exodus 15:26

Set Your Sights:

God promised the Israelites that if they did right, He would heal them. "Doing right" meant keeping 613 laws and performing sacrifices for every one they broke. Under the old system, healing was a big "if" dependent upon works. It was a never-ending cycle of works, failure, and sacrifice.

Healing is still an if-then promise but with one significant difference: Jesus. Through Jesus's sinless life and obedience unto death, He did all the "doing right" that needed to be done. He fulfilled the "if" for you by satisfying every requirement of the law (Matt. 5:17). There is now only one thing required for you to receive the "then" of His healing promise: Put your faith in what Jesus did. That's it.

Hit Your Mark:

It was impossible to earn and keep healing by works under the law, so why are you still trying to do it now? Your "if" for today is no longer contingent upon works but on believing in Jesus alone. You do the "if," and He'll do the "then." Stop stressing about what you're doing wrong or what you're missing. Stop. Breathe. Then tell yourself, *Jesus did all the doing that needs to be done, so all I have to do is believe in Him. I can do that!*

January 8

The Target:

Our God, will You not judge them? For we have no power against this great multitude that is coming against us; nor do we know what to do, but our eyes are upon You."

2 Chronicles 20:12

Set Your Sights:

The tribe of Judah was up against a powerful army that could wipe them off the face of the earth. With destruction looming on the horizon, they were overwhelmed with fear and cried to God, "We don't know what to do!"

At some point, most people have been in that place. It's the place of being at the end of themselves. They've checked all the boxes, done everything they know to do, and yet keep getting the same results: nothing, no change, no improvement.

But Judah did the one thing they knew to do in the wake of their destruction. They turned their eyes to God. They stopped looking at the advancing enemy and focused their eyes on the one who did know what to do. This has not changed. God still knows what to do.

Hit Your Mark:

If you are camped in the place of "I don't know what to do," then purpose to take your sights off your enemy—whether that be pain, symptoms, doctors' reports, confusion, bondage to sin—and look to the one who knows what to do. Let Him show you how to defeat the army you're facing. That is where the journey to leaving "I don't know what to do" Land begins.

January 9

The Target:

Your ears shall hear a word behind you, saying, "This is the way, walk in it," whenever you turn to the right hand or whenever you turn to the left.

Isaiah 30:21

Set Your Sights:

There are days you have done all you know to do, at a loss as to what comes next, not even knowing where to start. That sounds like "I don't know what to do" Land. (See yesterday's devotion for more on that place.) Maybe you're wandering aimlessly, or perhaps you're stuck. Paralyzed. Unsure. Everything you've tried has come to nothing, and there is no light at the end of the tunnel.

Let this promise from Father that He will never leave you stuck be the light for you today. It beautifully describes the gentle leading of the Holy Spirit in your life as a soft whisper in your ear. The Spirit is your constant companion no matter your direction—right, left, backwards, or nowhere. He is there to lead, guide, and get you moving again.

Hit Your Mark:

If you feel stuck today, not knowing which way to turn or what to do, with an overwhelming sense of hopelessness running through your heart, make it a point to stop and focus on the Lord. Then listen. Don't say a word, and just listen. When you listen—and this is important—expect to hear Him tell you the way. His job is to lead. Your job is to listen. Then follow.

January 10

The Target:

A man with leprosy came and knelt before him and said, "Lord, if you are willing, you can make me clean." Jesus reached out his hand and touched the man. "I am willing," he said. "Be clean!" Immediately he was cleansed of his leprosy.

Matthew 8:23 (NIV)

Set Your Sights:

Maybe your experience with healing has left you questioning if it's God's will to heal everybody … of everything … every time. Jesus answers that question with three words: "I am willing."

With absolute certainty, you can know that because Jesus was willing to heal on every occasion, God is also willing to heal on every occasion because Jesus perfectly represents how God speaks and acts (John 12:49, 5:19).

If Jesus said it, God says it. If Jesus did it, God does it. Jesus said, "I am willing," and immediately healed the leper. God says, "I am willing," and made healing available to you through the finished work of Jesus on the cross. It is God's will to heal you. Period.

Hit Your Mark:

If you don't believe it's God's will to heal, ask yourself why you think that. Did you hear it from a pastor, or are you basing it on experience? If either of those is the "why" of it, then your belief is not based on the word of God. Set aside your preconceived notions about healing and read through the four Gospels, paying particular attention to how Jesus addressed healing. Let that truth shape your belief. Spoiler alert: He healed everybody … of everything … every time.

January 11

The Target:

Who Himself bore our sins in His own body on the tree, that we, having died to sins, might live for righteousness—by whose stripes you were healed.

1 Peter 2:24

Set Your Sights:

There are two parts to what Jesus did for you on the cross:

1) He shed His blood for your sins. Believing for salvation was easy, right? You heard the gospel message that said He died for your sins, you believed, and you were born again. Now you are sure of salvation, even though you can't see it, because it is simply a matter of faith. Easy peasy.

2) He took the stripes for your healing. Healing was yours the moment you were saved, and you receive it into your body the same way you received salvation: by faith. (See the January 1 devotion for more.) And now you can be sure of your healing, even though you can't see it, because it is simply a matter of faith. Easy peasy.

Hit Your Mark:

Meditate on this throughout your day: *God saved and healed me, so I am saved and healed. Jesus didn't die just so my sins could be forgiven and I could go to heaven. He died so I could be free from sickness and disease. I recognize His sacrifice and the totality of what He did for me. Thank you, Jesus, for what you did. I receive it into my body by faith in Your name!*

January 12

The Target:

Immediately the father of the child cried out and said with tears, "Lord, I believe; help my unbelief!"

Mark 9:24

Set Your Sights:

This father witnessed his son experience violent seizure-type symptoms for many years. He believed Jesus could heal his son, but the things he had seen caused some major unbelief. Jesus's response in this situation is how to get rid of the unbelief caused by those natural senses. Even as the boy convulsed on the ground in front of Him, He asked the father a simple question: "How long has this been happening?" (v. 21)

A strange question to ask in that moment of chaos, but a question of extreme importance nonetheless. Why did Jesus ask it? Asking the question turned the father's eyes from the problem to the solution. He was saying, "Dad, look at Me, not at what's happening. Look at Me. I'm the solution. I'm the Healer. I will fix this."

Hit Your Mark:

If you believe in Jesus but what you're experiencing is causing unbelief, then like this father, stop focusing on the things thrashing around in front of you and turn your eyes to Jesus. Give Him your attention. Hear Him say to you, "Look at Me." Be totally distracted by Him. Distracted from the circumstances and unbelief and riveted to the Healer. In this, He can do what He does best: fix it and heal you.

January 13

The Target:

For all the promises of God in Him are Yes, and in Him Amen, to the glory of God through us.

2 Corinthians 1:20

Set Your Sights:

When someone makes a promise, they are declaring that they are definitely, most likely, to the best of their ability, if it's convenient, going to do what they said. It's true; people don't always keep their promises. But God is not people and He is incapable of lying. When He says it, He doesn't change His mind. And unlike people, He will never fail to follow through.

This is why you can put the total weight of your faith on what God says. It's why you can believe His Word above everything else, including symptoms in your body or adverse reports. Despite the facts staring you in the face and screaming in your ears, His Word is His promise. If you can find it in His Word, you can confidently stand on it.

Hit Your Mark:

Think about what a promise means when it comes from the mouth of your God. Feel the sheer weight of it. If you, as a mere human, do everything you can to fulfill a promise, how much more so the Creator of the universe? Find a promise in the Word that applies to your situation. That promise is for you. Imagine Him speaking it directly to you. Then He says, "Yes," and you say, "Amen. So be it."

January 14

The Target:

He has delivered us from the power of darkness and conveyed us into the kingdom of the Son of His love.

Colossians 1:13

Set Your Sights:

You have been rescued from the clutches of Satan's kingdom, where the power of darkness operates, and placed in Jesus's kingdom of abundant life. In other words, your feet may be firmly planted on the dirt of the earth, but you are not of this world any longer (John 17:14).

This means the fight is over and you don't have to battle with Satan one more day. It means Jesus is your King and Satan doesn't have an ounce of authority over you. You don't belong to Satan. You belong to Jesus.

If sickness has attached itself to you, it is there unlawfully. If oppression is tormenting you, it is doing so illegally. As a citizen of the Son's kingdom, you have all the rights of His kingdom, including freedom from the power of darkness.

Hit Your Mark:

The evil works that flow from the power of darkness are trespassers on the property of the King of Kings and Lord of Lords. Since you now live in Jesus's kingdom, they no longer have a right to you. They do not belong to you. In addition, they don't belong in you, on you, or anywhere in your vicinity. Identify them as trespassers, tell them to leave, and don't take "No" for an answer.

January 15

The Target:

And Moses said to the people, "Do not be afraid. Stand still, and see the salvation of the LORD, which He will accomplish for you today. For the Egyptians whom you see today, you shall see again, no more forever. The LORD will fight for you, and you shall hold your peace.

Exodus 14:13–14

Set Your Sights:

As the Israelites stood facing the Red Sea, Pharaoh and 600 of his chariots and about 15,000 infantry were closing in quickly behind them. In the heat of the moment, instead of focusing their eyes on God's promise of supernatural deliverance, they looked at the natural enemy forces closing in on them and cried out in fear.

When faced with a bad report or sickness, human instinct will naturally incline you to focus on the attack and cry out in fear, especially when it looks as if there's no hope. The Israelites' reactions were based purely on that instinct. Thankfully, Moses's response was not. He looked to God and encouraged them to do the same, urging them to stand firm on God's promise.

Hit Your Mark:

Standing firm doesn't mean denying the Egyptian enemy forces are in full attack mode or the presence of symptoms in your body. It means you keep returning to His promise no matter what you experience. The fact may be that sickness is affecting you, but those facts are subject to change at any moment. God's promise, which will never change, is that your deliverance from sickness came through the precious blood of Jesus Christ. Stand still on that truth and you will see it happen.

January 16

The Target:

Let us hold fast the confession of our hope without wavering, for He who promised is faithful.

Hebrews 10:23

Set Your Sights:

This verse is for one of those days you need a reminder to not quit. It encourages you to grab hold of what you believe with everything you've got and not let go of the hope (positive expectation) that you will see it come to pass.

You can secure your grip on hope by never forgetting that God is faithful. The Word assures you He will not lie (Num. 23:19), He cannot lie (Heb. 6:18), and He is faithful to His promises (1 Thess. 5:24).

He is God, not an indecisive man that regrets His decisions and changes His mind. He is the solid rock on whom you can boldly stand, professing your hope in the truth that you are healed, whole, righteous, and redeemed by faith in Him and the finished work of Jesus.

Hit Your Mark:

If you are losing hope because of your circumstances, as a cow chews its cud, let the verses above run over and over in your mind. Speak them out until they are ingrained on the inside how faithful your Father is. If He said it, it is a done deal. Think on that today and feel your grip tighten on what you believe. Then hold fast with the confession that He will never let you down.

January 17

The Target:

You will keep him in perfect peace, whose mind is stayed on You, because he trusts in You.

Isaiah 26:3

Set Your Sights:

God's promise is clear: to bring you to a place of perfect peace and keep you there. This means no matter what the situation might be, it doesn't have to wring you out and hang you out to dry. You can walk through the rough stuff without it stealing your peace, and this verse tells you how.

Look closely at what Isaiah 26:3 does and doesn't say:

It doesn't say you'll have peace when an occasional God-related thought is mixed with a flood of situation-related thoughts. It tells you you'll have peace when your mind is settled on Him, not yourself and your situation. God's peace, which passes understanding and guards your heart and mind (Phil. 4:7), is available 24 hours a day, 7 days a week, 365 days a year. All it takes to enjoy it is a little "staying" power.

Hit Your Mark:

Exercise your staying power and tackle the thoughts that come to steal your peace by doing three things: 1) Recognize the thought as a peace-stealer, 2) reject it by replacing it with God's word, and 3) set your mind on that Word and stay there. That is how you keep your mind stayed on Him, and the result is always perfect peace that remains.

January 18

The Target:

Beloved, I pray that you may prosper in all things and be in health, just as your soul prospers.

3 John 2

Set Your Sights:

God reveals His nature, character, thoughts, and intentions through the written Word. This verse gives insight into what He desires for your life: He wants you to prosper in everything you do and He wants you well. Whether you prosper little or much is directly linked to the prosperity of your soul (your mind, will, and emotions).

How do you cultivate a flourishing soul to achieve your goals of prospering much and being in excellent health? Line it up with what the Word says instead of what the world is bombarding you with daily. Value the truth of the Word above anything you see or feel, enabling you to be unmoved by any enemy attack. As your soul is focused on Him, prosperity and health will be inevitable.

Hit Your Mark:

As your soul prospers, so will your life and body. Nourish your soul today by picking a new verse to meditate on. Maybe even choose one that doesn't have anything to do with healing. Perhaps it has to do with faith or maybe it has to do with joy. Whatever it is, write it down and keep it with you. Think about that verse throughout the day and allow its truth to bring prosperity to your soul.

January 19

The Target:

Surely he took up our pain and bore our suffering, yet we considered him punished by God, stricken by him, and afflicted. But he was pierced for our transgressions, he was crushed for our iniquities; the punishment that brought us peace was on him, and by his wounds we are healed.

Isaiah 53:4-5 (NIV)

Set Your Sights:

The death of Jesus on the cross paved the way for you to be healed in spirit, soul, and body. He paid for your sins with His blood, the punishment He suffered was for the peace of your soul, and the stripes He took were for healing your body. He suffered and died once for it all, and that was enough (Heb. 10:10, 14).

His blood was so pure it didn't just cover your sins; it completely removed them. His stripes were so deep that no sickness or disease wasn't swallowed up within them. His punishment was so severe that not even the consciousness of sin, no guilt or shame, should ever torment your mind and steal your peace (Heb. 10:2). He covered it all: spirit, soul, and body.

Hit Your Mark:

You can't separate spirit, soul, or body from the cross. They are inseparable. When you were born again, you believed your sins were forgiven and you received forgiveness by faith in Jesus alone. Knowing now that healing and deliverance were provided for you on the cross, you can believe and receive them in the same way you received forgiveness … by faith in Jesus's blood, suffering, and stripes. Once and for it all.

January 20

The Target:

A furious squall came up, and the waves broke over the boat, so that it was nearly swamped. Jesus was in the stern, sleeping on a cushion. The disciples woke him and said to him, "Teacher, don't you care if we drown?"

Mark 4:37–38 (NIV)

Set Your Sights:

Before they pushed off from shore and encountered the fierce windstorm, Jesus gave this simple command to His disciples: "Let's go to the other side." Since this boat trip was on Jesus's agenda, God must have shown Him something important He needed Him to do (John 5:19). (In fact, read Mark 5:1–20 and see how Jesus radically changed a demon-possessed man's life there.)

Knowing Father told Him to go, when the storm came and threatened to sink the boat, Jesus wasn't restless and worried but asleep. He understood that with the command also came a promise. The command was to go and the promise was God would make sure He got there (1 Thess. 5:24). Sinking and drowning were not on Jesus's mind. He looked at the promise and didn't waste a second worrying.

Hit Your Mark:

You can rest during your storm, just like Jesus, by doing what He did: follow God's command and put your trust in the promise. For example, the command in Mark 11:23 to speak to your mountain carries the promise that it will move. There are many commands just like this one in the Word. Pick one and think about it today. That path will always lead to rest. No matter the storm.

January 21

The Target:

Bless the Lord, O my soul, and forget not all His benefits: Who forgives all your iniquities, Who heals all your diseases.

Psalm 103:2–3

Set Your Sights:

The word "benefits" conjures up thoughts of the packages offered by employers, such as medical, dental, and retirement. Some are good, some are not so good, and the best package with the most coverage typically commands a great price. Unfortunately, not everyone can afford the exorbitant premiums and is forced to settle for a less-than-best option.

As a believer, you are automatically enrolled in a benefits package with the best coverage. Ever. A great price is attached, but you don't owe a cent. Jesus paid the high premium with blood and flesh, and God reminds you to remember all its benefits—forgiveness of all sins and healing for everything. If you have a need, it's covered. Lifetime membership guaranteed.

Hit Your Mark:

Think about the best benefits package you've ever had. If you've never had benefits through a job, ask yourself what you would like covered if you did. Then realize the package you have because of Jesus goes above and beyond anything you've ever had or could ever imagine. It covers all sins, all diseases, all bondage, and all lack. If it's an issue, it's covered, and your premium has been paid. It's time to file a claim for benefits!

January 22

The Target:

Christ has redeemed us from the curse of the law, having become a curse for us (for it is written, "Cursed is everyone who hangs on a tree").

Galatians 3:13

Set Your Sights:

Deuteronomy 28 outlines the blessings for obeying the law (vv. 1–14) and the curses for disobeying it (vv. 15–68). Here are some of the curses: confusion, frustration, sickness, fever, inflammation, defeat by your enemies, tumors, madness, blindness, panic, stomach issues, rashes, infertility, and plague. Each curse is more horrible than the next. If not for one thing, that would be a terrifying list: Jesus.

Jesus's sacrifice turned the threatening list of curses into a list of all the things His blood covered and you are free from. Now you can scour the list to see everything you don't have to live with, everything that doesn't belong to you, everything with no power over you because Jesus redeemed you from it. He paid for every curse of death with the life in His blood.

Hit Your Mark:

Whatever comes against you today, see it for what it is, part of the curse, and recognize that Jesus paid the price for it. And by the way, no worries if the doctor doesn't know what's wrong with you or what you have isn't explicitly identified on the list. Verse 61 says you are also free from every sickness and disease that hasn't been named. There is absolutely nothing Jesus didn't cover. Nothing.

January 23

The Target:

Then they journeyed from Mount Hor by the Way of the Red Sea, to go around the land of Edom; and the soul of the people became very discouraged on the way.

Numbers 21:4

Set Your Sights:

God brought the Israelites out of slavery with great possessions, fed them with manna from heaven, satisfied their thirst with water from a rock, guided them with a pillar of fire by night and a pillar of cloud by day, and destroyed the Egyptian army in a marvelous display of power, crushing them with the Red Sea. What possible reason could they have for being discouraged?

The Israelites were intently focused on what they left behind and how far they still had to go, instead of how far they'd already come. They totally missed the encouragement of seeing the hand of God at work. Missing His handiwork can be easy when your journey is rough and long, but focusing on what you don't have and what hasn't changed will only discourage you.

Hit Your Mark:

Take a minute to think about the victories of your past, no matter how small they are, and focus on them today. See how God is moving you towards your goal and use that as ammunition to destroy the discouragement attacking you. When the enemy comes with his discouraging thoughts, boldly proclaim, "Satan, let me tell you what the Lord has done!" Then pull the good from the midst of the bad and let him have it!

January 24

The Target:

I will not die but live, and will proclaim what the Lord has done.

Psalm 118:17 (NIV)

Set Your Sights:

Can you see David standing on his balcony overlooking Jerusalem, stance fixed, beating the air with his fist, and at the top of his lungs making this proclamation for the world to hear? "I will not die but live!" Followed by a defiant, "So there!"

David had just recited everything his enemies had done in their attempts to defeat him (vv. 1–16). He spoke of hard places the Lord delivered him from, of not being afraid because God was with him, of trusting in the Lord above all else, and of victory over it all.

The Lord has delivered you. You don't have to be afraid and you can trust in Him. You have victory over anything that comes against you. David knew these things in his heart and it filled him with the confidence, determination, and power that propelled him to fearlessly proclaim, "I will not die but live!"

Hit Your Mark:

Stir yourself up with this today. Do as David did, remember God's faithfulness, and you will notice a spring in your step as your thoughts turn to victory. Think on it long enough and you will find yourself declaring: "I will not die but live and proclaim what the Lord has done!" And for good measure, end with a defiant, "So there!"

January 25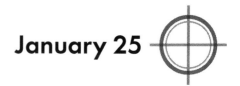

The Target:

Your salvation requires you to turn back to me and stop your silly efforts to save yourselves. Your strength will come from settling down in complete dependence on me.

Isaiah 30:15 (MSG)

Set Your Sights:

It may seem inconceivable to stop and let somebody else fight for you in a battle. There is a compulsion to constantly be doing something, and if you're not doing something, then you're not doing enough. If you're not exhausted and stressed out, it indicates you've been freeloading off somebody else's blood, sweat, and tears. And that's just not acceptable.

But God's instructions make it very clear that doing the exact opposite of your natural tendency, doing all the fighting yourself, is where rest and victory lie. God promises that your strength will come from complete reliance on the work—yes, the blood, sweat, and tears—of Jesus. Strength is a natural byproduct of being sure the work He did is enough.

Hit Your Mark:

Here's a rest exercise: Close your eyes, take a deep breath, and exhale slowly while mentally setting aside your "I have to do these things perfectly every day to be healed" checklist. Picture yourself where you find rest easy, maybe laying on the beach or reclining in your favorite chair. See it until you feel your body relax. The rest you feel is possible every minute of every day when you rely on the work of Jesus, and that's truly all you need to rest.

January 26

The Target:

If any of you lacks wisdom, let him ask of God, who gives to all liberally and without reproach, and it will be given to him.

James 1:5

Set Your Sights:

God instructs you to ask for wisdom and promises He'll give it. His heart is to lead you with wisdom in raising your kids, how to prosper, and the best road for your journey. If there's a problem, He wants to give you the solution. If you have relationship trouble, He wants to show you why you're having it and how to fix it.

Put His promise to the test. Without fail, He will give you the answer liberally and without reproach. In other words, He'll give you the wisdom you need without making you feel like an idiot for asking. The "I can't believe you just asked me that question" look, followed by the exaggerated eye roll, are things you will never get from God.

Hit Your Mark:

If you're at a fork in the road and don't know which way to turn, let this truth compel you to ask Him for wisdom and instill in you the confidence that He will give it to you. Ask Him, then listen expectantly for the answer. The answer may come in the sense of inner peace, a word from a friend, or a song, but He will most definitely answer. He never tires of your questions or runs out of answers, so ask!

January 27

The Target:

My son, give attention to my words; incline your ear to my sayings. Do not let them depart from your eyes; keep them in the midst of your heart; for they are life to those who find them, and health to all their flesh.

Proverbs 4:20–22

Set Your Sights:

These verses offer a guide on how to walk in life and health. However, your motivation for following the guide is equally important as having it. Is it a guide full of commands, a checklist to be meticulously completed, or a guide from a loving Father wanting to ensure you know the way?

The first motivation is empowered by fear and sheer willpower, and when your will runs out, so does your power. The second is empowered by trust in Him and the strength and endurance He supplies.

The first leads to exhaustion and defeat. The second keeps your eyes on the Word (gives attention), keeps your ears open to His voice (inclines your ear), enables you to meditate on His Word (not depart and keep), and leads you to life and health in your body.

Hit Your Mark:

With the proper motivation, here's how to actively follow your guide: On a 3x5 card, write a verse you're standing on. Look at it and read it throughout the day, silently and out loud, until it becomes a part of you, until it gets in your heart and becomes more real to you than what you see or feel. This guide will bring life and health to you. It's His promise.

January 28

The Target:

Because you have made the Lord, who is my refuge, even the Most High, your dwelling place, no evil shall befall you, nor shall any plague come near your dwelling.

Psalm 91:9–10

Set Your Sights:

As a child, do you remember the place you would escape to and hide when you were scared and the absolute safety you felt there? In childlike innocence, no matter how big the monster chasing you, you believed nothing could hurt you as long as you were in that place. That is a dwelling place, and when you enter, unexplainable peace overcomes you because you know you are safe.

That hiding place still exists, impenetrable to the ugliest of monsters, capable of restoring the childlike innocence of long ago that nothing can harm you, and envelop you with the same unexplainable peace. You don't have to fit into a tight space, climb a tree, or search the stars to enter that place because that place is no longer a where, but a who. You will find that place in Him.

Hit Your Mark:

Father has openly revealed Himself to you in His Word, so search for Him there. When you find Him, you will enter that place. Look for Him in every passage you read, seeing how He reveals Himself. Open the Book. Read the Book. Devour the Book. And you'll find yourself entering the place you are safe. The place where nothing can touch you. The dwelling place of peace.

January 29

The Target:

Therefore God exalted him to the highest place and gave him the name that is above every name, that at the name of Jesus every knee should bow, in heaven and on earth and under the earth, and every tongue acknowledge that Jesus Christ is Lord, to the glory of God the Father.

Philippians 2:9–11 (NIV)

Set Your Sights:

After Jesus was resurrected, God promoted Him to the highest rank of power and authority there is. His name became more powerful than any name in heaven (angels), under the earth (demons, principalities, powers, rulers of darkness, and spiritual hosts), and on the earth. If it is named, His name is higher.

Names on earth usually bring to mind the names of men, like John, Sandy, and Barbara. It is easy to accept His name is greater than Sandy and Barbara, but what about other names like cancer, diabetes, or bipolar disorder? Those are names, too, the identifying labels of Satan's evil works. He wants you to tremble at the mention of their names and forget you have the name above every other name. You don't have just any name. You have THE name. The name of JESUS.

Hit Your Mark:

Get a piece of paper. Go ahead, get it. On that paper, as tiny as you can, write the name of whatever you're standing against. Is it so little you can barely see it? Good. Now as big and bold as you can, write JESUS over the entire page. JESUS is now what you see. JESUS is covering that insignificant name. That other name means nothing compared to the name of JESUS.

January 30

The Target:

For if, by the trespass of the one man, death reigned through that one man, how much more will those who receive God's abundant provision of grace and of the gift of righteousness reign in life through the one man, Jesus Christ!

Romans 5:17 (NIV)

Set Your Sights:

Before the seminal event of the sin of Adam, there was only life on earth. After sin, death made its triumphant entry, and following close on its heels was sickness, pain, and mental torment. Adam, through sin, gave death and its evil works authority to rule and reign over humanity. Sickness had authority. Pain had authority. By that one man, Adam, death reigned.

But by the one man, Jesus Christ, you have received God's grace and the gift of righteousness and you now reign. This means you have authority and rule over your body, not death and sickness. Jesus ensured it was so in this: He laid down *His* life and body, so death and all its followers would lose the right to control *your* life and body.

Hit Your Mark:

Sickness and the symptoms in your body, no matter how big a fit they pitch, have no right to be there and no authority to stay. They can scream and yell as loud as they want, but they have been stripped of all power. They no longer reign. You do. If you don't know you have authority, there will be no reigning in life, so zero in on your target by meditating on this truth today.

January 31

The Target:

For if when we were enemies we were reconciled to God through the death of His Son, much more, having been reconciled, we shall be saved by His life.

Romans 5:10

Set Your Sights:

To understand the significance of "saved by His life," you must look back to the beginning. From the start, because of the fall of man, you were an enemy of God, cursed and incapable of making it right with Him. You couldn't fix it, and you were unable, in and of yourself, to close the immense chasm of death and darkness that separated you from God.

But in God's great love for you, He devised a plan to eliminate the chasm and bring you out of the clutches of darkness: Christ would give up His own life for yours. His life—the life He sacrificed and now lives at the right hand of God—closed the chasm and escorted you into the waiting heart of the Father of lights. No more darkness, just unspeakable joy as you stand in the light of being right with God.

Hit Your Mark:

Meditate on the magnitude of what being saved by His life means. You were once enslaved people to the darkness, but He rescued you and placed you in the safety and security of the light. You were once called God's enemy, but now you're called His son or daughter. You have been saved by His life. Totally. Completely. Forever.

FEBRUARY

February 1

The Target:

And by his one perfect sacrifice he made us perfectly holy and complete for all time!

Hebrews 10:14 (TPT)

Set Your Sights:

Old covenant law required repeated offerings of animal sacrifices to pay for sins. Once offered, the high priest would scrutinize it from top to bottom to ensure it was without spot or blemish. Though perfect on the outside, the sacrifice was imperfect because it could only cover sins, not remove them. Like throwing a clean robe over a dirty body, the robe doesn't make the body clean. Over time, the body will make the robe dirty again, hence the need for continual sacrifices. Until …

Jesus was offered as the sacrifice. Unlike all the other sacrifices, He was the last sacrifice because as God's holy, undefiled lamb, He didn't just cover your sins but took them away. He washed you white as snow before He covered you with His robe of righteousness. Nothing to hide and nothing to be revealed. Just perfection.

Hit Your Mark:

The supreme sacrifice of Jesus was so complete and all-encompassing that it even covered the guilt and condemnation associated with sin (Heb. 10:2). You don't have to be in bondage to guilt one more day. Think about that and let it bring you to a place of joy and thanksgiving. When you were washed with Jesus's blood, it was all washed away. All of it. Not a spot remaining.

February 2

The Target:

Then He touched their eyes, saying, "According to your faith let it be to you."

Matthew 9:29

Set Your Sights:

Jesus's encounter with these two blind men who cried out to Him for healing occurred shortly after another noted healing: the woman with the issue of blood (Matt. 9:20–22). The common thread is Jesus said their faith healed them, but that's not the only takeaway. His question in verse 28 reveals another: "Do you believe I can do this?" He didn't ask if they had faith in healing but if they had faith in Him.

What you put your faith in is paramount. You can have confidence in your hurting body, the doctor's report confirming the negative diagnosis, or the science that says what you have is incurable. The blind men didn't put their faith in any "other things"—the longevity of the situation nor the blindness of their eyes—and because of this, Jesus was able to heal them.

Hit Your Mark:

You have the faith to receive whatever you believe for, so make sure it is appropriately placed. Ask yourself if your faith is in Jesus, what you see and feel, or something else. Whatever the answer, and despite everything, you can determine to put the full weight of your faith in Him. He's the Healer. He's the one that does it. Put your faith in Him.

February 3

The Target:

What do you conspire against the Lord? He will make an utter end of it. Affliction will not rise up a second time.

Nahum 1:9

Set Your Sights:

In a previous devotion, you saw Moses encouraging the Israelites to not be afraid and declaring that after their victory over the Egyptians, they would see them "no more forever" (Ex. 14:13). In the same encouraging tone, Nahum boldly declares God is fighting for you and that affliction (anguish, distress, trouble) will not rise up a second time because He will crush it into oblivion the first time around.

When the enemy attacks, he is actually conspiring against (picking a fight with) God. The attack on your body is against God and the healing He stands for. Every battle belongs to the Lord, who has already won the war for healing. Only one battle belongs to you, the fight of faith, which is believing in the finished work of Christ in the face of the attack. He fought. You believe.

Hit Your Mark:

Rest and healing are available today in knowing that God has already fought the battle for you, crushing whatever you're facing into dust. That battle was fought and won in the spirit realm, and believing in Jesus will crush it into dust in the natural. Do not be afraid. Stand still. The victory is yours in Christ Jesus.

February 4

The Target:

So, it is impossible for God to lie for we know that his promise and his vow will never change! And now we have run into his heart to hide ourselves in his faithfulness. This is where we find his strength and comfort, for he empowers us to seize what has already been established ahead of time—an unshakeable hope!

Hebrews 6:18 (TPT)

Set Your Sights:

Fifty years ago, when a bank loan could be secured with a promise to pay and a handshake, you could put faith in a person's word. It meant a great deal if someone said they would be there through thick and thin or their help would be readily available. A man's word was a bond you could rely on. In this day and age, promises are often just empty words.

Does a place exist where you can find strength and comfort in a promise? This verse says it does. Only in the very heart of God can you whole-heartedly throw yourself upon the 100% guarantee that as the rain comes down from heaven and waters the earth, His promises will accomplish what they were sent out to do (Isa. 55:10–11). You can count on it.

Hit Your Mark:

Comfort and strength are found in knowing God's promises can be relied upon. This is an absolute truth because God does not lie and His promises cannot be changed or withdrawn. Search the Scriptures for God's promise addressing your situation and hide yourself in it by running it over and over in your mind. Think about the one who loves you and gave you that promise, taking refuge in His faithfulness.

February 5

The Target:

I shall not die, but live, and declare the works of the Lord.

Psalm 118:17

Set Your Sights:

In a desperate attempt to see healing in your body, you may try someone else's "formula." It usually goes like this: You hear someone was healed and ask them, "What did you do?" You then apply those steps to your situation and hope for the same results. That approach is rarely fruitful because the focus is squarely on you—what you've done, are doing, and can do next.

King David wasn't trying to make something happen when he uttered these words. They weren't part of some formula. He was speaking from the overflow of his heart. He intimately knew God and these faith-filled words flowed out of that relationship. He was confident God would deliver him, so he simply made a statement born of faith in his God.

Hit Your Mark:

Relationships take time, and a relationship with God is no different. If you are easily and frequently distracted, purposefully set aside time to read the Word, pray without interruption, and give Him thanks and praise every day. As your relationship with Him grows, from the overflow of your heart you will begin to declare with certainty what you know to be true of your God. No formulas. Just bold statements born of your faith in Him.

February 6

The Target:

A vast crowd brought to him people who were lame, blind, crippled, those who couldn't speak, and many others. They laid them before Jesus, and he healed them all.

Matthew 15:30 (NLT)

Set Your Sights:

When you combine today's verse with Mark 1:40–41, every hole in thought or belief about the scope of healing promised in God's word gets filled. Too often, the doubt-filled "If it's Your will to heal" prayer is prayed when the Bible clearly teaches that Jesus, the perfect representation of God, is always willing to heal. Jesus said it Himself: "I am willing." No minced words there.

There may also be uncertainty as to whether there is anything God can't or won't heal, restore, or correct. This verse says Jesus healed them all. Lame, blind, crippled, deaf, mute, it didn't matter then and it doesn't matter now. He even healed a severed ear (Luke 22:50–51). Healing is provided whether you have cancer or a cold. It's all covered. Every thing, every time.

Hit Your Mark:

God's word will keep you walking in truth and out of uncertainty (2 Tim. 3:16). Diligently search the Scriptures concerning what God says about healing. Don't be swayed from the truth by hastily taking someone else's word. Dive in and see for yourself, letting it shape what you believe. And remember, no matter what they say, it's what He says that matters. And He says whatever you need, whenever you need it, is covered by the precious blood of Jesus.

February 7

The Target:

For a mere moment I have forsaken you, but with great mercies I will gather you.

Isaiah 54:7

Set Your Sights:

This is an Old Testament truth that holds a New Testament reality. The truth is that the Jews were forsaken by God after sin caused Him to turn away (Isa. 59:1–3). The reality (what you live in today) is that because of His abundant love and mercy and His son's obedience, you are no longer forsaken and He is passionately drawing you to Himself.

Here's another encouraging way to view this verse, especially for those of you who spent years in rebellion against God: The amount of time in your life you were away from God and running from Him was just a mere moment when compared to the time you will spend with Him in eternity. Don't lament the time lost. Look forward to the time that is and is yet to come.

Hit Your Mark:

It's not easy to stop looking at lost time and mistakes, how you can't imagine God would still want you after all that garbage, and how you can't imagine His promises would still apply to you. Thoughts acknowledged. But the only way to move beyond those thoughts and feelings is to focus on the fact that the God of the universe has gathered you to Himself. You. The God of the universe. Together.

February 8

The Target:

They that observe lying vanities forsake their own mercy.

Jonah 2:8 (KJV)

Set Your Sights:

It is not uncommon after receiving healing for symptoms to return days, weeks, or even years later. This verse reveals what those symptoms are and will supply you with the strength you need to resist them.

Based on biblical definitions, "observe lying vanities" could be translated as giving heed to the falsehood of breath. In other words, giving the light of day to someone lying through their teeth and full of hot air. God is saying the returning symptoms are a lie, a mirror image of what you experienced during your sickness.

The enemy has no new tricks. He will try to bring old symptoms back on you to deceive you into thinking you were never really healed in the first place, opening the door for him to come back in. If you know you're healed, don't entertain a single thought trying to convince you otherwise. See those symptoms for what they are—lies.

Hit Your Mark:

If you know you're healed and symptoms have once again returned, revisit the exact moment you knew sickness was finished in your body. Remember the confidence you felt, the freedom. If it was true then, take heart that it is still true now, and reject the lying vanities of the enemy.

February 9

The Target:

Now when He had said these things, He cried with a loud voice, "Lazarus, come forth!"

John 11:43

Set Your Sights:

Just four verses earlier, Martha, one of the sisters of the recently deceased Lazarus, said to Jesus, "He's been in the grave four days! He's going to stink!" Of course, she was right because the decomposition process would have already begun by this time.

Lazarus's body was going to require more than simple healing. It needed a creative miracle, a healing involving the appearance of something previously nonexistent. In Lazarus, that "something" was life itself.

Creative miracles are no problem for Jesus; Lazarus's resurrection and restoration are documented proof of that. The same power that worked through Jesus to raise Lazarus from the dead is the same miracle-working power present in His name today.

Hit Your Mark:

It doesn't matter if you need emotional healing, physical healing, or a creative miracle; His name holds His power to overcome it. Envision whatever you're facing as an insignificant speck of dust in the shadow of your Savior, and don't be deceived by the lie of the enemy saying the minute particle is too big or impossible for the name of Jesus to conquer. All the power of the Man is now contained in His name, and when it is uttered, even death itself must obey.

February 10

The Target:

He was delivered over to death for our sins and was raised to life for our justification.

Romans 4:25 (NIV)

Set Your Sights:

You might think, *What's this got to do with healing?* Simply put, everything, because sin brought death and every evil thing into the world (Rom. 5:12). Think about it. Before Adam sinned, did he experience death or sickness? Nope. God even warned him that if he sinned, he would surely die (Gen. 2:17). Sin and death are inherently linked.

That's why this verse has everything to do with healing. Jesus was sent to His death to pay for your sins. When He was raised to life again, He broke the power of sin. And because sin includes death … and sickness … and disease … and every evil thing, when He broke the power of sin, He also broke the power of sickness (Rom. 6:6).

Hit Your Mark:

Sin handed you a bill you couldn't pay, but Jesus could. He paid your entire sin bill, plus an infinite amount more than what was due, to ensure you would never owe a thing. When your sin bill was paid, so was your sickness bill. Visualize this truth by cutting out a piece of paper in the shape of a receipt. Title it "Sickness Bill." On it, list anything you need healing for today. Now write "PAID" in big letters over it. He paid for it. All.

February 11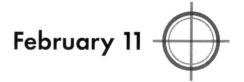

The Target:

This hope is a strong and trustworthy anchor for our souls. It leads us through the curtain into God's inner sanctuary.

Hebrews 6:19 (NLT)

Set Your Sights:

This verse compares your soul to a boat. If not buried deep in the river's floor, a boat's anchor will drag along, allowing the tide to carry the vessel adrift. Unanchored, your soul will meander aimlessly like that boat, directed by the ebb and flow of life. However, when anchored securely, it will be unaffected by the wind and changing tides you encounter.

Hope is the soul's anchor and comes from confidence in God's promises and faithfulness. When hope is secured firmly in the depths of His Word, it keeps you positioned in the inner sanctuary, His very presence, soundly trusting in Him. It is great to get guidance and be encouraged by others, but your anchor will be most steadfast and you most immovable when it is lodged deeply in God's word.

Hit Your Mark:

The rougher the waters of life, the more critical your anchor is to keep you from getting off course and wrecking. When surrounded by agitated waters, set your anchor by knowing His promises and thinking about them often. Every time you choose His word over what you see and feel, your anchor digs in a little deeper. That is the hope that will anchor your soul.

February 12 – Part I

The Target:

Now in the morning, as He returned to the city, He was hungry. And seeing a fig tree by the road, He came to it and found nothing on it but leaves, and said to it, "Let no fruit grow on you ever again." Immediately the fig tree withered away.

Matthew 21:18–19

Set Your Sights:

This is a powerful example of how to put your faith to work. Jesus didn't just think in faith; He spoke in faith. And what happened? The fig tree died, demonstrating that death and life are in the power of the tongue (Prov. 18:21). If you speak life over your body and death into what is attacking it, those things must respond, just like the fig tree.

Words are important because faith is released when you speak. Faith for life or faith for death, it works the same for both. Believing in the importance of your words is essential to seeing things change, so start believing it by placing value on all your words. If you make a promise, keep it. If you say you'll be somewhere at a specific time, be there. Take your words seriously.

Hit Your Mark:

Your words can change things, so start using them. (Remember: It's not the words, but God's power flowing through your words that does the changing. It's not you; it's Him.) Speak to your problem out loud. What does that look like? "Arthritis, be gone." "Cancer, die." No long-winded prayers filled with eloquent words are needed. Recognize your words as the powerful weapons they are and fire them at the enemy today.

February 13 – Part II

The Target:

Now in the morning, as He returned to the city, He was hungry. And seeing a fig tree by the road, He came to it and found nothing on it but leaves, and said to it, "Let no fruit grow on you ever again." Immediately the fig tree withered away.

Matthew 21:18–19

Set Your Sights:

When Jesus spoke, the fig tree withered immediately. Looking at the parallel account in Mark 11, however, it says the disciples didn't see any difference in the tree until the following day (v. 20). Is this a discrepancy? Not at all because the tree withered from its roots. When Jesus cursed it, it died, but the change happened under the surface first, where it was invisible to the eye.

You know from Part I that your words change things when you speak, so let's build on that truth with this: When you speak, even if it appears nothing is happening, you can have confidence the power from your words is actively working. If you spoke to it, it is changing. Because it has to. When you speak, your circumstances are immediately affected.

Hit Your Mark:

If you have spoken life into your body or death to sickness, no matter what you see or feel, those words are at work within you, even now. And when Satan tries to tempt you to doubt because you don't see anything yet, go to the promise the fig tree represents: Something is happening under the surface, and if you continue to believe the promise, what is hidden will be revealed. Take courage in that today.

February 14

The Target:

Therefore God also has highly exalted Him and given Him the name which is above every name, that at the name of Jesus every knee should bow, of those in heaven, and of those on earth, and of those under the earth, and that every tongue should confess that Jesus Christ is Lord, to the glory of God the Father.

Philippians 2:10–11

Set Your Sights:

"Every" is to the exclusion of none. Not a single thing can stand up against His name. Jesus was given this name by the Father, He inherited it as the Son (Heb. 1:4), and He earned it through His victory over death, making a public spectacle out of Satan (Col. 2:15). There has never been, nor will be, a name like it. No other name compares.

JESUS.

If you don't understand there is power in His name, it will have as much impact as a rabbit's foot when you use it. You might as well be saying, "Twinkle, twinkle, little star." However, when you trust in its power and speak it, it will accomplish what it was sent out to do. Whether sickness, mental illness, or demons, His name will dominate and bring you to complete victory.

Hit Your Mark:

His name is more significant than what you're facing. Settle that truth in your heart, then call out those things that don't belong in your body. Command them to go in the mighty name of Jesus. When you speak to them, they must submit to His name. No competition exists (no matter how hopeless the doctors say your situation is) between His name and your problem. Take courage in that today.

February 15

The Target:

No weapon formed against you shall prosper, and every tongue which rises against you in judgment you shall condemn.

Isaiah 54:17

Set Your Sights:

It's easy to get so excited about the weapons not prospering part of this verse that you skip right over the vital second part, condemning the voices against you. Voices come against you with words, and since life and death are in the power of the tongue (Prov. 18:21), words most definitely qualify as weapons and can prosper against you.

When word weapons are fired at you, your job is not to sit there and take them, accepting them as truth and allowing them to shape what you believe. On the contrary, your job is to condemn them by declaring them wrong and countering them with the truth. The truth in God's word is your built-in missile defense system against the flying word missiles of the enemy.

Hit Your Mark:

If negative words have been spoken over you, or if the people around you are speaking death and not life, don't be timid in declaring those words wrong. You can say things like, "I appreciate your concern, but I don't accept that for myself," or "I know you may think that way, but the Word says _____, so that's what I believe." Go ahead. Don't be shy. Shoot down those word missiles with your own truth-filled words.

February 16

The Target:

Praise the Lord, my soul; all my inmost being, praise his holy name. Praise the Lord my soul, and forget not all his benefits — who forgives all your sins and heals all your diseases.

Psalm 103:1–3 (NIV)

Set Your Sights:

Imagine King David, the weight of the kingdom on his shoulders, thoughts of his enemies and their plans bombarding his mind, exhausted from the unrelenting battle raging in his soul.

David needed to strengthen himself in the Lord, so when despair and fear threatened to overwhelm him, he seized control of his thoughts and dictated to his soul what it would think. It would not control him; he would control it.

Persistent anxiety-producing thoughts and nagging symptoms can weigh heavily on your mind. They will control you if left unchecked, but David's solution will still work for you today. There is no better cure for anxiety and fear than praising the Lord in good times and bad, remembering what He has done for you through the powerful blood of Jesus.

Hit Your Mark:

Command your soul to praise Him because sometimes it needs a reminder. Demand it. And don't take no for an answer. Despite what you think or how you feel, whether you want to or not, praise Him. Praise Him as you've never praised Him before. Shout His name, dance before Him, and don't stop until all His benefits are running through your mind. Rejoice because you know it, not because you feel it. It's not easy. But it's worth it.

February 17

The Target:

That if you confess with your mouth the Lord Jesus and believe in your heart that God has raised Him from the dead, you will be saved.

Romans 10:9

Set Your Sights:

You have probably heard this verse a dozen times, but do you know the full extent of what it means to be saved? It's more than simply going to heaven when you die. While that is true about the eternity to come, it also significantly impacts the life you are living right now.

"Saved" means to save, deliver, and protect, but it also means to heal, preserve, and make whole. When you believe, not only are you delivered from an eternity in hell, separated from your loving Father, but in this life, healing and wholeness are provided in the form of the Holy Spirit living inside you (Rom. 8:11). When you received forgiveness of sins (know it or not) you also received the gift of the Holy Spirit (Acts 2:38), and with the Holy Spirit came healing.

Hit Your Mark:

Let's cover the bases: If you haven't confessed Jesus as Lord with your mouth, confess. If you haven't believed in your heart that He was raised from the dead, believe. And if you haven't accepted that healing and wholeness were a part of what you received when you confessed and believed, accept it. Acknowledging that truth is the first step to receiving the healing the Holy Spirit is itching to make your reality.

February 18

The Target:

They will not live in fear or dread of what may come,
for their hearts are firm, ever secure in their faith.

Psalm 112:7 (TPT)

Set Your Sights:

There may be days on your healing journey when temptation comes to fear what might lie ahead. Maybe disease is breaking down your body a little more each day. Perhaps in the natural, according to the doctors, there is nothing you can do but "Wait and see."

Those three little words imply you have no control over anything and can generate debilitating fear. Despite that, you can live a fear-free life no matter what you're going through, and the second part of this verse reveals how.

Your heart (referring to the soulish part of you) will not fear what may come when it is firm in your faith, fixed and established in the Lord. When you trust Him, your mind, will, and emotions are strong and you will not fear.

Hit Your Mark:

If you are fearful, evaluate what your trust is in. Is it in yourself, the words you're speaking and your actions? Is it in the worst-case scenario given to you by your doctors? Both of those will lead down a path to fear. Ask the Holy Spirit to reveal the actual target of your trust. If it is not squarely focused on Jesus, expect Him to help you adjust your target and watch the fear disappear.

February 19

The Target:

Suddenly a violent storm developed, with waves so high the boat was about to be swamped. Yet Jesus continued to sleep soundly.

Matthew 8:24 (TPT)

Set Your Sights:

A superstorm arises, the waves batter the boat, the water inside is dangerously high, and Jesus sleeps. The perfect example of how it is possible to rest in any situation, even in the middle of a savage storm. With the rain beating down on Him and the boat lurching violently, how did Jesus maintain His peace in such a dangerous situation?

First, by knowing who He was. Second, by knowing whose He was. He was the Son of God and He belonged to His Father. This gave Him the confidence that He wasn't alone no matter what came against Him. He knew He had the Spirit of the Father inside Him, so when that storm threatened Him and those He loved, that's all He needed to know to speak to the storm and overcome.

Hit Your Mark:

You are a child of God and you belong to the Father. Just like Jesus. You have the Spirit of the Father inside you. Just like Jesus. No matter what you face, you are not alone. So in the threatening storm, experience the quiet confidence and perfect peace that comes from knowing He is with you. Then from that place of confidence and peace, speak to the storm and watch the Spirit overcome.

February 20

The Target:

Unless the Lord builds the house, they labor in vain who build it; unless the Lord guards the city, the watchman stays awake in vain. It is vain for you to rise up early, to sit up late, to eat the bread of sorrows; for so He gives His beloved sleep.

Psalm 127:2

Set Your Sights:

This verse talks about relying on yourself and what you do to receive from God. It's the formulas you apply to your healing journey. For example: "If I quote this verse ten times a day, fast two days a week, and make sure to go to church every Sunday and Wednesday, then that should do it." This is you working, laboring in vain, for healing.

To labor in vain means to do things without achieving the desired results. It is a waste of energy that leads to exhaustion and frustration, and it definitely doesn't lead to God's beloved experiencing rest and healing. Rest and healing will evade you as long as you rely on your own labor, but they will be your reality when you trust in God as your source.

Hit Your Mark:

Throughout the day, stop and think about this verse. Ask God to show you areas you are unwittingly laboring in. As He is faithful and reveals something to you, ask Him to show you how to turn that vain labor into a life-producing work of faith. Make the decision you will not labor in vain but will trust in Him. And He will give you rest. Guaranteed.

February 21

The Target:

For indeed Christ, our Passover, was sacrificed for us.

1 Corinthians 5:7

Set Your Sights:

This refers to Exodus 12, a beautiful foreshadowing of what Jesus would do for you on the cross. In that account, the Israelites were still in bondage in Egypt, and God was going to send a great plague of death on all firstborns to encourage the Egyptians to let them go. For death to "pass over" the homes of the Israelites, the blood of spotless lambs was required to cover them.

The Israelites took the blood of the lambs and spread it over their doorposts (Ex. 12:7), and when the Lord passed through and saw the blood, He kept going and did not destroy their firstborns with the plague. Jesus is your spotless Lamb (John 1:29). The blood He shed on the cross covers and protects you, causing death to pass over you, and enables you to walk free of sickness and disease.

Hit Your Mark:

Read Exodus 12:1–13 and think about the power in the blood spread on the doorposts. It had the ability to turn away death. If the blood of a little lamb had that power, try to fathom the power contained in the blood of the Lamb of God who was sacrificed for you. Death must pass you by.

February 22

The Target:

For I know the thoughts that I think toward you, says the Lord, thoughts of peace and not of evil, to give you a future and a hope.

Jeremiah 29:11

Set Your Sights:

God's thoughts towards you are full of peace and intended to surround your future with hope. Since His thoughts towards you are only good, that means whatever it is you're butting heads with directly contradicts what the Creator of the universe has in mind for you and your life. His thoughts don't include sickness, disease, or early death, and they are saturated with peace, goodness, health, and a future full of hope.

If you're experiencing symptoms to the contrary or being bombarded with thoughts that are the opposite of peace- and hope-producing, then recognize they are not coming from God. This verse says it outright: His thoughts are not of evil. He is a good God and He can think no other way. He thinks peace. He thinks future. He thinks hope. That is what He has planned for you and what He wants for you.

Hit Your Mark:

Experience the peace and hope He has for you by making His thoughts your thoughts today. Purpose to think only about things that revolve around peace, hope, and your future. Don't let symptoms or pain snuff out your dreams for the future. God hasn't stopped thinking about it, He hasn't changed His mind about it, and neither should you.

February 23

The Target:

Your hearts can soar with joyful gratitude when you think of how God made you worthy to receive the glorious inheritance freely given to us by living in the light.

Colossians 1:12 (TPT)

Set Your Sights:

No matter what is happening in your body, you have much to be thankful for and joyful about. For starters, you were made worthy to receive the benefits and blessings of a glorious inheritance. When you accepted Christ, you became God's child (John 1:12), and He made you worthy to receive. Nothing you did made you worthy, and nothing you do now can make you more or less worthy of that inheritance.

If that's not enough to make you thankful and joyful, then look at what you inherited. In addition to the assurance of eternal life in His presence, you also inherited everlasting life for the here and now. Jesus defined everlasting life as knowing and experiencing the only true God and His Son, Jesus Christ (John 17:3), and that is where you will walk in the blessings of your glorious inheritance ... including in healing.

Hit Your Mark:

Start every day with joyful gratitude, thanking God that you didn't have to earn your position as His son or daughter and that your glorious inheritance is accessible today. You don't have to wait for it, only enjoying the benefits when you get to heaven someday. It is in your hands here. Now. Healing is available to you here. Now.

February 24 – Part I

The Target:

For we walk by faith, not by sight.

2 Corinthians 5:7

Set Your Sights:

Here's a fact about faith that must be understood before discussing how to walk this verse out in everyday life (which is tomorrow): You have the faith you need to receive everything you believe for.

Faith is a gift you received when you heard the gospel and accepted Christ as Lord and Savior (Rom. 10:17, Eph. 2:8). When you did, God gave you the same amount of faith He gives to everyone who believes (Rom. 12:3).

Take Peter, for example, who declared that your faith is identical to his (2 Peter 1:1). He walked on the water and he raised a woman from the dead (Matt. 14:29, Acts 9:40). The faith you have is the exact same faith Peter used to perform healings and miracles. You don't need more faith. Your faith is enough.

Hit Your Mark:

Change your thinking today to reflect that you have all the faith you need to receive everything God has promised and block out the voices that may tell you otherwise. Look at the verses above and think on them until they become ingrained in your heart and mind. Think about them until no one, including yourself, can talk you out of the truth: You. Have. Faith. And it is more than enough.

February 25 – Part II

The Target:

For we walk by faith, not by sight.

2 Corinthians 5:7

Set Your Sights:

In light of yesterday's devotion, your question might be: How do I walk by faith? Walking by sight is easy because life is typically dominated by how you feel and the facts the world professes (lab results, diagnoses, science). It comes naturally to act on what you see.

Walking by faith (acting on what you *can't* see) may seem foreign and downright impossible, but it is essential because it is how you receive from and please God. Why does it please Him? Because when you believe and receive His blessings, He is very pleased.

Whether you walk by faith or sight is determined by your focus. If you focus on what your five senses perceive, you will walk by sight. You will walk by faith if you focus on the Word's wisdom. Your words, actions, and emotions are a great indicator of which walk you're walking.

Hit Your Mark:

Don't beat yourself up if you've been walking by sight and are filled with fear and doubt. Instead, refocus on God's promises. Whatever you're believing for, see it in your mind. Believing to pick up your child without pain? See that. Believing for an excellent report from the doctor? See that. That's a practical way to start walking by faith.

February 26

The Target:

Who being the brightness of His glory and the express image of His person, and upholding all things by the word of His power, when He had by Himself purged our sins, sat down at the right hand of the Majesty on high.

Hebrews 1:3

Set Your Sights:

Jesus was the "express image" of God. This means the Son of Man perfectly represented who God is. The only difference is Jesus came to this world in human form. Without ceasing to be God, He became man. He shed blood. He faced hard decisions. He experienced emotions. He experienced betrayal. And He experienced death.

There is not a single thing in this world you can go through that Jesus can't relate to (Heb. 4:15). When you're going through a trial and someone comes to you and says, "Listen, I have been through this too. I completely understand how you're feeling," that gives you comfort. And then when they say, "Not only have I been through it, but I got through it unscathed and better for it on the other side," that gives you hope.

Hit Your Mark:

You are not alone. Jesus is right there with you. He's been through it and He understands. Reject the enemy's lie saying you're facing this situation alone and no one understands what you're going through and how you feel. Take comfort and find hope in the fact that Jesus has been there and is now by your side to walk with you, hand in hand, step by step, to victory.

February 27

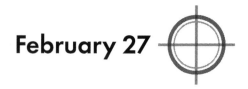

The Target:

They will take up serpents; and if they drink anything deadly, it will by no means hurt them; they will lay hands on the sick, and they will recover.

Mark 16:18

Set Your Sights:

Let's look at healing from the angle of you being the carrier of healing for someone else. As a born-again believer, this verse says you will lay hands on the sick and they will recover, and recovery means getting better.

"Get better" can mean slow as molasses or quick as lightning. Regardless of speed, the promise is they will get better. For this to come to pass, however, something fundamental has to take place: You have to lay hands on people.

You might ask, "How can I do that when I haven't received my own healing yet?" The answer is simple: Because it's not about you. It's about God's healing power flowing through you to them. It doesn't say only healthy believers will partake of this promise, but "those who believe" will (v. 17). So whether you have received your healing or not, that includes you.

Hit Your Mark:

Accept the challenge to pray for someone who needs healing today, whether over the phone or in person. It can be someone you know or a complete stranger in the store. Don't think about it, and don't question it. Just do it. Then expect them to get better, whether molasses or lightning, because that is God's promise to you.

February 28

The Target:

Then Jesus answered and said to them, "Most assuredly, I say to you, the Son can do nothing of Himself, but what He sees the Father do; for whatever He does, the Son also does in like manner."

John 5:19

Set Your Sights:

To paraphrase: If Jesus saw the Father do something, that's what He did. The following are a few things Jesus did concerning healing: "healed all that were sick" (Matt. 8:16), "healed them all" (Matt. 12:15, Luke 6:19), "laid his hands on every one of them and healed them" (Luke 4:40). The point being, everyone Jesus touched was healed.

Jesus no longer lives on the earth in the flesh to physically touch and heal you, which sounds like bad news, but think about what that would mean from a practical standpoint. Still in the flesh, you would have to fight through crowds of sick, dying, desperate people to touch Him. If you can't reach Him, you may never get another opportunity. Healing would be a possibility at best, not a certainty. You now have something far better than Jesus in the flesh: He lives in you, touching you every minute of every day (Col. 1:27).

Hit Your Mark:

Jesus brought healing everywhere He went. He was and is the carrier of healing. Jesus is in you, which means healing is in you too. Change your thinking today to reflect that healing isn't something you need from some outside source, but it is already inside you in the person of Jesus.

February 29

The Target:

An honest witness tells the truth, but a false witness tells lie.

Proverbs 12:17 (NIV)

Set Your Sights:

When you think of a witness, the first thing that probably comes to mind is a person in a courtroom on a witness stand who is testifying to what they know, saw, or heard. That person can either be honest and tell the truth or deceitful and tell a lie. There is no in-between.

In life, there are only two witnesses to choose from: The Spirit, the honest witness, who only speaks what is in the heart of the Father (1 Cor. 2:10–11), or Satan, the deceitful witness, who was given the name Father of Lies (John 8:44). He will spread his lies through whatever means available. If it has a mouth and an audience, he's probably used it. The witness of the Spirit is your weapon against the witness of the liar.

Hit Your Mark:

It matters what witness you listen to. The witness of the Holy Spirit will tell you that you are healed and whole. The witness of the enemy will tell you you're not worthy of healing, that Jesus didn't die for physical healing, and that God doesn't necessarily want you well. Like in a courtroom, you can choose which witness you believe. Choose the Holy Spirit. He speaks only the truth.

set your sights

MARCH

March 1

The Target:

There is one who speaks like the piercings of a sword, but the tongue of the wise promotes health.

Proverbs 12:18

Set Your Sights:

The words you take into your ears and heart are very important, so do a deep dive and identify the individuals you allow to speak into your life. Who are they, what are they saying, and how do their words impact you? Do they cut like sharp swords, opening old wounds and creating new ones, or are they words of life and wisdom that bring you one step closer to healing?

Whether from your lips or the lips of those you surround yourself with, life and death are carried in the power of the tongue (Prov. 18:21). Seek out people who are speaking what you believe. Especially in times of difficulty, you need people who will reinforce the truth you are standing on, not tear it down with words filled with unbelief.

Hit Your Mark:

Evaluate the words being thrown at you from those in the circle around you. It may be time to build a new circle if they are not words of life. Seek out fellowship with like-minded believers in your surrounding physical community, your local church, or the online community of believers. Ask God to help you find people who will build you up and offer you wisdom. Ask Him and He will be faithful to do it (1 John 5:14–15).

March 2

The Target:

Have I not commanded you? Be strong and of good courage; do not be afraid, nor be dismayed, for the Lord your God is with you wherever you go.

Joshua 1:9

Set Your Sights:

You are commanded to be strong and courageous, not afraid or discouraged. This won't be easy to hear, but even during sickness, pain, and heartache, this command applies. It doesn't say, "When everything is going great, be strong and courageous." In fact, if everything was going great, He wouldn't have to encourage you to be strong and courageous.

You might think this command is impossible, but He wouldn't give you an order He hasn't equipped you to carry out. Your circumstances may exert a strong influence on your soul. Still, they can't take away what's in your born-again spirit: joy, peace, and hope in the power of the Spirit (Rom. 15:13). Everything you need to fulfill this command doesn't come from you and your strength, but from Him.

Hit Your Mark:

Yield your will to the Spirit today instead of letting your emotions and mind run the show. Choose words of love over offense and retaliation. Joy over sadness. Courage over fear, knowing God is with you wherever you go. Even if you don't feel like it, thank Him for the Holy Spirit and what He supplies, and He will bring out those characteristics of joy, strength, and hope that you need to be strong and courageous!

March 3

The Target:

And he said to him, "Son, you are always with me, and all that I have is yours."

Luke 15:31

Set Your Sights:

This statement comes from the story of the prodigal son who demanded his inheritance, left home, and spent every penny on scandalous living. When he returned home, he was met by an overjoyed father and a not-so-happy brother.

There is something significant and easily overlooked in this passage: The oldest son received his inheritance at the same time as the younger (v. 12). At his disposal the whole time, he grew angry as he waited to be given what he already possessed, missing out on his father's love and provision.

Asking God for things you've already been given is no less common today, and His response is still the same: "You are always with me, and all that I have is yours." You say, "God, heal me," and He says, "I am always with you and healing is yours." If He promised it in His Word, it is yours. No exceptions.

Hit Your Mark:

As you meditate on this today, think about how God never leaves you and is always by your side. Think about the magnitude of His statement that all He has is yours. He has healing, freedom, prosperity, unlimited strength, and authority. These things, and much more, are your inheritance through Jesus Christ. Walking in it begins with believing it.

March 4

The Target:

But Christ came as High Priest of the good things to come, with the greater and more perfect tabernacle not made with hands, that is, not of this creation. Not with the blood of goats and calves, but with His own blood He entered the Most Holy Place once for all, having obtained eternal redemption.

Hebrews 9:11–12

Set Your Sights:

Every year under the old covenant, the high priest was required to sacrifice goats and calves to pay for the sins of the people. Their blood was enough to cover the sins but not to take them away. Think of putting a clean robe over a dirty body.

That practice was a foreshadowing, an indication of an event yet to come, which was the death, burial, and resurrection of Jesus Christ. Unlike the yearly practice of the past, however, shedding Jesus's blood was a one-time event. One. And. Done.

Jesus's blood did for you what the blood of animal sacrifices could not: it eradicated your sins. You are clean inside and out. And because His sacrifice was once and for all, your redemption is not temporary but permanent. You can't lose it because His blood paid for it ... and it was enough.

Hit Your Mark:

Think about the fact that you are eternally redeemed today. Your salvation is sure. Not only are your past, present, and future sins paid for, and healing, freedom, and prosperity yours, but more importantly, you have a seat at the Father's table. You have a mansion prepared for you. Those facts cannot be changed no matter what is going on in your life. You are redeemed. Forever.

March 5

The Target:

Now the Lord is the Spirit; and where the Spirit of the Lord is, there is liberty.

2 Corinthians 3:17

Set Your Sights:

The Spirit has liberated you from the law of sin and death and everything evil attached to it (Rom. 8:2). Bondage to sickness and disease, oppression and depression, and anything designed to steal, kill, and destroy, the moment you accepted Jesus, the Spirit set you free from every bit of it.

Before you had Jesus, you were a prisoner to the law, locked up in a dark dungeon, secured with heavy chains with no hope of escaping. Every effort you made on your own to escape only caused the chains to become tighter. The prison warden doesn't like it, but you are allowed one phone call. Your phone call is to Jesus. You call. He answers. What happens next? He sends His Spirit. The chains fall off. The prison door swings open wide. You are free.

Hit Your Mark:

You are no longer bound and held captive by the enemy's works. You have the Spirit of the Lord inside you and that means freedom. Freedom from pain. Freedom from sickness. Freedom from depression. The prison doors are wide open before you, so move towards freedom by stepping out in faith. Faith will look different for every person, so ask Father to light the way. Then take that step today.

The Target:

Behold, God is my salvation, I will trust and not be afraid; "For Yah, the Lord, is my strength and song; He also has become my salvation." Therefore with joy you will draw water from the wells of salvation.

Isaiah 12:2–3

Set Your Sights:

These verses have many good takeaways, such as trust leads to freedom from fear and God is your strength, but focus your attention on this one: He is your salvation. Salvation encompasses deliverance, health, and victory. In other words, everything good and desirable is available in the "wells of salvation."

God keeps the wells full, but you must pull up the water you need. If you've ever pulled a whole bucket of water up from a well, you know it takes effort. Drawing from the well of salvation is no different. It takes effort, but your effort is as simple as renewing your mind to God's word. As you do, your beliefs will be established, your faith will be activated, and that draws life from the well.

Hit Your Mark:

Everyone is at a different stage of drawing up water. Where are you in the process? Do you need to start lowering your bucket into the well by discovering what God's word says about your situation? Is your bucket full and now you need to start speaking and acting in faith to draw it up? No matter where you are in the process, the well is there. The water is there. And salvation is at your fingertips.

March 7

The Target:

And those who know Your name will put their trust in You; for You, Lord, have not forsaken those who seek You.

Psalm 9:10

Set Your Sights:

This verse identifies two components of trust in God: He shows Himself faithful by not abandoning you (the "not forsaken" part), and you experience His faithfulness (the "know Your name" part). Experience can be in the form of deliverance from or through something, like a sudden manifestation of healing (deliverance from) or a supernatural infusion of strength and joy as you walk through a treatment plan (deliverance through).

In both cases, He showed Himself faithful, you experienced it, and trust is the result. God understands trust has to be earned. Knowing you can't trust someone unfaithful to their word, He gains your trust by being faithful to His. When He shows Himself faithful, the Word becomes your reality and trust is established. More experience leads to more trust and more trust leads to more experience. It's a beautifully crafted circle.

Hit Your Mark:

If you are struggling to trust God today because of the magnitude of your situation, fuel your trust in Him again by remembering the times when you experienced His faithfulness. Look closely for His hand at work even now, no matter what it looks like on the surface. He has not, nor will He ever, let you down because He is faithful (2 Tim. 2:13).

March 8 – Part I

The Target:

Then the Lord said to Moses, "Make a fiery serpent, and set it on a pole; and it shall be that everyone who is bitten, when he looks at it, shall live."

Numbers 21:8

Set Your Sights:

The stage: The Israelites are journeying to the promised land, complaining profusely about the provisions God was, and wasn't, giving them. Because they were stubborn and rebellious, fiery serpents were sent among them. Whether fiery in appearance or their bite felt like fire, it doesn't say. What it does say is their bite was deadly.

The target verse is God's solution for the Israelites' problem with the snakes, but it is also a foreshadowing of God's solution for the problem with sin.

When Moses held up the snake on the pole, he demonstrated how Jesus would one day be lifted up on the cross. And just like this instance where everyone who was bitten and looked to the pole lived, everyone who is bitten today (by sin, sickness, or bondage) and looks to Jesus will be restored to health. They "shall live"!

Hit Your Mark:

On the cross, Jesus took what you were (sinner, sick, slave) and gave you what He is. He took your sin and gave you righteousness. He took your sickness and gave you health. He took your chains and gave you freedom. That is the great exchange no man can explain. As a born-again believer, you are what He is (1 John 4:17). No matter what.

March 9 – Part II

The Target:

And Moses made a serpent of brass, and put it upon a pole, and it came to pass, that if a serpent had bitten any man, when he beheld the serpent of brass, he lived.

Numbers 21:9 (KJV)

Set Your Sights:

To avoid certain death from a snakebite, the Israelites were instructed to behold the brass serpent, which meant taking their eyes off the slithering, hissing snakes and looking at the brass one. Just imagine the snakes wrapping around their ankles, biting them, people screaming hysterically, and Moses calmly telling them to look at a pole instead. That could not have been easy.

It took more than just a glance at the brass serpent to be healed. Those bitten had to fix their eyes on it. A sideways glance from the periphery wouldn't do. They had to gaze at it, be absorbed by it, and expect their healing to come. It was a committed turning away from one thing and turning toward another. God is inviting you to turn away from the serpent and gaze intently and expectantly at Jesus.

Hit Your Mark:

It is hard to take your eyes off the snakes. To do it well, you must rely on the strength and endurance the Father supplies. Envision your symptoms as snakes today. If that snake of a negative report comes, don't read and reread it until you have it memorized, but fix your gaze on Jesus. He'll get you through it as you keep looking to Him. Eyes off the snakes. Eyes on Jesus.

March 10

The Target:

For God so loved the world that He gave His only begotten Son, that whoever believes in Him should not perish but have everlasting life.

John 3:16

Set Your Sights:

God sent Jesus so you could have everlasting life, which includes more than the eternity you will spend with Him after death. Jesus defines everlasting life in John 17:3: "And this is eternal life, that they may know You, the only true God, and Jesus Christ whom You have sent." This knowing is a personal relationship for the here and now, not just the sweet by-and-by.

This verse gives a clear picture of the character of God. He is not some far-away power keeping track of everything you do wrong, waiting for the opportunity to drop the hammer. He sacrificed His only Son so you could intimately know Him. He is not harsh but gentle (Matt. 11:29). He is not your enemy, but your ally (Ps. 54:4). He is not judgmental, but merciful (Heb. 8:12). In short, He is good.

Hit Your Mark:

The purest motive behind why Jesus suffered was to give you the incredible opportunity to have a personal relationship with the Creator. You are missing that point if you are consumed with chasing after healing. He is the one to be pursued, not healing. It makes perfect sense to go after what you need, but instead of being led by your head, let your heart lead you … straight to Him.

March 11

The Target:

From now on, therefore, we regard no one according to the flesh. Even though we once regarded Christ according to the flesh, we regard him thus no longer. Therefore, if anyone is in Christ, he is a new creation. The old has passed away; behold, the new has come.

2 Corinthians 5:16–17 (ESV)

Set Your Sights:

This verse encourages you to look past the messy, flawed, often unpleasant exterior of people and see them as God sees them: people He loves and sent Jesus to die for (vv. 14–15). Sometimes the hardest person to see in this way (loved and worth the ultimate sacrifice) is yourself because the mess is in your face every moment of every day. Wherever you go, there you are.

But make no mistake, this verse's "no one" also applies to you. God is encouraging you to see yourself through your new identity in Christ, where you are one with Him and identical to Him (1 John 4:17). In God's eyes, you are forgiven, unblameable, and perfect. He doesn't see your messes, flaws, or bad attitude. Regardless of what you see on the outside, you are perfect inside, and that's the only truth He sees.

Hit Your Mark:

No matter what you see or feel today, focus on the fact that you are a new creation who is perfect, just as you are, in His eyes. You might not physically, emotionally, or mentally display this new creation every day, but that doesn't change the fact that He thinks you are magnificent. That's how He sees you. And that's how He wants you to see yourself.

March 12

The Target:

When evening had come, they brought to Him many who were demon-possessed. And He cast out the spirits with a word, and healed all who were sick that it might be fulfilled which was spoken by Isaiah the prophet, saying: "He Himself took our infirmities and bore our sicknesses."

Matthew 8:16–17

Set Your Sights:

In the New Testament, Jesus healed everyone who came to Him. Not a single person left Him sick or possessed. That may be a common fact, but this verse takes it one step further, directly linking healing to the cross.

By healing all who came to Him, Jesus demonstrated what He would do for all humankind. For example, Jesus healed the blind man with His touch, but by taking blindness into Himself on the cross, He made healing for the eyes available to all. He exhibited in them tangibly what He would secure for you permanently.

Jesus proved He had the power and authority to take away sickness and disease during His earthly ministry. When He was lifted up, He extended the reach of His healing power beyond those in His immediate vicinity. Because of that, you no longer have to touch Jesus in the flesh to be healed. Now all you have to do is believe.

Hit Your Mark:

Read through the Gospels and pay special attention to when Jesus healed people. Look at the people. Look at the circumstances. Look at the problems. Then recognize He healed them all as a demonstration of the powerful truth that He would heal you too. What He showed you in the natural, He finished on the cross.

March 13

The Target:

So then faith comes by hearing, and hearing by the word of God.

Romans 10:17

Set Your Sights:

In context, this verse refers to the gift of faith God gives a person when they hear the gospel message, which enables them to believe. But like an onion, when you peel back the layer of context, there is a layer of concept hidden beneath.

The verse says faith comes "by hearing," not "by having heard." The difference is significant. It is a common misconception that once you receive healing, you have heard all you need to hear to walk in healing for the rest of your life, but keeping your healing is directly connected to keeping your hearing.

Hearing keeps your faith alive and active. Unfortunately, the distractions of life can plug your ears, stop your hearing, and allow symptoms to return. You can keep healing secure by hearing God's word daily. Hearing today means faith today, means healing every day.

Hit Your Mark:

Think about the importance of hearing and dedicate today as a day for listening. Block out some time for a one-sided conversation with God. Tune your ears to hear Him. Set aside any distractions and then be still. Know He's with you and just listen. Whether you hear anything or not, smile. Enjoy His company. His very presence will fuel your faith and heal you.

March 14

The Target:

Come on, everyone! Let's sing for joy to the Lord! Let's shout our loudest praises to our God who saved us! Everyone come meet his face with a thankful heart. Don't hold back your praises; make him great by your shouts of joy!

Psalm 95:1–2 (TPT)

Set Your Sights:

God saved you. Let that sink in. He rescued and delivered you. He's concerned about your welfare, prosperity, and victory. Since He is on your side, whether in life or death, you can't lose. That's something to shout about!

Despite this truth, it's easy to hold back praise when nothing seems to be going your way, when you want to cry out, "It's not supposed to be this way!" But the psalmist reminds you that no matter what circumstance you're in, there is always something to praise God for.

If nothing else, the very heart of the gospel says He sent His only Son to die so He could have an intimate relationship with you. With you. Sometimes that's all you've got. But if you'll grab hold of it, it's also all you'll need.

Hit Your Mark:

So praise Him today for all He has done for you and all He is. Don't focus on what you lack or need, but on the things He has already provided. Praise Him for who He is. Praise Him because He has delivered you. Praise Him because He has given you victory. Go ahead. Whether you feel like it or not, don't hold back your praises because He is worthy of them all!

March 15

The Target:

So, what does all this mean? If God has determined to stand with us, tell me, who then could ever stand against us?

Romans 8:31 (TPT)

Set Your Sights:

This statement is frequently rattled off but not thought about. Like a knee-jerk reaction, it is often shouted out in fear. It's a go-to when face to face with a person who is hurting and nothing else comes to mind. But it is meant to be a gold mine of encouragement and strength.

There are no words to describe God's power and glory. If you commissioned the most talented writer in the world to construct the most eloquent prose and offered it up to Him in praise, it wouldn't even come close to what He deserves. And yet … He has determined to stand with you. Yes, you.

Your God, the all-knowing, ever-present, very God of life itself, has promised to go before you in every situation, to rescue you from every pit, and to never leave or forsake you (Deut. 31:8, Ps. 40:2, Heb. 13:5). So ask yourself: Since God is for you, who could ever stand against you?

Hit Your Mark:

Compared to the one who stands with you, your mountain is a mere speck of dust. So lift up your chin, square your shoulders, and stand with confidence in the face of it all, side by side with the Maker of the universe, knowing He is with you and victory is assured.

March 16

The Target:

But let him ask in faith, with no doubting, for he who doubts is like a wave of the sea driven and tossed by the wind. For let not that man suppose that he will receive anything from the Lord; he is a double-minded man, unstable in all his ways.

James 1:6–8

Set Your Sights:

This verse is frequently taught in the context of healing, implying if a person wavers, they shouldn't expect to be healed. If you have a terrible day and worry about the symptoms in your body, God isn't going to do anything for you. Stating it plainly: If you can't believe perfectly, God won't be faithful to heal you. Ouch. That's pretty harsh theology.

So what is this verse saying if it isn't saying that? The heart of the matter is this: Not wavering means not doubting God's ability to do what He says He'll do. Not wavering means not questioning whether Jesus died on the cross for you. If you waver in your head because of what you're experiencing in your body but don't waver in your heart about Jesus, healing is still yours. Just ask the father of the epileptic boy (Mark 9:14–27). He'll tell you.

Hit Your Mark:

If what you've been taught about wavering has caused you to throw up your hands in defeat and disqualify yourself from healing, then today is the day to change your thinking. First, God doesn't expect you to be perfect in your faith. Second, there is only one He expects you to be single-minded about. And that's Jesus. That's all. Just Jesus.

March 17

The Target:

So Jesus answered and said to them, "Assuredly, I say to you, if you have faith and do not doubt, you will not only do what was done to the fig tree, but also if you say to this mountain, 'Be removed and be cast into the sea,' it will be done."

Matthew 21:21

Set Your Sights:

Many will read this and become discouraged as they think *If I doubt, I won't receive, so it's hopeless.* But in light of Jesus's words in John 1:13–14, you could rewrite this to say: "I'm telling you, if you have faith in Me and don't doubt I will do what I say, when you tell something to move, I will move it." When you don't doubt His ability to do what He says, the burden isn't on you to see it come to pass. It's on Him.

When your faith is securely in Jesus, you can expect Him to move, eradicate, and fix things. And since He can move a mountain fueled by your faith in Him, He can move a cold or those pesky allergies that return year after year or that irritatingly persistent pain in your hip. It doesn't matter how small or big, He can do it.

Hit Your Mark:

Jesus is the one who does the "it will be done" part. You just have to trust in Him to do it. This is your focus for today: See yourself speaking to your mountain. Now don't just see it move. See *Him* move it, casting it into the sea. Watch it sink and disappear. Out of sight. Never to return.

March 18 – Part I

The Target:

Who, contrary to hope, in hope believed, so that he became the father of many nations, according to what was spoken, "So shall your descendants be."

Romans 4:18

Set Your Sights:

Over the next few days, a great roadmap to healing will be unfolded using a passage about Abraham. Your first stop: *Focus on the promise.*

Today's verse reveals God's promise to Abraham that he would be the father of many nations. What hasn't been told yet is that Abraham was 75 years old and his wife Sarah was barren. There was no hope in the natural of fatherhood. But in the face of the impossible nature of the promise, his hope was fueled by "what was spoken." In other words, Abraham drew his hope from God's promise alone.

God's spoken and written words contain all the power necessary to accomplish what they are sent out to do (Isa. 55:11), and Abraham put his hope in that. Despite the opposition in the natural (their age, her barrenness, being ridiculed by naysayers for believing) he chose to focus on the promise.

Hit Your Mark:

You have a book chock-full of what-was-spokens, a.k.a His promises. Today is another day to focus on His promises because you can never do that too much. Despite your circumstances, despite how your body feels, choose to keep your eyes focused on one thing: What He said. And that's it. Welcome to your first stop.

March 19 – Part II

The Target:

And not being weak in faith, he did not consider his own body, already dead (since he was about a hundred years old) and the deadness of Sarah's womb.

Romans 8:19

Set Your Sights:

Abraham had strong faith. After reading that statement, your question is most likely: How did he have strong faith, and how do I have faith like his? The answer lies in one word: consider. To consider means to think carefully about something. What you consider is important because it becomes what you have faith in.

As you saw yesterday, Abraham only considered God's promise. Equally important to what he did consider is what he didn't. He didn't linger on his age or the impossibility of the promise.

Thinking about God's promises will activate God's "call those things which are not as though they were" kind of faith. Considering the symptoms and negative reports will only bring unbelief and fear and hinder you from receiving God's best.

**The second stop on your roadmap to healing:
Don't look at the problem.**

Hit Your Mark:

It can be challenging to not look at something that is wrong, such as the swelling in your hands or the protruding lump, but to instead stay focused on the Word. Not looking doesn't mean you're denying the symptoms are there. It means you're choosing to look at the answer, not the problem. It is hard, but you can do it with His strength. Welcome to your second stop.

March 20 – Part III

The Target:

He staggered not at the promise of God through unbelief; but was strong in faith, giving glory to God.

Romans 4:20 (KJV)

Set Your Sights:

We'll cross stops three and four of the roadmap today. First, Abraham "staggered not" because of unbelief. Despite the facts, he didn't bat an eye at the truthfulness of the promise. His faith remained strong, overpowering any unbelief that reared its ugly head by keeping his eyes focused squarely on the promise.

The third stop: Let the promise reign over everything.

Identifying stop four is Abraham, in the face of all opposition, giving glory to God. The powerfully simple act of praise kept his faith in God strong, and it will do the same for you. When you praise with your whole heart, it is impossible to be worried simultaneously. When your focus is praise, your faith will thrive.

The fourth stop: Give God the glory and praise!

Hit Your Mark:

With four stops complete on your roadmap to healing, your mind is probably fighting to stay focused and on course. It's not easy to give God's promise the loudest voice amid all the other voices, so imagine Him shouting it over a bullhorn, drowning out everything else. Keep your mind on the promise and give Him all the glory for it. As you do, you'll find your faith becoming stronger and your footing more secure.

March 21 – Part IV

The Target:

And being fully convinced that what He had promised He was also able to perform.

Romans 4:21

Set Your Sights:

Abraham didn't stop at being convinced. He focused on God's promise until he was *fully* convinced God could do what He said He would do. It is possible to believe He promised something but at the same time not believe He can actually do it. Not that He won't do it, but He can't do it. This kind of errant thinking comes by focusing on the problem, magnifying it until it becomes more prominent than your God.

There is nothing more powerful than God Almighty. The Israelites sang this song after crossing the Red Sea: "And with the blast of Your nostrils the waters were gathered together; the floods stood upright like a heap; the depths congealed in the heart of the sea" (Ex. 15:8). What a fantastic word picture of the magnitude of His power. He snorted and the waters of the sea parted.

The fifth stop on your roadmap to healing: Be fully convinced.

Hit Your Mark:

There is nothing that won't crumble and fall to its knees in God's presence. Before continuing your day, read 2 Samuel 22:5–16 and imagine the power it describes. The earth shook. The heavens quaked. Devouring fire. Thunder. Lightning bolts. That is your God. Whatever you're facing, it's nothing compared to Him.

March 22 – Part V

The Target:

And therefore "it was accounted to him for righteousness."

Romans 4:22

Set Your Sights:

Today is the final stop. These last four days of devotions culminate here as God gives Abraham righteousness and fulfills His promise. All this talk about Abraham wasn't to convince you how great he was but to give you an example of an average, flawed guy who received what was promised through faith and righteousness (v. 23). Faith was Abraham's part, but righteousness and the promise fell to God.

As faith led Abraham to righteousness, so your faith in Jesus leads you to righteousness. Being righteous (right with Him) isn't a position you earn. When you believe, God makes you righteous (2 Cor. 5:21). You become righteous. You are righteous. Following closely behind becoming righteous is Him saying yes to everything He promised (2 Cor. 1:20). Every promise is yours, approved, and fulfilled.

**The final stop on your roadmap to healing:
Recognize your righteousness.**

Hit Your Mark:

Your position of righteousness is permanent, and no matter what you have done, are doing, or will do in the future can change that. God's faithfulness to fulfill His promises is as fixed and secure as your righteousness. You are always righteous and healing is always approved. This is the final stop as you recognize that healing follows righteousness. Welcome to your destination.

March 23

The Target:

You are my hiding place; You will protect me from trouble and surround me with songs of deliverance.

Psalm 32:7 (NIV)

Set Your Sights:

There is a special place, only open to an elite group, called The Hiding Place. Once a member, you can stay as often and as long as you'd like. While on premises, you will be free from all forms of trouble, including, but not limited to, sickness, poverty, oppression, offense, slander, and backbiting.

Also during your stay, there's a Guard who sticks with you like glue. You can stay without fear, knowing every inch of the property is under His watchful eye. He has proven Himself faithful and has even gone so far as to defeat death. We can't say enough about Him.

Membership is open to all and only has one requirement: accepting Jesus Christ as Lord and Savior. When you accept, The Hiding Place will welcome you with open arms.

Hit Your Mark:

The Hiding Place is available right now. It is a place of peace, comfort, safety, and healing. You enter by abiding in the Word, keeping your mind fixed on Him (Isa. 26:3). You withdraw by allowing your thoughts to go to worldly things that cause fear and unbelief. If you wander and find yourself outside the walls of The Hiding Place, don't worry. Simply knock on the door, and it will swing wide open every time, welcoming you back again.

March 24

The Target:

He gives strength to the weary and increases the power of the weak. Even youths grow tired and weary, and young men stumble and fall; but those who hope in the Lord will renew their strength. They will soar on wings like eagles; they will run and not grow weary, they will walk and not be faint.

Isaiah 40:29–31 (NIV)

Set Your Sights:

Have you ever stood on a verse that gave you hope but nothing more? No change. No nothing. Frustrating. Here are two explanations that may help:

One: When reading His promises, often all that's seen is what God will do for you, but your role in fulfilling those promises is overlooked. Using this verse as an example, God promises strength and power to the weak. That sounds great. But the part that says the promises belong to those who hope in Him is skimmed over.

Two: You may read this verse and think you are trusting God when you're really not. Unbeknownst to you, your trust is actually in what you're doing. It's not in the Word you're reading and quoting at all but in the physical acts of reading and quoting. It's in successfully checking all your faith boxes and "doing everything right." It's in your doing, not His.

Hit Your Mark:

These things are sometimes not easy to recognize or admit but could quite possibly be what's holding you up on your healing journey. The good news? They're easy to remedy. Ask the Holy Spirit to open your eyes to the truth and show you how to change your ways. And don't beat yourself up. Just keep moving forward.

March 25

The Target:

But now Jesus the Messiah has accepted a priestly ministry which far surpasses theirs, since he is the catalyst of a better covenant which contains far more wonderful promises!

Hebrews 8:6 (TPT)

Set Your Sights:

Under the old covenant, God promised the children of Israel His protection and immeasurable blessing as long as they obeyed the rules. A purely works-based system. In addition to the Big Ten, there were 613 rules they had to follow. If they broke even the least of those rules, severe punishment followed. Think of picking up sticks on the Sabbath and being stoned to death for it (Num. 15:32–36).

You, however, don't live under the old covenant. Through Jesus's shed blood, He fulfilled the old and brought about the new (Luke 22:20). Under the new covenant, God promises grace and salvation through one thing and one thing alone: faith in Jesus (Acts 16:31).

You don't have to exhaust yourself trying to earn it. Because Jesus did all the work. You don't have to be perfect. Because Jesus was. When you mess up, God's not waiting with His rod to punish you. Because Jesus took all the punishment. That's your covenant.

Hit Your Mark:

Having a bad day? Meditate on the fact that your covenant with God is new, not old, and think about the stark difference between the two. That reflection alone can bring heartfelt thanksgiving and joy to your day!

March 26

The Target:

For the Lord God is our sun and our shield. He gives us grace and glory. The Lord will withhold no good thing from those who do what is right.

Psalm 84:11 (NLT)

Set Your Sights:

After reading this, you might think, *do I have to do everything right to get good things from God? That must be why I'm not healed, because I'm not doing everything right.* When it was written, that was true because they were under the old works-based system. (Remember that you live under a new system when you read the Old Testament.)

Under the new system, there's only one thing you need to "get right" to receive God's grace and promises (including healing): to believe in and accept Jesus as Lord and Savior. That's it. No amount of work can earn the promises.

Don't get me wrong, there are works you do, but they don't come from a heart of fear that you aren't doing enough. They come from a heart of faith. You don't work to make faith; you work because you have faith. Your belief propels your actions.

Hit Your Mark:

Are you trying to live up to the unattainable do-everything-right standard of the old system? God doesn't expect that, so why are you expecting it from yourself? Give yourself a break. Stop being so hard on yourself. In God's eyes, as His kid who believes in Jesus, you've already done everything right. He is well pleased with you!

March 27

The Target:

You will keep him in perfect peace, whose mind is stayed on You, because he trusts in You.

Isaiah 26:3

Set Your Sights:

This promise of peace consists of two parts you and one part God.

Your parts: First, you trust God. Like with your fellow man, you trust Him by getting to know Him. Where to start? If you wanted to know someone and there was a book about them, wouldn't you read it to find out who they are? Second, your mind is stayed on Him. This means consistently refocusing your scattered, doubt-filled thoughts on His Word.

God's part: As you learn to trust God and practice the art of directing the mayhem in your mind back to Him, He promises to keep you in perfect peace. You'll never do this perfectly and that's okay. He knows this and won't withhold His peace when you miss it. More than anything, He longs to be your peace and can be when you trust and cling to His promises.

Hit Your Mark:

Peace is yours in every situation because God is with you. He is your peace in the middle of pain and sickness, alarming reports, and unmet expectations. It doesn't make any sense in the natural world, but that's why it's called peace that passes understanding. Peace doesn't come from everything being right and rosy. It comes from Him. And He is always with you.

March 28

The Target:

When You said, "Seek My face," My heart said to You, "Your face, Lord, I will seek."

Psalm 27:8

Set Your Sights:

The desire to seek after something is fueled by the heart's longing to find and possess it. Examples may be a man on a life-long quest to find a priceless buried treasure or a woman searching for her long-lost love. Their searches have a passionate intensity because they have placed a high value on what they're seeking.

God says, "Seek My face." His face. Just Him. You may view seeking Him as taking precious time away from pursuing what you need until you realize He is what you need. He is inviting you to value Him above all others, to make Him your priceless treasure, your long-lost love, because He knows that in pursuing Him, you will lack for nothing (Matt. 6:33).

Hit Your Mark:

Open the door to your heart to see what it's after. If it's been in hot pursuit of healing, that's a great answer and something you can change. Changing your heart's desire is a process you can start by doing this simple thing: Every time you think about healing, recognize Jesus as the source of that healing. Over time, as you see that all healing flows from Him, your heart will naturally pursue Him. And in Him is where everything you need lies.

March 29

The Target:

Therefore we do not lose heart. Even though our outward man is perishing, yet the inward man is being renewed day by day.

2 Corinthians 4:16

Set Your Sights:

Not losing heart is one of the biggest challenges on any healing journey. It is a daily ... hourly ... sometimes minute-by-minute struggle to not focus on the things that usher in discouragement, like pain and symptoms.

Paul declares that his endurance didn't come from an absence of trouble (he was beaten, stoned, and whipped) but from the fact that his inward man received fresh encouragement daily. Though his physical body was suffering, he was thriving on the inside. That's what mattered most to Paul and it's how he carried on.

If you are stressed out and depressed, that's a sure sign you're trying to make it on your own. Not losing heart isn't something you do, but that's done through the Holy Spirit working in you. The same Spirit that refreshed Paul lives inside you to daily fill you up and encourage you.

Hit Your Mark:

You aren't on this journey alone, and that's the only reason it is possible to not lose heart. There will be bad days, and everyone has them. But regardless of your situation or how long you've been in it, God wants to renew your strength and joy. Let Him encourage you by simply recognizing that He is with you and thanking Him for working in your life.

March 30

The Target:

For our light affliction, which is but for a moment, is working for us a far more exceeding and eternal weight of glory.

2 Corinthians 4:17

Set Your Sights:

The word "affliction" means burden, persecution, tribulation, and trouble; in context, it refers to the affliction you will face for being a Christian. However, suppose you ask anyone suffering from a sickness or disease. In that case, they will probably tell you it feels like a burden, a tribulation, *and* a trouble. No surprise there.

Looking at sickness as just that—a burden and a trouble—a fundamental principle can be applied from this verse: as you walk through your healing journey, keep everything in perspective.

Paul's afflictions included beatings, stonings, imprisonments, and shipwrecks, yet he could label them as "light." How? Because of his perspective. What you focus on becomes big. What you don't focus on becomes small. Focus on your problem and it becomes big. Focus on the Word, not your problem, and it becomes small. It's simple, and that's why it's called a simple truth.

Hit Your Mark:

If you want to dig a little deeper and really appreciate the significance of Paul's words, read 2 Corinthians 11:23–28 for a complete list of the afflictions God delivered him through. Put yourself in his shoes, and then put yourself and your problem in his frame of mind: Word big. Problem small.

The Target:

While we do not look at the things which are seen, but at the things which are not seen. For the things which are seen are temporary, but the things which are not seen are eternal.

2 Corinthians 4:18

Set Your Sights:

Over the last two days, you've seen that Paul viewed the trials and tribulations he encountered as light afflictions and that because of his perspective, he could find contentment in even the most brutal circumstances (Phil. 4:11–13). Today he gives you another way of thinking that will help you endure: temporary versus eternal. He saw his troubles as short-term when viewed in the light of eternity, and he invites you to do the same.

Paul recognized and embraced that his life on earth was but a vapor (James 4:14), just his temporary residence, and this kept him focused on what mattered most. He knew everything he was experiencing was trivial compared to the eternity he would spend in God's presence. He looked at the unseen and was able to finish his race strong.

Hit Your Mark:

It's impossible to see the unseen with your physical eyes. You have to use your spiritual eyes. How do you do that? Keep your mind focused on the things of God, such as His Word, what He's already done for you, and the eternity you will spend with Him. This takes practice and is often quite challenging, but the payoff is totally worth the effort.

APRIL

April 1

The Target:

But when the fullness of the time had come, God sent forth His Son, born of a woman, born under the law, to redeem those who were under the law, that we might receive the adoption as sons.

Galatians 4:4–5

Set Your Sights:

God sent Jesus to redeem you from the law, meaning He paid the price to buy you out from under its legal ownership. It owned you. You weren't a hostage being held against your will. You were property, born into slavery with a debt you could never work off, hopeless until Jesus came and paid it for you. His passion assured your freedom and eliminated all claims of the law to return you to a life of slavery.

Freedom is something you receive. Don't over-spiritualize it. It simply means you believe you are no longer under the law and stop trying to live by it. You throw off the "must work for God's blessing" shackles and step out into the freedom of being the child He adores and cares for. It's letting Him do the work and loving Him for it.

Hit Your Mark:

A mentality of needing to earn healing will make receiving it difficult because the thought will perpetually haunt you that if you don't do enough, you don't deserve it. The truth is, you don't and never would … except for Jesus. But now, as His beloved child, you can live unbound by the law and its requirements. Think about His works, not yours, and experience His freedom today.

April 2

The Target:

And because you are sons, God has sent forth the Spirit of His Son into your hearts, crying out, "Abba, Father!" Therefore you are no longer a slave but a son, and if a son, then an heir of God through Christ.

Galatians 4:6–7

Set Your Sights:

The instant Jesus became your Lord and Savior, you were born again. Your old man died and a new man was born (2 Cor. 5:17). Into that newly-created spirit God placed the Spirit of His Son and the two became one (1 Cor. 6:17). You instantly became as Jesus is (1 John 4:17). Not in your mind and flesh, but in your spirit. That part of you is perfect.

Here and now, you are as Jesus is. Jesus isn't a slave. Neither are you. Jesus isn't sick. Neither are you. Jesus isn't defeated. Neither are you. In the natural, those things may not be your reality, but they are immutable spiritual truths.

Jesus is an heir, however, and so are you. If you were still a slave, you wouldn't have a right to anything the Master has. But as an heir, you have a right to everything. Every possession of the Father, which includes healing and freedom, belongs to you.

Hit Your Mark:

Take possession of the inheritance that is rightfully yours by stepping out of the old man's shackles and putting on the identity of an heir. You are His child, not His slave, and He has given you a vast inheritance. Recognize it. Own it. Expect it.

The Target:

Then they journeyed from Mount Hor by the Way of the Red Sea, to go around the land of Edom; and the soul of the people became very discouraged on the way.

Numbers 21:4

Set Your Sights:

On the tail of a miraculous deliverance from Egypt, the Israelites wander and are discouraged in the desert. After such a supernatural rescue, why were they discouraged? Was it because the journey was longer than expected and they were tired? Possibly. But even more so stands out the striking disparity between the rock water and manna sustaining them and the milk and honey God had promised.

They were measuring the faithfulness of God and the truthfulness of His promises with their circumstances, and He was coming up short in every way. Instead of the promises being a source of hope, they became a source of discouragement. They were comparing the two and blaming God for not matching up, which will always lead to disappointment.

Hit Your Mark:

It is tempting to react like the Israelites when it doesn't seem like you will ever reach your destination. If that is you today, return to the promise of healing that God has given you. Let it be your source of hope today, knowing that no matter what you are experiencing, His promise was true, is true, and will always be true until the day you receive it.

April 4

The Target:

Jesus Christ is the same yesterday, today, and forever.

Hebrews 13:8

Set Your Sights:

Other than Jesus, this statement cannot be applied to anyone who has ever walked this earth because everyone changes. Family members change. Friends change. You change. Whether for the good or the bad, shaped by life's experiences, inevitably, people change. They change their minds, their attitudes, their actions. But where people can be unpredictable, Jesus is not.

With this assurance that He doesn't change, you don't have to second-guess His intentions toward you regarding healing. Instead, you can have confidence that because He healed all who came to Him then, He will undoubtedly heal you now. If He did it then (yesterday), He is doing it now (today) and will continue to do so until He comes again (forever). He has not, and will not, change.

Hit Your Mark:

This knowledge is essential because if you're unsure if Jesus is still healing today, the question mark that lingers may keep you from receiving what He has to give. Jesus healed all through His word and His touch. Unchanged, He longs to do the same for you. Use this thought to erase the question mark in your mind: *Jesus is unchanged, so healing is available to me every day for the rest of my life … including today.*

April 5

The Target:

Now when He had said these things, He cried with a loud voice, "Lazarus, come forth!"

John 11:43

Set Your Sights:

Imagine the mourners watching as the stone was rolled away, their eyes and hearts overflowing with disbelief, so quiet you could hear a pin drop. Then, when Jesus cried out, "Lazarus, come forth!" you can bet every single person jumped out of their skin, letting out an audible gasp as His commanding voice cut through the thick silence and Lazarus appeared before them. Just imagine!

The same power that filled Jesus's words that day and brought breath into the lifeless body of Lazarus is the same power that fills your words today. It is the power of the Holy Spirit. Jesus knew the importance of the Holy Spirit and instructed you not to do life without Him (Acts 1:4–5). With the Holy Spirit, your words, like Jesus's, can accomplish what you send them out to do.

Hit Your Mark:

As a born-again believer, you have the Holy Spirit within you. So as your words align with God's words, He fills them with the power to change things. Change the atmosphere around you. Change that thing in your body. The power to change the unchangeable. Your words carry his power. Know it and put them to work.

April 6

The Target:

And he who had died came out bound hand and foot with graveclothes, and his face was wrapped with a cloth. Jesus said to them, "Loose him, and let him go."

John 11:44

Set Your Sights:

Shock and awe must have been the prominent expression on the spectators' faces as they witnessed the bandaged-wrapped Lazarus emerging from the clutches of death, covering their noses as the stench of decay radiated from the recently opened tomb. With thoughts of zombies and the walking dead flooding their minds, they were probably afraid of what they'd find after removing the graveclothes.

But consider this scene from another's perspective … the perspective of Lazarus.

From the moment Jesus called him out and he took his first breath, still lying on the slab in the tomb, he knew he was healed. He knew he was alive. All the people saw when he shuffled out of the tomb was graveclothes, the remnants of death. They couldn't see healing or life. All they could see and smell was death, but that didn't change what Lazarus knew to be true: Jesus had healed him.

Hit Your Mark:

It doesn't matter what anyone else thinks about your healing. It doesn't matter if they can see it or not. It doesn't matter if they agree with you or not. It doesn't matter if they think you're crazy for believing. All that matters is what you know, so don't let the opinions of others change what you know to be true: you are healed!

April 7

The Target:

Therefore He is also able to save to the uttermost those who come to God through Him, since He always lives to make intercession for them.

Hebrews 7:25

Set Your Sights:

Many think Jesus sat down at the Father's right hand after His earthly ministry and "clocked out" from His job as Savior. It's the "He's done everything He can do" philosophy, which heaps unwarranted and unbiblical pressure on the believer to perform perfectly. Let me assure you, Jesus is still very active on your behalf as He saves you completely, perfectly, and for eternity ("uttermost").

Jesus was active on the earth, dying on the cross for all your sins—past, present, and future. Now, in heaven, Jesus is active as your advocate. He is always standing on your behalf, His shed blood offered as the defense for your every misstep. There will never be a day, hour, minute, or second when you are not saved completely and forever because of His intercession.

Hit Your Mark:

Sometimes forgiving yourself for present sins is less challenging than past sins, and you feel you deserve whatever you get as a consequence or penance to pay. Sin has consequences, and a price must be paid, but every consequence was covered and every price was paid by Jesus, who continues to save you completely, perfectly, and forever.

April 8

The Target:

Then God saw everything that He had made, and indeed it was very good. So the evening and the morning were the sixth day.

Genesis 1:31

Set Your Sights:

When God created the earth and everything in it, it was very good. In fact, it was perfect. Sickness and disease were not mentioned when He spoke our reality into existence. God never said, "Let there be seasonal allergies!" Why? Because He didn't create them. You don't see the first hint of anything "not good" until after Adam and Eve sinned.

So where did the bad come from? When Adam sinned, he turned over the keys to the earth to Satan, giving him the authority to occupy and control it. He became the god (tiny "g") of this world (2 Cor. 4:4). Adam turned our earthly home over to the most horrible landlord that will ever exist, and when Satan took possession of his new property, he brought all his junk with him, including sickness and death.

Hit Your Mark:

Sickness does not ever come from God. Ever. It is the devil that comes to steal, kill, and destroy, and one of the ways he does that is through sickness (John 10:10). All God has to give you is life, and He has delivered it to you through the sacrifice of His Son, Jesus Christ. Know that today.

April 9

The Target:

But he who is joined to the Lord is one spirit with Him.

1 Corinthians 6:17

Set Your Sights:

When you were born again, God sent Jesus's spirit into your heart (Gal. 4:6). When that happened, your spirit and His spirit became one and the same. Since the Word and your spirit are one, you have an assurance that you are never alone. No matter how alone you feel, He is a permanent part of you, with you always, never to be separated.

It also means the Word, and all His healing power, is alive and active in your spirit man. Like a cauldron of water on the verge of boiling, the healing power of God simmers day and night. As you focus on the truths of the Spirit, healing power boils hotter and hotter until one day, it reaches the boiling point and spills over into your flesh, purifying all it touches.

Hit Your Mark:

How do you turn up the heat? By focusing on verses such as 2 Corinthians 5:16–17, Galatians 4:6, today's verse, and 1 John 4:17. They reveal you are one with Him and He is one with you. Don't miss this next point. It also means healing isn't coming from somewhere on the outside but from the Spirit working on the inside. Think about that today.

April 10

The Target:

The next day John saw Jesus coming toward him, and said, "Behold! The Lamb of God who takes away the sin of the world!"

John 1:29

Set Your Sights:

"Listen up!" John exclaimed. "What I'm about to say is important, and I don't want you to miss it!" He identified Jesus as the Messiah, the one God sent to cover your sins (think clean robe over a dirty body) and thoroughly take them away (clean robe over a squeaky-clean body) so you can rightly stand before God. This distinction is so crucial as you approach God regarding healing.

If you don't know you're right with God, you'll think you must work your tail off to earn the right to be in His presence. When you finally get there, cowering in shame at your imagined covered dirtiness, you'll plead your case on why He should heal you and then question whether you did enough to earn it. But when you know you are right with Him, squeaky clean outside and in, you'll run to Him boldly, confidently claiming your inheritance of healing (Heb. 4:16). And you'll get it.

Hit Your Mark:

Set aside what you feel today and focus on what you know. Your feelings are fickle and will seldom lead you down the path to truth. Only God's Word holds the truth about your standing with Him. You are right with Him. Completely clean. Today and always.

April 11

The Target:

Therefore take heart, men, for I believe God that it will be just as it was told me.

Acts 27:25

Set Your Sights:

To set the stage, Paul is speaking to a ship full of men in a dire situation. A terrible storm had been blasting them for two weeks straight. Their provisions were gone, their boat ripped apart, and they had lost all hope of survival. All the men were terrified except Paul. Why was he so confident they weren't all going to die? Because Paul believed God's word and knew it would come to pass.

God told Paul he would go to Rome and testify (Acts 23:11). He couldn't do that if he died in the storm, so he sailed through it unafraid, encouraging those around him. That is what a word from God will do. It will bring you joy and confidence through any storm and positively impact those around you. Your attitude will be contagious.

Hit Your Mark:

Are you in the middle of a storm today? What has God said to you? Has He given you images of teaching, dancing, working, or preaching? Has He called you to pastor or marketplace evangelism and it hasn't happened yet? Focus on those things and believe God that it will be just as He told you. And like Paul, you will see it come to pass.

April 12

The Target:

For we who have believed do enter that rest, as He has said: "So I swore in My wrath, 'They shall not enter My rest,'" although the works were finished from the foundation of the world.

Hebrews 4:3

Set Your Sights:

Maybe you're thinking *I don't even know what rest is.* Perhaps you've been trying to receive healing for so long that you are not resting and are exhausted. Maybe you've never experienced rest and have difficulty grasping the concept. Paul tries to help by comparing your rest to God's rest on the seventh day of creation.

Think about that day. God rested because He finished His work, not because He was exhausted. There wasn't a single thing left to do. Now think about a time you completed a big project—maybe you renovated a house or restored a classic car—and when you did that "last thing" to it, you stepped back, sighed in relief, and declared, "It's finished." Nothing left to do but relax and enjoy the finished project. That is rest.

Hit Your Mark:

On the cross Jesus said, "It is finished." Taking the liberty to paraphrase, He said, "That's it. The project is complete, and there's no more work for me to do." His spoken words are intended to lead you to rest. When you believe He did all the work, you will rest from yours, and that is when you will experience proper rest. (Insert big sigh of relief.)

April 13

The Target:

And He said, "My Presence will go with you, and I will give you rest."

Exodus 33:14

Set Your Sights:

The word "presence" in this verse translates as a face, so God is saying, "My face will go with you." What does He mean? He's painting a picture of His eyes fastened on you with industrial-strength glue, impressing that He's always watching out for you. He wants you to know there will never be a day when He'll be distracted and looking elsewhere. He'll never have to say, "Oops. Sorry about that. I wasn't paying attention."

Knowing God always has you in His sights should bring you rest. No matter what lies the enemy whispers in your ear, you are never alone. Sometimes you'll be tempted to believe that nobody cares and nobody sees you, that your life doesn't matter. This verse tells you otherwise. If He didn't love and care about you, He wouldn't have His eyes fixed on you.

Hit Your Mark:

Let this verse sink in today. As you meditate on the truth that God's eyes are fixed on you and you are never alone, feel the rest and peace that truth brings. Fix your eyes on Him because His are ever fixed on you.

April 14

The Target:

Brethren, I do not count myself to have apprehended; but one thing I do, forgetting those things which are behind and reaching forward to those things which are ahead, I press toward the goal for the prize of the upward call of God in Christ Jesus.

Philippians 3:13–14

Set Your Sights:

This verse holds the secret ingredient of Paul's success in his Christian walk and a key to the door of victory in yours: "but one thing I do." One thing. Paul was laser-focused and single-minded. He set his sights on the bullseye, not the rings around it. In other words, he was not distracted by anything happening to him or around him.

Distraction is one of Satan's favorite tactics. He skillfully uses his "Weapons of Mass Distraction" to keep you from receiving. Distractions will keep you running here and there, doing this and that, checking off your to-do list from morning to night, and they will eat up all your time for the Word and prayer. If he can distract you by keeping your sights focused on the minutia of life, he can keep you from hitting your target every time.

Hit Your Mark:

No matter how busy your schedule is, spend time with God in the Word and prayer. Make Him a priority and don't let anything interfere. Block out everything else. Turn off the phone and close the laptop. Shut the door on his distractions. Do this "one thing" every day and the distractions will get easier to ignore and your target easier to hit.

April 15

The Target:

For I am persuaded that neither death nor life, nor angels nor principalities nor powers, nor things present nor things to come, nor height nor depth, nor any other created thing, shall be able to separate us from the love of God which is in Christ Jesus our Lord.

Romans 8:38–39

Set Your Sights:

You can hear in Paul's words that he was fully convinced there was nothing he could do to make God stop loving him. He was secure in their relationship, confident God's love would never change. The following statement is an important concept to get deeply rooted in your heart: God loves you and nothing in the world will change that.

Knowledge of His love for you will cause uncertainty and fear to leave (1 John 4:18), resulting in a life free from the constant dread that you're not good enough and not doing enough. Not a single thing (including your past, present, or future actions) has the power to diminish His love. He loves you despite your flaws, failures, and shortcomings. Always and forever.

Hit Your Mark:

Like every other promise God has made, you will experience His unconditional love by accepting it as truth and letting it change how you think. His love and healing cannot be separated, so walking in His love means walking in His healing. And just as His love is an unchangeable promise, so is healing, and nothing in the world will change that. It is yours just as His love is yours … unconditionally.

The Target:

And Moses said to the people, "Do not be afraid. Stand still, and see the salvation of the Lord, which He will accomplish for you today. For the Egyptians whom you see today, you shall see again no more forever. The Lord will fight for you, and you shall hold your peace."

Exodus 14:13–14

Set Your Sights:

It is easy to miss the "suddenly" component of these verses. Moses was the bearer of God's message that the Israelites would see deliverance from the Egyptians today. Today, not tomorrow or the next day. To the people, it probably seemed as if the Egyptians had been pursuing them forever, until they were suddenly gone. In the blink of an eye, the waves of the Red Sea came crashing down and washed the enemy away. Never to be seen again.

You can expect the same. Your healing journey may seem long, but your today will come. Your suddenly will come. As God instructed the Israelites in verse 15—"Tell the children of Israel to go forward"— keep moving forward in faith, knowing that your enemies will be washed out of your life forever as the mighty waves of God's healing power come crashing down on them.

Hit Your Mark:

Look forward today. Don't look back on your enemy. Pay him no attention. It is just a matter of time before all of a sudden, you will see him no more forever. Eyes forward.

April 17

The Target:

The thief does not come except to steal, and to kill, and to destroy. I have come that they may have life, and that they may have it more abundantly.

John 10:10

Set Your Sights:

Keep it simple: If it is bad, it's from the devil. If it is good, it's from God. Using this reasoning, answer this question: Is sickness good? Easy answer. No, it's bad. Then sickness isn't from God because He gives the good, not the bad. Period. Ergo, all sickness is from the devil.

Deuteronomy 28:59–61 says sickness is a curse. Jesus calls sickness a form of bondage (Luke 13:16). Peter calls sickness satanic oppression (Acts 10:38). Sickness steals everything it can—life, money, families, joy.

In contrast to the curse, bondage, and satanic oppression the devil brings through sickness, God sent Jesus to bring you the zoe life, the life as He has it. If God has it, you can have it. He is incapable of giving you anything else. God is not to blame for sickness. It is the work of the devil.

Hit Your Mark:

See for yourself what the Word says about God giving you sickness for any reason, maybe to teach you something or make you more "Christ-like." Go ahead and ask God about it. He isn't afraid of your questions, and He's got all the answers you'll ever need.

April 18

The Target:

You watched me as I was being formed in utter seclusion, as I was woven together in the dark of the womb. You saw me before I was born. Every day of my life was recorded in your book. Every moment was laid out before a single day had passed. How precious are your thoughts about me, O God. They cannot be numbered!

Psalm 139:15–17 (NLT)

Set Your Sights:

Even if you've been told you were an "accident," you were no accident to God. Your parents didn't plan for you; He did. He knew everything about you before you existed in your mother's belly. You are His child, deeply cherished, the apple of His eye, and He crafted a beautiful, abundant life just for you (Jer. 29:11).

God's plan includes health and freedom, and He sent Jesus to ensure that the plan could be implemented. The enemy will try to steal any hope of that promised life by bringing sickness or disease, but those are not part of His plan for you and you don't have to accept them.

Hit Your Mark:

Think about what God has planned for your life—health, wholeness, peace—and recognize the bad stuff you may presently be experiencing is not in that plan. Since it's not in His plan, it shouldn't be in your plan either. Plan to be healthy. How do you do that? Start by seeing yourself healed and whole. Think as He thinks. Think healthy.

April 19

The Target:

The Lord has appeared of old to me, saying: "Yes, I have loved you with an everlasting love; therefore with lovingkindness I have drawn you."

Jeremiah 31:3

Set Your Sights:

God said to the Israelites and is telling you now that He will draw you with His grace, mercy, and favor. Romans 2:4 reflects this truth when it says God's goodness brings men to repentance. It is His goodness that draws men to Him. This is a truth that needs to be proclaimed with boldness throughout the whole world.

It is wrongfully alleged that sickness is initiated by God to teach you something, to make you stronger, or build your relationship with Him when there isn't a single instance in the New Testament where the sick were given anything other than healing when they came to Jesus. Jesus demonstrated the goodness of God every time, and people were drawn to Him because of it.

Hit Your Mark:

God longs for an intimate relationship with you and continually woos you with His goodness. Don't allow the work of the enemy, sickness and disease, to blind you to His goodness and separate you from His love. Instead, poke a stick in Satan's eye by using that sickness to propel you even deeper into the arms of your Father. The Father of all goodness.

April 20

The Target:

Moses was 120 years old when he died, yet his eyesight was clear, and he was as strong as ever.

Deuteronomy 34:7 (NLT)

Set Your Sights:

This is prime ammunition in combat against the world's view of aging. The world says as you get older, your eyesight will fade, your metabolism will slow down, your muscles will atrophy, your joints will ache, and your memory will deteriorate. That's not what the Word says, so you don't have to accept it.

You don't have to age the way the world ages. As a child of God, you are not of this world and, therefore, not bound to its rules of aging (John 17:16). You are part of the kingdom of God, operating under the rules of the King of Kings. Those rules are demonstrated in Moses, who had clear vision and unrelenting strength when he died at 120. That is what you can and should expect in your kingdom.

Hit Your Mark:

Get out of the "this is what happens when you get older" mentality. Purpose to never utter those words ever again. If what you're experiencing isn't part of your kingdom, go to your King and stand against it. You don't have to accept something just because science and the rest of the world say it is inevitable. The only inevitable thing is health as you keep your sights fixed on Him.

April 21

The Target:

A man with leprosy came and knelt before him and said, "Lord, if you are willing, you can make me clean." Jesus reached out his hand and touched the man. "I am willing," he said. "Be clean!" Immediately he was cleansed of his leprosy.

Matthew 8:2–3 (NIV)

Set Your Sights:

Reflecting the heart of the Father, Jesus told the man who had leprosy He was willing to heal him. Not only was He willing, but He healed him immediately. This may sound nonsensical, but as in this account, not only was God willing to heal you, but He healed you immediately. When you accepted Jesus, He touched and healed you. He came into your heart and immediate healing occurred as your old man was crucified and a new spirit was born.

Many people believe God is willing to heal them but that He hasn't done it yet because there's no evidence of it in their bodies. They discount the complete spiritual healing that took place and fail to recognize the importance that their born-again spirit is where all healing now flows from. Healing began there. Because that's where Jesus is.

Hit Your Mark:

You aren't waiting for healing. You have healing. You aren't waiting to be healed. You are healed. Despite what your body may tell you, this is an indisputable truth in your spirit man. Renew your mind to that truth, and you will draw the healing power of the Holy Spirit right out of your spirit man and into your body. No more waiting. Healing is for now.

April 22

The Target:

The mind governed by the flesh is death, but the mind governed by the Spirit is life and peace.

Romans 8:6 (NIV)

Set Your Sights:

This verse is very straightforward. If your mind is ruled by your physical senses, it will bring about things related to death, such as sickness, disease, depression, and lack. If your mind is ruled by the things of the Spirit, it will lead to something that relates to life and peace, such as health, prosperity, and freedom.

This verse echoes the vital truth that renewing your thinking changes you physically and mentally (Rom. 12:2). This change can be for the better or the worse. So if you are experiencing signs of death in your body (worsening condition) and soul (anxiety, fear), then you may be spending too much time thinking about the wrong things, the things that are at war with the truth in God's Word (Rom. 8:7).

Hit Your Mark:

That might sound like bad news, but it's not! It means you direct the changes in your body and soul with what you think. You can choose to allow death and fear or life and peace into your life. You are not at the mercy of anyone or anything when it comes to your thoughts. You decide. Choose life and peace by fixing your sights on the things of the Spirit (Phil. 4:8).

April 23

The Target:

My sheep hear My voice, and I know them, and they follow Me.

John 10:27

Set Your Sights:

Sheep are amazing creatures to observe while out to pasture. When they hear the voice of their shepherd, they respond immediately. They trust him because he is their leader. They follow him because they know he will lead them to food, shelter, and safety. Jesus, your Good Shepherd, leads you by His voice.

Notice it's not just some of His sheep who hear His voice. He's not picking and choosing a select few to experience the pleasure of His voice and the benefit of His leading. When He says, "My sheep hear," He means all His sheep hear. If you are His sheep, you can hear Him. Maybe His voice will come through a verse, a song, or another believer, but you can be confident He is speaking.

Hit Your Mark:

God will never speak anything outside of what is written in His Word, making the Word the best gauge to determine if the voice you hear is the voice of your Shepherd or the voice of another. The more familiar you are with His Word, the quicker you will recognize Him. Listen intently for His voice today and don't be surprised when you hear it. When you do, He will lead you into everything you need, including healing.

April 24

The Target:

He also brought them out with silver and gold, and there was none feeble among His tribes.

Psalm 105:37

Set Your Sights:

When God delivered the Israelites out of Egypt, there wasn't a feeble one among them. This means that of the millions of men, women, and children, from oldest to youngest, not a single one was worn out, weary, or about to fall down for lack of strength. Since sickness causes a person to be exhausted, you can infer that every Israelite was free from illness as they were escorted from bondage to freedom.

This event is a picture of the new birth. Just as God delivered the Israelites out of bondage with abundant provision and health, when you accept Jesus, you come out of Satan's bondage with nothing less. The way the Israelites were the day they left Egypt is the way you are the minute you are born again: Free from sickness. Free from poverty. Free indeed.

Hit Your Mark:

Meditate on this today and see the reflection of your life in this event. See God bringing you out of Egypt. See Him fixing what is broken and infusing you with the strength for life's journey ahead. God fulfilled His will for freedom and health in the Israelites and will do the same for you.

April 25

The Target:

You make known to me the path of life; you will fill me with joy in your presence, with eternal pleasures at your right hand.

Psalm 16:11 (NIV)

Set Your Sights:

The path of life is where you live life to the fullest. It's the path that leads to a robust, thriving, and successful life. If you are not on that path but instead find yourself trapped on the treacherous path of sickness, let me assure you there's another better path, and God wants to get you to it and keep you on it. You are not trapped.

God has a way off the dark path, which He'll show you through the leading of the Holy Spirit (John 16:13). It's His job to reroute you from one path to the other. He can show you the way as you spend time with Him in the Word and in prayer. As you do, you will hear His directions and the path of life will become clear before you. It is inevitable.

Hit Your Mark:

If you've spent enough time on the path of sickness and are ready for a change of scenery, the Holy Spirit is prepared to help you do that. Ask Him to show you the next step and to point you in the right direction. Maybe you need a revelation of His love or will to heal you. Whatever it is, He promises to make known to you the path of life.

April 26

The Target:

I will worship toward Your holy temple, and praise Your name for Your lovingkindness and Your truth; for You have magnified Your word above all Your name.

Psalm 138:2

Set Your Sights:

A powerful message is conveyed in this verse: God magnified His word above His name. The name of Jesus is so powerful that every knee will bow in heaven, on earth, and under the earth (Phil. 2:10), yet He elevates His Word above it. He places such emphasis on His Word for your benefit, so you can know the extent of your inheritance and His promises.

You have the words of God in written form, and they are just as powerful today as they were the day He spoke them and they were written. His Word holds all His promises and He is bound to keep them. It contains every answer to every question you will ever have. It holds all the healing you will ever need. If there's anything you need, you have it in the Word.

Hit Your Mark:

His Word is the most powerful thing on earth, yet it seems as if when a problem arises, people first run to the internet or the doctor for the solution. Those things are not wrong, but you have something far more effective and powerful to turn to. He has literally given you His words. Search for your answers there first and let Him show you the way through.

April 27

The Target:

The Lord is my light and my salvation;
*   Whom shall I fear?*
The Lord is the strength of my life;
*   Of whom shall I be afraid?*

Psalm 27:1

Set Your Sights:

David kicks this Psalm off by proclaiming God is his salvation, his deliverer, so he will not fear. He goes on in the chapter to paint a beautiful picture of God's faithfulness to deliver him from all the hazards and pitfalls of life. He had confidence that no matter what situation he got himself into or was plunged into by evil men, God would come through and rescue him. The certainty he had, you can have today.

David was called the man after God's own heart (Acts 13:22). He knew God, His nature and character. His relationship with God enabled him to face the lion, the bear, Goliath, and all the enemies that outnumbered and outpowered him without fear. David wasn't afraid to meet the challenge in front of him because he knew and trusted his God.

Hit Your Mark:

If you are facing a challenge and experiencing fear, you may be placing more weight on the challenge than on the faithfulness of your God. There is a straightforward remedy for this type of fear: Spend time with Him. Get familiar with His Word. Get familiar with Him. Fear will have no place and you'll confidently tackle every challenge when your sights are set on Him.

April 28

The Target:

Do you not know? Have you not heard? The Lord is the everlasting God, the Creator of the ends of the earth. He will not grow tired or weary, and his understanding no one can fathom.

Isaiah 40:28

Set Your Sights:

Sometimes on a healing journey, especially the long one, you can begin to feel as if you're getting on God's nerves. You may even hesitate to approach Him again for fear He will look at you in disgust and say, "Enough! You are really getting on my nerves! Stop bugging me with all your questions!"

If that has ever been your thinking, you are not alone, but let's bury that thought permanently. Notice what it says about God and growing weary. It says He won't. He will never become fed up with you or exhausted because of you. Not ever. You can't wear Him out. It doesn't matter how many questions you have or how long it takes; He is always in your corner and ready to fight for you.

Hit Your Mark:

Think about what that means today. You have a God who never gets tired of standing beside you through thick and thin, good times and bad. Through times of triumph and utter defeat, He is always with you and wouldn't have it any other way.

April 29

The Target:

For you are my hiding place; you protect me from trouble. You surround me with songs of victory.

Psalm 32:7 (NLT)

Set Your Sights:

The purpose of hiding is to not be seen. When you are in The Hiding Place, it's the devil who can't see you. He may be roaming around outside the security gates like a roaring lion, waiting for an opportunity to devour you (1 Pet. 5:8), but as long as you are hidden inside, he's completely blind to your existence.

People don't usually leave The Hiding Place intentionally. They check out when the trials of life or symptoms in their bodies scream for attention and they give in to them. When they believe the trial or the symptom above God's word, they step out from the bastion of safety with flashing neon signs around their necks that say, "Here I am, devil! Come and get me!" Focusing on the problem will expose you to the enemy.

Hit Your Mark:

If you've poked your head out of The Hiding Place and taken a few hits, if you've stuck an arm out to test the direction of the wind and been pierced by a dart of the enemy, that's okay. The Hiding Place is always open and filled with understanding, wisdom, and healing, so refocus your attention on Him and step back into hiding.

April 30

The Target:

My brethren, count it all joy when you fall into various trials, knowing that the testing of your faith produces patience. But let patience have its perfect work, that you may be perfect and complete, lacking nothing.

James 1:2–4

Set Your Sights:

Perfect doesn't mean flawless. Perfect means you're complete, whole, lacking nothing. Trials, in and of themselves, don't bring about wholeness. If that were so, everyone who faced a trial would be perfect. But two people can face the same problem, one coming out of it tougher and the other totally destroyed. It's not the trial, but their response to it, that determines whether patience works through them or the trial works them over.

Your God-given patience can work when you stick with the Word despite what you see or feel. Patience is easily understood as consistently enduring. Don't get me wrong. Enduring a trial and counting it all joy doesn't mean you should enjoy it. It means you don't cower away from it but face it head-on with a dogged determination to see it through. That is patience. And it will work.

Hit Your Mark:

The key word to think about today is patience. Consistently endure. Have patience by turning your eyes from the problem and onto God's word. As you do, you will feel yourself rest, and in that rest your patience will have its perfect work. Leaving you complete and whole, lacking nothing.

MAY

May 1

The Target:

And one of them, when he saw that he was healed, returned, and with a loud voice glorified God ... And He said to him, "Arise, go your way. Your faith has made you well."

Luke 17:15, 19

Set Your Sights:

Ten lepers had called on Jesus for healing and they all received it. But one of them, just one, was made whole because he returned to worship God for what Jesus had done. Jesus demonstrates through the one that healing is available for your body and soul, and wholeness and restoration are also.

This means whatever the enemy has stolen, Jesus paid the price to have it returned in full. In the case of the lepers, healing meant the leprosy was gone. But for one man, wholeness meant missing fingers, ears, or toes grew back in place. So for you, if a car accident left you with pain in your back, healing takes the pain away, but wholeness restores your spine to its original condition. Recognizing the difference is essential so you know what belongs to you.

Hit Your Mark:

God is not a God of halfway. Don't be content with just healing for a specific thing. Expect wholeness in your body. Don't just expect the outward symptoms to be healed; expect all the inward working parts to be made whole and restored to their God-designed function. Don't settle for anything but healing and wholeness.

The Target:

Oh, taste and see that the Lord is good;
Blessed is the man who trusts in Him!

Psalm 34:8

Set Your Sights:

Taste and see! David implores you to get it through your noggin that God is good and can be no other way. He isn't judgmental or unjust, and His thoughts about you are only good (Jer. 29:11). He isn't punishing you for your sins with sickness, and His goodness leads you to repentance (Rom. 2:4). He is good. All the time.

When you think of Him this way, you will begin to trust Him. Trust is vital because, as this verse says, it leads to His blessings flowing in your life. One of the definitions of "blessed" is happiness. Trust leads to happiness, which is desperately needed on any journey. Not the temporary enjoyment of the world but the sustaining joy of the Holy Spirit that will carry you through.

Hit Your Mark:

If you are unhappy today, you may not be putting your trust in God. Maybe you don't know what trusting looks like, so let's get you started. Begin by becoming rock solid in your mind that God wants you well more than you want to be well. That is a giant step for some and a baby step for others, but it is a step in the right direction to walk in His goodness.

May 3

The Target:

Therefore, since we are receiving a kingdom which cannot be shaken, let us have grace, by which we may serve God acceptably with reverence and godly fear.

Hebrews 12:28

Set Your Sights:

A kingdom represents dominion and authority, is ruled by a king, and has an established system of principles by which all its subjects live. If Jesus is your Savior, your King, you have already received and become a part of His kingdom (Luke 17:21). Through it, you are meant to rule and reign in this life with Him (Rom. 5:17).

Unlike the kingdoms of this world, yours cannot be shaken, which means it can't be overthrown. It is firm and stable. Possessing the kingdom within you means you have a source of order when your life is in chaos. You have a source of stability when you feel you're about to stumble and fall. If you'll choose to dwell there, the kingdom inside of you offers security, peace, and healing.

Hit Your Mark:

How do you dwell in the kingdom? First of all, recognize it's there. Second, receive by faith the security and peace it provides by not allowing the enemy to steal it from you through worry and anxiety. If Satan can keep you focused on what's happening around you and in your body, he can keep you from abiding in the blessings of the kingdom.

May 4

The Target:

Then the channels of the sea were seen,
The foundations of the world were uncovered
At Your rebuke, O Lord,
At the blast of the breath of Your nostrils.

Psalm 18:15

Set Your Sights:

After David was delivered from Saul's attacks, he artfully described God's unfathomable power to defeat his enemies and yours. The word "blast" describes the panting of someone who is infuriated. Imagine a bull letting off fierce warning snorts as it prepares to charge. When God snorts, a shock wave exposes the sea's valleys and lays the earth's foundations bare. With one snort.

Unlike David's many human enemies, your enemies are no longer flesh and blood (Eph. 6:12). You have one enemy, Satan and his evil works. God's anger towards his works has not changed, and His snort still lands the same devastating punch on them: it totally decimates, lays bare, and defeats them.

Hit Your Mark:

Play this verse out like a movie in your head. See God snort and envision the sea being pushed back and restrained, just like the parting of the Red Sea. Now see the same thing happen to whatever is trying to overtake you. See God snort and the power of the blast drive that evil far away from you, completely separating it from you. See yourself walking free as that thing shrivels up into dust. Totally decimated. Totally defeated.

May 5

The Target:

For I, the Lord your God, will hold your right hand,
Saying to you, "Fear not, I will help you."

Isaiah 41:13

Set Your Sights:

When holding someone's hand, you are generally right beside them. This is the picture God is trying to paint for you. He wants you to see He's not a distant God floating around in outer space somewhere, oblivious to you and your life. He is right there by your side.

For this very reason, He says to you, "Fear not. I've got you. Hold on tight to my hand and we'll walk through this together. I am here to help you every step of the way." You have no reason to fear anything. Don't let the enemy deceive you into thinking you are all alone and get you walking hand-in-hand with fear. Drop the hand of fear and reach again for the hand of the one who will help you.

Hit Your Mark:

You can choose fear today or focus on the fact that the God of the universe is holding your hand. When fear tries to rear its ugly head, speak this verse to it. Speak it until it becomes a part of you and you start to believe it. When you believe it, fear will flee and reveal the truth … you are never alone and there is no need to fear.

May 6 – Part I

The Target:

The hand of the Lord came upon me and brought me out in the Spirit of the Lord, and set me down in the midst of the valley; and it was full of bones. Then He caused me to pass by them all around, and behold, there were very many in the open valley; and indeed they were very dry. And He said to me, "Son of man, can these bones live?" So I answered, "O Lord God, You know."

Ezekiel 37:1–3

Set Your Sights:

God set Ezekiel in the middle of a valley full of skeletons and asked him if they could live again. Don't miss this. What Ezekiel thought mattered to God and ultimately to the outcome of this encounter. God was really asking: "Ezekiel, do you believe I can raise these bones up, put flesh on them, and breathe life into them again?"

In the natural, this was a ridiculous question. Most would have looked at the bones and replied, "No, Lord. Nothing can be done. The bones are too far gone." But Ezekiel believed God could do the impossible, so he acted on what God told him. And by the end of verse 10, an exceedingly great army stood before him. Resurrected. Restored. Ready to fight for their God.

Hit Your Mark:

You may be facing a situation that resembles a valley full of very dry bones, with no hope in the natural. But there is always hope with God. Today, purpose in your mind to believe your situation is not too far gone, you're not done yet, you will live and not die, and there is more than enough power in His word to heal you. See those dry bones rising today!

May 7 – Part II

The Target:

Again He said to me, "Prophesy to these bones, and say to them, 'O dry bones, hear the word of the Lord!'"

Ezekiel 37:4

Set Your Sights:

Yesterday we saw God set Ezekiel in the middle of a bunch of skeletons and ask him if he thought they could live again. Ezekiel said yes and that's where we pick up today, with God telling him what to do next.

God instructs Ezekiel to speak the word of the Lord to the bones. To speak His words, the words of life (Prov. 4:22), directly to that impossible situation. "Speak, Ezekiel, and I will back your words with My power and bring those dry bones back from the grave!"

The instruction to speak to things is seen frequently throughout the Word. You are told to speak to the mountain (Mark 11:23). Jesus demonstrates the power of speaking when he curses the fig tree and it shrivels up and dies (Mark 11:12–20). The power of the spoken Word subdued Satan in the wilderness (Luke 4:1–13). There is power in the Word when you speak it.

Hit Your Mark:

When you speak the Word to things, it has the power to usher in change. Today, speak to your situation and expect it to change. Speak to your mountain and expect it to move. Tell your dry bones to hear the Word of the Lord and live!

May 8 – Part III

The Target:

So I prophesied as I was commanded; and as I prophesied, there was a noise, and suddenly a rattling; and the bones came together ... the sinews and the flesh came upon them ... skin covered them ... but there was no breath. Also He said to me, "Prophesy to the breath...'Thus says the Lord God: "Come from the four winds...and breathe on these slain, that they may live."' "So I prophesied as He commanded me ... and they lived...an exceedingly great army.

Ezekiel 37:7–10

Set Your Sights:

From the last two days, you know Ezekiel believed in God and received instruction from Him. Today you see him follow God's instructions, acting on what he believed. Ezekiel spoke as God directed and the dried-up bones started to rattle. Then they came together. Then tissue and muscle appeared. Then skin covered them. Just imagine!

Ezekiel didn't just speak and *BAM!* perfectly whole people were standing there. It took place in steps. Small improvements. And even when the bodies looked human again, they were still empty shells devoid of life. Ezekiel could have given up there, not acknowledging what God had already done, but he saw it through to the end. God told him to speak breath into their lifeless bodies, so he did, and God did the impossible.

Hit Your Mark:

On your way to healing, it is easy to miss the minor improvements and call it quits. When you get discouraged, read this account of Ezekiel. Then find one little area of improvement and use it as ammunition to keep going. If you continue to believe and speak like Ezekiel, you will see what you believe for. You will see those dry bones live!

May 9

The Target:

For this purpose the Son of God was manifested, that He might destroy the works of the devil.

1 John 3:8

Set Your Sights:

From before the beginning of time, God knew dominion of the earth would go to Satan when Adam sinned and that every evil work would follow (2 Cor. 4:4). But God had the plan to save humankind and strike a death blow upon Satan's malicious schemes. The Word was His weapon, Jesus (John 1:1, 14), and His sights were set on defeating the devil.

Jesus's marching orders were to incapacitate and obliterate the works of Satan, and that's precisely what He did. He came into this world as flesh, lived a sinless life, and then gave that life for you, setting you free from the clutches of Satan. Jesus took every evil work imaginable into His body as He hung on the cross so you wouldn't have to.

Hit Your Mark:

You don't have to tolerate Satan's evil works. If you're experiencing contrary to what God has promised, remember that Jesus carried that very thing in His body for you. See Him hanging on the cross. See the evil work in you being transferred to Him. He took it and He destroyed it. You don't have to keep it.

The Target:

Jesus said to him, "Have I been with you so long, and yet you have not known Me, Philip? He who has seen Me has seen the Father."

John 14:9

Set Your Sights:

Hebrews 1:3 says that Jesus is the "express image" of God, an exact copy. He is the perfect representation of God, so what God would do is what you'll see Jesus do. Whatever you hear Jesus say is precisely what God would say. That's what these two verses mean.

When Jesus stretched out His hands and touched people, did He give them sickness and pain? Did He withhold healing from anyone? Did His words reflect a God of punishment or love and forgiveness? In His thirty-three-and-a-half years on this earth, Jesus took sickness and disease. Not once did He give it. All God has to offer is good and Jesus is proof of that.

Hit Your Mark:

If you are unsure of God's stance on sickness, slowly read through the Gospels of Matthew, Mark, Luke, and John, paying close attention to what Jesus says and does when presented with it. See for yourself how God views and responds to sickness. He is so against it He sacrificed His only Son to destroy it. Solidify that in your heart today.

May 11

The Target:

For with You is the fountain of life; in Your light we see light.

Psalm 36:9

Set Your Sights:

God is the fountain, meaning the source, of all life. All things were made through Him, and in Him all things are held together (John 1:3, Col. 1:17). Everything pertaining to life flows from Him. He is your source of nourishment, strength, refreshing, and healing. As you dwell in Him, He holds it all together. He maintains it. He sustains it.

God is also your light. What does light do? It reveals the things hidden in darkness. It illuminates the path ahead. It brings about the promise of a new day. His Word is the light that breaks you free from the darkness that binds you, lights your path so you can walk confidently without stumbling, and gives you hope with the dawning of each new day. His Word is your source and the light of your life.

Hit Your Mark:

If you are stuck, frustrated, or weary today, take time to meditate on this verse. Whatever you need, see it flowing freely from God's fountain of life. Feel the warmth of His light as it gently caresses your face. When you sit and rest by His fountain, spending time in His presence and drinking from its refreshing waters, you will be satisfied, you will prosper, and you will be healed.

May 12

The Target:

Whatever I tell you in the dark, speak in the light; and what you hear in the ear, preach on the housetops.

Matthew 10:27

Set Your Sights:

The revelations you receive during your journey are not meant to be kept to yourself but shouted from the rooftops, so think about how you can share what you have "heard in the ear" with others. Some people will take your revelations, apply them to their lives, and get healed even if you haven't seen it for yourself yet.

When it comes to sharing what you know, it doesn't matter if you have received healing or not. If God has revealed something to you through the Holy Spirit, it is up to you to spread that word like wildfire. Don't be stingy with it and don't be afraid to share it. Your revelation could be the final piece of someone's puzzle that enables them to receive, and that's what it's all about.

Hit Your Mark:

It is easy to fall into the trap of thinking you have to be outwardly healed before sharing what the Holy Spirit has taught you. The enemy whispers that people won't believe the message or tell you you're a hypocrite if you share, but that makes the message all about you. And it's not about you. It's about Him and the message He has given you to share, so be bold and share it!

May 13

The Target:

Do not be deceived, my beloved brethren. Every good gift and every perfect gift is from above, and comes down from the Father of lights, with whom there is no variation or shadow of turning.

James 1:16–17

Set Your Sights:

James is giving a stern warning to not be deceived. He knows if Satan can get you to believe something that isn't true, he can wreak havoc in your life. The specific deception James is warning about remains a prevalent lie that keeps many from receiving healing, namely, that God gives the good and also the bad.

James is vehement that God only puts good and perfect opportunities in your path. Trials may come, but not from God. Sickness may come, but not from God. If any doctrine teaches you otherwise, it's in error. When James says, "There is no variation or shadow of turning," that is his way of saying it's an absolute truth. No exceptions and they are not subject to change.

Hit Your Mark:

Sickness is not a good and perfect gift God will ever give you. He can't. It's not a part of His covenant with you, and He is all about keeping His covenant. Today, see yourself taking whatever you're standing against and putting it in a box with a nice bow. Hand it to the enemy and say, "Thanks, but no thanks. I'm returning this gift to you. I hope you kept the receipt." If it's not good, it's not God. Give it back.

May 14

The Target:

How God anointed Jesus of Nazareth with the Holy Spirit and with power, who went about doing good and healing all who were oppressed by the devil, for God was with Him.

Acts 10:38

Set Your Sights:

Building on the truth in yesterday's devotion, Jesus demonstrates what the good gift from above is by doing the good. What is the "good" He did? He healed everyone who came to Him. Healing is good. If sickness was good, Jesus would have given it to all the people and would have been doing wrong by healing them. That's just backward.

This verse clearly states where sickness comes from. Jesus healed all that were oppressed by who? The devil. The devil is the author of the bad, of sickness and disease. Whatever the devil has to offer is the complete opposite of what God has to offer. God offers to heal and the devil offers illness.

Hit Your Mark:

You can never return to this point enough: God is good. Sickness is bad. Thinking what you're struggling against came from Him can cause a hang-up in your healing, making it hard for you to resist, and maybe even lead you to accept it. Meditate on this verse today and know that what is plaguing you is from the devil. Reject it, turn to God, and expect the good.

The Target:

Yea, though I walk through the valley of the shadow of death, I will fear no evil; for You are with me; your rod and Your staff, they comfort me.

Psalm 23:4

Set Your Sights:

The valley of the shadow of death can be described as a land of pits and drought which no one has ever crossed (Jer. 2:6). Scary. But keep reading. David tells you not to fear because God is with you and will comfort you with His rod and staff.

David (once a shepherd) used his rod to count sheep as they came out of, and returned to, the fold. He also used it to protect his flock from predators. The staff was used to direct the sheep where to go, which was always the greenest pastures and purest water, and to rescue fallen or trapped sheep.

For you, the rod symbolizes how God counts you as His and is watching over you. The staff represents His guidance and assurance that He will pick you up when you fall and provide you with everything you need. His rod protects you and His staff delivers you.

Hit Your Mark:

Your Shepherd sees and protects you. When you need it the most in the valley, let that comfort you. When you think on this—not on the part where you're walking through a valley, but that He is with you and He's for you—you'll get through it. Together.

May 16

The Target:

Who has believed our report? And to whom has the arm of the Lord been revealed?

Isaiah 53:1

Set Your Sights:

Isaiah asked these questions because his report about the Messiah was too good to be true. He knew it would be difficult for people to comprehend that not only would He pay for all their sins, but He would be beaten so severely as to be unrecognizable as a human, suffering to ensure healing for their bodies and peace for their souls (Isa. 52:14, 53:5).

The "arm of the Lord" refers to the day warriors would "roll up their sleeves," baring their right arm up to the shoulder so they could fight without any hindrance. The arm represents God's omnipotence and power and was revealed through Jesus's death, burial, and resurrection. Jesus was God's arm and He fulfilled Isaiah's too-good-to-be-true report, making the power of God to save and heal available to everyone who believes.

Hit Your Mark:

Believing the correct report is essential. It's not a matter of positive thinking but accepting God's declaration over any symptom, doctor's statement, or circumstance. The world's report spreads only death and despair, but God's report says He saved you spirit, soul, and body. Put the world's report in the shredder today and choose to believe the report of your God. No matter what.

May 17

The Target:

For by grace you have been saved through faith, and that not of yourselves; it is the gift of God, not of works, lest anyone should boast.

Ephesians 2:8–9

Set Your Sights:

Grace is God's unmerited favor. Do you remember merit badges from the Scouts? They weren't handed out for nothing but had to be earned by completing specific tasks. God doesn't work on the merit-badge system, so He saved you by His unearned favor alone. Paul wanted to make sure you understood this, as evidenced by his two comments that being saved is "not of yourselves" and "not of works." Plain and simple.

Self-effort will not earn any aspect of God's grace. It is a gift, which means forgiveness, healing, and deliverance are gifts too. When you were born again, you freely received the gift of forgiveness by faith. It was a done deal and nothing could convince you otherwise. The same is true for healing. As surely as your sins are forgiven, healing is yours.

Hit Your Mark:

Believe it or not. It's up to you. Decide if you believe there's more to God's grace than forgiveness of sins and an eternity in heaven. Decide if you believe healing is yours because of the stripes Jesus took for you (1 Pet. 2:24). There is a difference between knowing and believing. Thinking about it is the first step to believing it.

May 18

The Target:

So Jesus answered and said to them, "Have faith in God. Truly I tell you, if anyone says to this mountain, 'Go, throw yourself into the sea,' and does not doubt in their heart but believes that what they say will happen, it will be done for them."

Mark 11:22–23

Set Your Sights:

The disciples just saw the fig tree Jesus had cursed withered and dead and they were astounded, so Jesus used it as a teachable moment.

First: Faith in God comes first. Not in your eloquent words, the number of times you speak, or the authority resonating in your voice. When your faith is in Him, you can have what you say. Speaking the Word will cause change, and when you feel like it the least, you usually need to do it the most.

Second: If you doubt when you speak, your mountain will not move. It is normal to have doubt and belief simultaneously (Mark 9:24), so the goal isn't to eliminate the unbelief. The enemy will continue to barrage you with thoughts of unbelief, but you can overcome them by meditating on His Word and through prayer and fasting (Matt. 17:20–21).

Hit Your Mark:

Don't rent space in your mind to any thought contrary to His promise of healing. Those thoughts are carriers of unbelief and need to be quickly evicted. Set your sights on any unbelief you may have today and begin to pick them off one by one by telling them exactly what God's Word says.

May 19

The Target:

Therefore I tell you, whatever you ask for in prayer, believe that you have received it, and it will be yours.

Mark 11:24

Set Your Sights:

Jesus continues the teachable moment from yesterday and tells you to believe that whatever you asked for is yours now. In other words, after you speak to your mountain and tell it to go, believe it's on its way out the door. Jesus demonstrated this very thing with the fig tree (Mark 11:12–25).

When He cursed the tree and seemingly nothing happened, He didn't say, "Well, that didn't work. I'll try something else." No. He spoke, believed, and moved on because He knew it was done, seeing it wither with His spiritual eyes.

Likewise, there's no need to try this and that. Simply put your faith in the Word you speak and see it as good as done. See it with your spiritual eyes first, even though you may not see it with your natural ones.

Hit Your Mark:

Believing you have received your healing starts with imagining you're healed and envisioning your body whole. As you saturate your mind with God's Word, you will reach a point where you don't even care what your body tells you because you know you're healed. That is seeing with your spiritual eyes, and that is when you know … that you know … that you know … you are healed.

May 20

The Target:

Though he fall, he shall not be utterly cast down; for the Lord upholds him with His hand.

Psalm 37:24

Set Your Sights:

There are times on your journey when you fall. Things aren't going the way you believe, so you give up. You feel lost and overwhelmed, so you stop believing. You stop resisting and start putting up with the symptoms in your body. You stop speaking and reading the Word. You have fallen.

In those times, run to this verse and find strength in that even though you've fallen, you won't be "utterly cast down" (in other words, left flat on your face and defeated) because God will lift you up with the power of His mighty hand. He will bring you help through a verse, an encouraging word from a friend, or a beautiful sunrise that gives you hope in the dawning of a new day. Another day to fight. Another day to live. One day closer to victory.

Hit Your Mark:

Be encouraged today that although you feel defeated, God will lift you up and sustain you. He has all the strength you need to continue the battle, so once again, fix your sights on Him. See yourself getting up off the ground and brushing yourself off. You will feel His strength and resolve return to stand another day as you do. You. Can. Stand.

May 21 – Part I

The Target:

Therefore, put on the complete armor of God, so that you will be able to [successfully] resist and stand your ground in the evil day [of danger], and having done everything [that the crisis demands], to stand firm [in your place, fully prepared, immovable, victorious].

Ephesians 6:13 (AMP)

Set Your Sights:

Yesterday we talked about falling and getting back up. It is no fun being knocked flat on your face, so Paul gives you the key to standing your ground once you are back on your feet: "Put on the complete armor of God." Not some of it. All of it. A warrior doesn't go into battle missing a piece of armor because that would leave vital parts exposed and vulnerable to the enemy.

As you look at each piece of armor over the next several days, you'll notice that the armor to protect your back is conspicuously missing. This is because you have to stand and face the enemy. Turning around in retreat will leave you wide open to his attack, so Paul tells you several times to stand. Stand your ground. Stand.

Hit Your Mark:

After you put on the armor, then you stand. You put it on and you stand. It's one thing to know what the armor is and another to know how to put it on and use it. If you don't know how to use it, it will be ineffective in protecting you. That's not what you want, so read Ephesians 6:14–17, familiarize yourself with the armor, and prepare to use it.

May 22 – Part II

The Target:

Stand therefore, having girded your waist with truth, having put on the breastplate of righteousness.

Ephesians 6:14

Set Your Sights:

During Bible times, men wore robes, not pants and shirts. When they fought, they would tuck their robes into their belts so they wouldn't get tangled up and fall down. Your enemy aims to trip you up by removing your belt (God's Word), which he does through deception. Your belt of truth keeps you from being tangled up by the enemy's lies.

The breastplate protected the heart and vital organs of the warrior and was attached to the belt. If the belt was loosened, the breastplate would fall off. It was only secure when the belt was firmly in place. When you know the truth, you know your right standing with God, and your breastplate is secure and your heart protected, propelling you boldly into battle with complete confidence He is on your side.

Hit Your Mark:

You put on and utilize the belt of truth by knowing what God's Word says about your situation and keeping your eyes fixed on that. The breastplate is secured by knowing who you are in Christ and by approaching Him boldly, knowing you are fully known, fully loved, and unconditionally accepted.

May 23 – Part III

The Target:

And having shod your feet with the preparation of the gospel of peace.

Ephesians 6:15

Set Your Sights:

In combat, balance and stability for the Roman soldier were vital components in avoiding an untimely death. To anchor themselves to the ground, they wore nail-studded sandals. When these military shoes were "shod" (bound on the foot), they provided traction for quick movement and the stability essential for successful hand-to-hand combat against the enemy.

The "preparation of the gospel of peace" is a call to have a firm knowledge of the gospel message. Knowing you are saved by grace and at peace with God will give you a firm foundation to set your feet on, even when standing on rocky ground. Knowing the gospel lets you quickly side-step the enemy's attacks and grounds you against whatever he may bring.

Hit Your Mark:

To put your gospel shoes on and experience His peace, get it in your heart that there is only peace between you and God because of what Jesus did. That gospel message will fasten your shoes snuggly in place, your footing secure and saturated with His peace, fully prepared to crush Satan under your armor-clad feet (Rom. 16:20).

May 24 – Part IV

The Target:

Above all, taking the shield of faith with which you will be able to quench all the fiery darts of the wicked one.

Ephesians 6:16

Set Your Sights:

The shield of apostle Paul's day, called a "door shield," was about two-and-a-half feet wide by four feet high. Made of heavy wooden planks that were glued together (as thick as a man's palm), it weighed between 13 and 22 pounds. When advancing in battle and overlapping their shields, soldiers created a massive wall that protected them from the most advanced weapon of that time: the flaming arrow.

Faith is the substance of your spiritual door shield, capable of stopping every one of Satan's fiery darts. Every. Single. One. Total victory in every situation. That's not to say you won't experience attacks from the enemy and get hit once in a while—this verse says you will—but it means you can triumph through Christ every time (2 Cor. 2:14).

Hit Your Mark:

Notice you take this piece of armor. It isn't handed to you, nor is it held for you. You take it and you hold it. You take it by continually placing God's word above everything you see or feel. You hold it up by speaking His word, especially when you don't feel like it, and believing even when you haven't seen it. Take up your shield and continue the good fight of faith.

May 25 – Part V

The Target:

And take the helmet of salvation, and the sword of the Spirit, which is the word of God.

Ephesians 6:17

Set Your Sights:

The helmet protects the most vital part of a soldier's body: the brain. The rest of the armor is useless in battle if the brain is damaged. Your helmet is the assurance of salvation, and it will protect your mind (the battlefield) against any lie the enemy throws at you, enabling you to take captive every thought that comes against what you know is true (2 Cor. 10:5).

The sword is the offensive weapon in God's armor that will kill the enemy. It is the spoken word of God, the words He speaks to you, that apply to your situation. If you'll notice, it is the Spirit's sword and He wields it. When you speak God's word in faith, you bring the Holy Spirit out swinging, and He is laser-focused on destroying the enemy's works.

Hit Your Mark:

You fasten and keep your helmet firmly in place by renewing your mind to what God's Word says about you, enabling you to reject doubt, replace old ways of thinking, and combat any confusion from the enemy. You take up the sword by speaking the Word in faith. After you speak, stand back because all that's left to do is watch as the sword of the Holy Spirit obliterates the enemy.

May 26 – Part VI

The Target:

Praying always with all prayer and supplication in the Spirit, being watchful to this end with all perseverance and supplication for all the saints.

Ephesians 6:18

Set Your Sights:

Paul reveals the final and least acknowledged piece of His armor: prayer. Prayer is a powerful part of your armor, so he instructs you to pray without ceasing (1 Thess. 5:17). That doesn't mean you shut yourself in your prayer closet from morning until night, which wouldn't be practical, but praying without ceasing is possible.

Prayer comes in many different shapes and sizes. There are prayers of thanksgiving and praise. Silent prayers and spoken prayers. Prayers of intercession. Prayers of faith and agreement. Prayers about something in a broad sense and prayers about something specific (supplication).

Always praying is possible when you see it as having a conversation with your God. It doesn't have to be with eloquent words, your eyes closed, and your hands folded. When you talk to Him with a heart directed towards Him, that is prayer.

Hit Your Mark:

Today, imagine God sitting in the chair next to you at your kitchen table or in the car or at work with you. Whatever you are doing, imagine Him there. Then simply talk to Him. Share your thoughts with Him. Share your ideas with Him. Share your concerns with Him. Share your life with Him. Pray. Always.

The Target:

Therefore submit to God. Resist the devil and he will flee from you.

James 4:7

Set Your Sights:

Notice the sequence of events: First, submit to God. Second, resist the devil. Third, he will flee from you. Many skip the submitting part and attempt to resist the devil in their own strength, then wonder why he's not fleeing. Submitting means surrendering your human viewpoint to His supernatural view. God doesn't want your submission because He's a dictator but because He's a loving Father who knows what's best.

After you submit, you resist. You resist the enemy by holding up your shield of faith (1 Pet. 5:9), activating the spiritual weapon of prayer, and employing the sword of the Spirit as Jesus did in the wilderness. How? Each time Jesus was tempted, His response began with "It is written." When you submit your thoughts to God and actively resist the devil by utilizing your full armor, he has to flee.

Hit Your Mark:

Submit to God by changing your natural thinking about your situation to reflect His supernatural thinking. Submit your thoughts to Him in every way. Then resist the devil. Don't accept what the enemy has given you. Don't give up and you will see the enemy's backside as he runs away, screaming like a little girl. Picture that today and smile.

May 28

The Target:

Brood of vipers! How can you, being evil, speak good things? For out of the abundance of the heart the mouth speaks.

Matthew 12:34

Set Your Sights:

The words you speak are a reflection of what's in your heart. If there is doubt in your heart, your words will be full of doubt. If there is life in your heart, they'll be full of life. Proverbs 18:21 says that life and death are in the power of the tongue. Put these two verses together and you see that power isn't present in idle words but only when what's spoken from your mouth is what you believe in your heart.

Speaking something that's not in your heart won't change anything. If you confess "By His stripes I'm healed" a million times but don't believe healing is for you, your words will be empty and powerless. But when you speak words that are charged by belief, words that flow out of you on the raging river of faith, they will bring about what you believe.

Hit Your Mark:

If you don't 100% believe something yet, don't stop speaking it. Your natural ears hear the Word you declare and can change what's in your heart. If your words fall flat, stop talking and look at your heart. Ask yourself if you really believe what you're speaking. If not, ask Him how to change that. If so, keep believing and keep speaking!

The Target:

Jesus said to him, "Rise, take up your bed and walk."

John 5:8

Set Your Sights:

Jesus told this man who hadn't walked for 38 years to do what was physically impossible. Jesus didn't lay hands on him or speak healing into his body. There was no prayer for healing and no touch. There was nothing tangible, just a simple command that, when followed, activated this man's faith and led to his healing.

In the Bible, people acted on their faith in different ways. For example, by stretching out a hand or walking blindly to a pool to wash their eyes (Matt. 12:13, John 9:7). The woman with the issue of blood determined how she would be healed. Then she acted on that belief (Matt. 9:20–22). She said, "If I can just touch the hem of His garment, I'll be healed." They all believed. They all acted. They were all healed.

Hit Your Mark:

An active response to Jesus's command will bring your faith to life. Sometimes it's difficult to know what "acting in faith" looks like. There's no canned response to this, and it will change from one person to the next, but what is universal is asking God to show you what it looks like for you. Just as He instructed these, He will instruct you. Go ahead. Ask. Then dance. Bend. Run. Jump. Stand. Speak. Have faith and do.

May 30

The Target:

And when Jesus came to the place, He looked up and saw him, and said to him, "Zacchaeus, make haste and come down, for today I must stay at your house."

Luke 19:5

Set Your Sights:

This verse says Jesus "looked up" and saw Zacchaeus. In Greek, the words mean more than tilting His head up to see him better. In other verses, the terms refer to people who are blind receiving their sight. Jesus wasn't blind, so what other sight of Zacchaeus was He looking for? A spiritual sight to see him the way God saw him.

When Jesus looked up, He didn't see what everyone else saw: a tax collector hated by all. He saw a humble heart and a man who believed in Him. That's what God does. He doesn't look at your physical appearance but your heart (1 Sam. 16:7). He doesn't look at your physical limitations but at who He created you to be and the plan He has for you.

Hit Your Mark:

If you were up in that tree and Jesus "looked up," He wouldn't see a weak, defeated, sick son or daughter. He would look right through the exterior to the heart of your being, where you are strong and whole. Look at yourself the way Jesus looks at you. "Look up" and use your spiritual sight to see past everything you see in the natural. See yourself strong and whole … just as He does.

157

May 31

The Target:

The centurion answered and said, "Lord, I am not worthy that You should come under my roof. But only speak a word, and my servant will be healed."

Matthew 8:8

Set Your Sights:

This centurion had a servant near death who Jesus was willing to lay hands on, but the centurion said, "Don't bother yourself to come, Jesus. Your word will be enough." Notice the words Jesus spoke weren't of healing over the sick man, but instead, He told the centurion to go his way and he would have what he believed. The centurion heard the words of Jesus, believed his servant would be healed, and acted in faith on what he was told.

He heard, believed, and acted. Simple, not complicated. Healing boils down to taking God at His word. It believes if He said it, He'll do it and bring it to pass (Num. 23:19). Don't let circumstances leave you questioning His faithfulness to do what He said He would do, because at the root of all faith is believing, unquestionably, His word.

Hit Your Mark:

It's easy to say, "Yes, I believe the Word," but have you made the conscious decision that if God's Word says it, that settles it no matter what? The centurion's servant was healed because the centurion believed the words Jesus spoke and acted on them. You have God's words to you. Hear, believe, and act on them. Then expect it to be done for you, just as He said.

JUNE

June 1

The Target:

For I also am a man under authority, having soldiers under me.

Matthew 8:9

Set Your Sights:

The man speaking to Jesus in this account was a centurion (Matt. 8:8). A centurion was a captain of 100 soldiers, so he had a working knowledge of authority. When he commanded his soldiers, they responded, "Yes, sir." Nothing more, nothing less. They wouldn't ask questions or second-guess him. He'd give the order and they'd carry it out.

The centurion knew Jesus had this kind of authority over sickness, to speak and see it obey. Authority to speak and see a fever leave, leprosy cleansed, or the dead raised. Through His passion, Jesus granted this same authority to you, backed by the power of His name, to destroy the works of the devil. He delegated you to rule over the enemy (Luke 10:19).

Hit Your Mark:

His name holds the authority, His Word contains the power, and He has given you both. Knowing you have authority over the devil should ignite your faith and change your attitude. You are not defeated. On the contrary, you can tear down and utterly destroy the enemy's plots against you. When you believe it and use your God-given authority, sickness will listen like a good soldier.

June 2

The Target:

Now this is the confidence that we have in Him, that if we ask anything according to His will, He hears us. And if we know that He hears us, whatever we ask, we know that we have the petitions that we have asked of Him.

1 John 5:14–15

Set Your Sights:

You don't have to ask God for healing because He has already given it to you through the stripes of Jesus (1 Pet. 2:24). Past tense. Already done. Asking Him for healing would be like asking Him to give you a beating heart. You don't ask Him for it because you know you already have one. But that's not the takeaway.

This is: He hears you. When you speak, He hears you. When you pray, He hears you. When you snore at night, He hears you. There is never a time when He is not listening for your voice. He hears you from when you mumble your first groggy word in the morning until your last sleepy word before you drift off at night. You can speak and be confident that He is always listening.

Hit Your Mark:

Believing He hears you is an important factor in you hearing Him. If you don't believe He's listening, this is a great verse to stand on to get that truth rooted deep within you. If you have asked anything according to His will—maybe for wisdom or next steps (James 1:5, Isa. 30:21)—believe He heard you and He will respond. Expect Him to hear you. Then expect to hear Him.

The Target:

*Cause me to hear Your lovingkindness in the morning,
for in You do I trust;*

*Cause me to know the way in which I should walk, for
I lift up my soul to You.*

Psalm 143:8

Set Your Sights:

This verse is built on two if-then statements: If you do this, then you receive that. The first statement says that if you trust in God, you will hear His lovingkindness in the morning. Only by putting your confidence and belief in God can He bring you into the knowledge of the grace, goodness, and devotion He feels toward you.

The second statement says if you lift up your soul to Him, you will know how you should walk. Lifting up your soul means you desire Him above all else in the deepest recesses of your mind, will, and emotions. It means you yield your thoughts to His thoughts and your will to His will. Your path will be clearly laid out before you as you do that.

Hit Your Mark:

By nature, your soul doesn't naturally trust or desire Him. It is independent, depending only on itself, and cannot lead you to love and victory. As you train your soul to think and respond like Him, growing in trust through time spent in His presence, you will understand His deep affection for you and confidently put one foot in front of the other, the way to healing coming into focus in front of you.

The Target:

"And often he has thrown him both into the fire and into the water to destroy him. But if You can do anything, have compassion on us and help us."

Jesus said to him, "If you can believe, all things are possible to him who believes."

Mark 9:22–23

Set Your Sights:

This man brought his demon-possessed son to Jesus and asked Him if He could do anything. Jesus knew it wasn't a matter of if He could do it or not—He knew He could—but rather a matter of what the man could believe. The boy's healing didn't depend on the ability of Jesus but on the father's faith in Jesus to heal him.

Faith was the common denominator when people were healed in Jesus's day, and that principle has not changed today. Unfortunately, many are praying the faithless "Oh, God, heal me" prayer, but God's response to that prayer will always be, "Healing is yours. And if you can believe in what my Son did, you will have it." It is inevitable because it is the Word.

Hit Your Mark:

It's a fact. Believing can be challenging. If it wasn't, faith wouldn't be called a fight (1 Tim. 6:12). So when the battle drags on, and you're finding it hard to believe, turn your eyes to this promise that says if you do this one thing, believe in Him, anything is possible. Then no matter how dark the situation, your belief will release Jesus's healing power inside you to permeate every cell of your body. Just believe.

The Target:

Wherefore seeing we also are compassed about with so great a cloud of witnesses, let us lay aside every weight, and the sin which doth so easily beset us, and let us run with patience the race that is set before us.

Hebrews 12:1

Set Your Sights:

Hebrews 11 starts with this: "Now faith is the substance of things hoped for, the evidence of things not seen." The chapter gives numerous examples of people who put that God-kind of faith into action—Noah, Abraham, and Moses (just to name a few). They were ordinary people with nothing special about them except they believed in God, but their actions demonstrated the powerful combination of God's word and faith.

You are surrounded by this vast array of witnesses who proved the strength and genuineness of their faith through their actions. They faced impossible situations, terrible odds, and severe opposition and yet stood firm because they believed in God and the power of His word. They are there for you to study and learn from, encouraging you to keep the faith. They are there to tell you to never quit believing.

Hit Your Mark:

Read through Hebrews 11 and ask the Holy Spirit to highlight one example. Maybe it will be Sarah, Enoch, or Gideon. Whoever it is, take the time to read about their life. Look at the trial they faced and pay particular attention to how they responded to it. They are your example today of how to stand in faith.

June 6

The Target:

For what if some did not believe? shall their unbelief make the faith of God without effect? God forbid: yea, let God be true, but every man a liar.

Romans 3:3–4 (KJV)

Set Your Sights:

Paul used the phrase "God forbid" to express a passionate denial of the question: If people don't believe God, does that nullify His faithfulness to His word, making His promises untrue? His answer was an emphatic no. He is faithful and His promises are irretractable even when you are faithless (2 Tim. 2:13).

Paul said, "Let God be true." The understood subject of this sentence is "you" let God be true. You choose the truth of His faithfulness over everything else. Let God's word be true over the symptoms in your body. Let it be more true that by Jesus's stripes, you were healed (1 Peter 2:24), than the negative lab report you received. Don't let your problems be your truth. Let God's word be true and everything else a lie.

Hit Your Mark:

When anyone or anything (including your body) speaks something contrary to a promise in God's Word, recognize it as a lie from the enemy and reject it. In every part of your life—health, finances, freedom—believe His word above whatever you hear, see, or feel. Speak this declaration over yourself today: I don't care how I feel. I choose to believe God's word is the truth.

The Target:

And Peter answered Him and said, "Lord, if it is You, command me to come to You on the water." So He said, "Come." And when Peter had come down out of the boat, he walked on the water to go to Jesus.

Matthew 14:28–29

Set Your Sights:

Peter had grit and wasn't afraid to ask for the impossible from Jesus. When he got out of the boat, he didn't walk on the water by his own power, and the water didn't instantly turn into a solid surface that kept him from sinking. Two things kept Peter from going under: Jesus's word and his faith in that word.

Jesus said, "Come." That one word generated enough power to defy the law of gravity and hold a full-grown man out of the water, and the power would have gone untapped if Peter hadn't taken a literal step of faith. But as Peter fixed his eyes on Jesus and stepped out onto the water, every step he took was held up by the power of Jesus's word and brought to life by his faith in it.

Hit Your Mark:

Acting in faith on the healing God provides ensures that the power of the Word to work in your life doesn't remain dormant. I don't know what acting on faith looks like for you, but God does. Spend some time with Him and ask Him to give you your word, the word you can put your faith in, and then act on it. Go ahead ... step out of the boat.

June 8

The Target:

To those who have obtained like precious faith with us by the righteousness of our God and Savior Jesus Christ.

2 Peter 1:1

Set Your Sights:

Peter is talking to you. Yes, you. When you were born again, you were given a gift of faith (Eph. 2:8). When he says you have "like precious faith," he means your faith is equal to his. The same. Identical. Whether you feel like it or not, it is true. Need another verse to convince you?

Romans 12:3 says you have been given the/a measure of faith. Whether it's "the" or "a" doesn't really matter because God doesn't play favorites. The measure He gives to one, He gives to all. And that measure is enough.

Peter's faith is a mirror of your faith. What his faith did, your faith can do. For starters, Peter walked on water and raised a woman from the dead (Matt. 14:29, Acts 9:40). Not too shabby! You have that same miracle-working faith that enables you to receive every single promise of God.

Hit Your Mark:

Stop trying so hard to get more faith. Satan will lie and tell you your faith isn't enough, convincing you to get on an endless cycle of chasing what you already have. Meditate on these verses until you realize you already have all the faith you need. Once you believe it, start using your faith by acting on the Word you know.

June 9 – Part I

The Target:

But when he saw that the wind was boisterous, he was afraid; and beginning to sink he cried out, saying, "Lord, save me!"

Matthew 14:30

Set Your Sights:

Over the last several days, you learned Peter had water-walking faith, and today you see him sinking. The cause of his faith failure is something to take careful note of. When Peter first stepped out of the boat, his eyes were fixed on Jesus, pushing out all doubt that the impossible was not only possible but doable. But the moment he turned his eyes to the boisterous wind, fear rushed in like a tidal wave and overcame his faith, making it ineffective; hence, the sinking.

Keeping your eyes on Jesus is the most important factor in receiving God's promises. As Peter demonstrated, that one thing determined whether he walked on water or got wet. You have all the faith you need to receive your healing, but as long as you are constantly focused on something other than the Word (the symptoms, lab reports, what others say about your healing), you will continue to sink, or at the least tread water and remain unchanged.

Hit Your Mark:

Don't be content to tread water. Get your eyes fixed again on Jesus, on God's promises, and take your focus off of the wind whipping around you. Rise up out of the water and walk.

June 10 – Part II

The Target:

But when he saw that the wind was boisterous, he was afraid; and beginning to sink he cried out, saying, "Lord, save me!"

Matthew 14:30

Set Your Sights:

Peter walked on the water and then promptly sank. One moment, victory. The next, failure. What was Jesus's response to Peter? Did He say, "You really messed that up, Peter, so you can get back to the boat yourself"? How about, "That will teach you. Choke on some water and maybe you'll do better next time."

No. Jesus immediately reached out His hand (v. 31), took hold of him, and pulled him out of the water. Then they walked back to the boat ... together.

Everyone has moments of victory and moments of defeat in their journey. That's completely normal, so don't come under condemnation when you have a bad day and miss it. God doesn't expect perfection from you, and He won't let you sink. He will always take hold of you and keep you from going under.

Hit Your Mark:

If you're down because you think you've failed and it feels like you're rapidly sinking, spend some time thinking about Matthew 14:28–31 today. Tell yourself that God is not condemning you, so neither should you. Allow Jesus to reach out His hand and pull you out of the water. Then walk with Him, hand in hand, back to the boat ... back to safety ... back to healing.

June 11 – Part III

The Target:

And immediately Jesus stretched out His hand and caught him, and said to him, "O you of little faith, why did you doubt?"

Matthew 14:31

Set Your Sights:

Peter walked on the water, yet Jesus called his faith "little." Mindboggling! His great faith turned little when he took his eyes off Jesus and focused on the raging wind swirling around him. That will cause water-walking faith to become "little" every time. Little compared to the fear and unbelief that will surely come from focusing on what is contrary to what you believe.

Abraham, on the other hand, got it right. Romans 4:19 says, "And not being weak in faith, he did not consider his own body, already dead (since he was about a hundred years old)." He was strong in faith because he didn't focus on the problem but on the promise (Rom. 4:17, 20). As demonstrated by these two godly men, what you look at directly impacts the effectiveness of your faith, and looking at anything but Jesus will cause you to sink every time.

Hit Your Mark:

Don't allow physical circumstances to empower fear and unbelief to hinder your ability to effectively use your faith to receive. Look to Abraham as your inspiration, stop thinking about the storm within or around you, and put your eyes back on Jesus and the promise. Looking at Jesus results in great faith. Set your sights, once again, on the Word.

June 12

The Target:

Then Abram fell on his face, and God talked with him, saying: "As for Me, behold, My covenant is with you, and you shall be a father of many nations. No longer shall your name be called Abram, but your name shall be Abraham; for I have made you a father of many nations."

Genesis 17:3–5

Set Your Sights:

God told Abraham, "I have made you a father of many nations." Notice His word choice. He didn't say I will make you, but I have made you. That's how God's faith works. He calls things that are not as though they already were (Rom. 4:17). According to God's promise, and in God's eyes, Abraham was the father of many nations, so that's what He called him.

In his old age, Abraham could have responded, "This is a great promise, God, but we are way too old. Maybe try the young couple living down by the well." But Abraham knew God, so he believed what God said and then became what God said. He spoke what God spoke, calling himself Abraham, and became the father of many nations. He lived the promise.

Hit Your Mark:

Just like Abraham, God gave you a promise and called you "healed" (1 Pet. 2:24). Follow Abraham's lead and call the things that are not as though they were. Even if your body disagrees, you can confidently declare, "I am healed because that's what God has declared about me." That's not denying the symptoms or being a hypocrite; it's simply speaking a truth that God has already spoken.

June 13

The Target:

On the last day, that great day of the feast, Jesus stood and cried out, saying, "If anyone thirsts, let him come to Me and drink. He who believes in Me, as the Scripture has said, out of his heart will flow rivers of living water."

John 7:37–38

Set Your Sights:

There are days the journey seems long and hard. Maybe it *has* been long and hard. Perhaps it's a fight every single day to hold up your shield of faith, and it's tempting to lay on the couch and binge-watch your favorite show on those rough days. If it's one of those days, this verse is for you. If not, lock it away in your memory bank so it's there when you need it.

Jesus says rivers of living water will flow out of the hearts of those who believe in Him. The Holy Spirit is the river (John 7:39), and what will flow is His fruit—in particular, joy, peace, and endurance (Gal. 5:22–23). The fruit isn't something you have to conjure up or fake, but it will freely flow when you believe in Jesus and focus on God's word.

Hit Your Mark:

This truth will set you free (John 8:32) to walk through the day with a joy that comes from deep within, a peace the world could never understand, and a renewed determination that will give you more than enough strength to hold up your shield of faith another day. Don't stay on the couch. Get up. Start speaking the Word and feel the fruit of the Spirit stirring inside you as you believe in Him.

June 14

The Target:

You have also given me the necks of my enemies, so that I destroyed those who hated me. They looked, but there was none to save; even to the Lord, but He did not answer them. Then I beat them as fine as the dust of the earth; I trod them like dirt in the streets, and I spread them out.

2 Samuel 22:41–43

Set Your Sights:

This passage's picture, framed by the preceding verses, is one of strength, domination, and power. It displays utter victory in battle, not just somehow managing to barely eke out a win by the skin of your teeth.

Victory is yours because you don't wage this battle under your own power. God is your strength and power (v. 33), He teaches you how to fight (v. 35), and He makes sure your feet won't slip in battle (v. 37). Best of all, He has given you the necks of your enemies.

Whatever you are experiencing that is contrary to the blessings of God is your enemy. Notice it says He has given you their necks, so there's no need to strive against them in an attempt to overcome them on your own. Their defeat is a gift from the God who has conquered them all.

Hit Your Mark:

Today, see yourself clutching your enemy in your hand and carrying out verse 43. Beat it until it is nothing more than dust. Throw it on the ground and stomp on it until it is absolutely pulverized under your feet. This is the power and authority you have from Him and through Him. He has given you your enemies. Accept it. Receive it. Finish it.

June 15

The Target:

For we are His workmanship, created in Christ Jesus for good works, which God prepared beforehand that we should walk in them.

Ephesians 2:10

Set Your Sights:

Even before you were a thought in your parents' minds, God knew your story from beginning to end, including every good work you would do in His name to show His love to a lost and dying world. He created you to be uniquely you and perfect. This can be said with certainty because you are His workmanship, and everything He crafts is perfect.

Perfection means no pain and weakness, no sickness and disease. God prepared good works for you and intended you to walk in health, with a strong mind and body, as you accomplished them. His plan never included a storyline of sickness. Sickness is the antagonist, the evil villain, that was written in by the enemy and was never a part of your original story.

Hit Your Mark:

Pull out the original storyline God wrote for your life, with plans to walk in health and strength. If those characteristics don't define your life, somewhere as the plot thickened, the enemy hijacked and rewrote part of your story. But his story is not set in stone. God's is. Disregard the devil's revised version, and begin to read, once again, the perfect storyline of your God.

June 16 – Part I

The Target:

The Lord is not slack concerning His promise, as some count slackness, but is longsuffering toward us, not willing that any should perish but that all should come to repentance.

2 Peter 3:9

Set Your Sights:

The sovereignty of God is among the most dangerous doctrines in circulation. It wrongly contends that God is exerting His supreme power by controlling everything. Everything. If it happens, He did it. Cancer, rape, abortion … all Him. This doctrine is not scriptural and creates passive, come-what-may believers. Today's verse demolishes that false doctrine.

It says God isn't willing that anyone should perish, but many are perishing. If God controlled everything, especially since it's His will, He'd force everyone to be saved so they didn't perish. But He doesn't. Because He's not sovereign in that way.

Absolute, the most exalted, and having supreme authority and power are all words rightly describing the sovereignty of God. Under those definitions, God is absolutely sovereign. Without a doubt. No questions asked.

Hit Your Mark:

God is sovereign, but He does not control everything. If you've been taught this, get in the Word and let it reveal the truth. Don't sit back and let the world happen to you and attribute it to Him. Don't let the enemy run over you one more day because of this lie. God isn't the cause of your problem. He's your solution.

June 17 – Part II

The Target:

For You, Lord, are most high above all the earth; You are exalted far above all gods.

Psalm 97:9

Set Your Sights:

Let's apply the sovereignty of God specifically to healing. A wrong belief says God gives you sickness, but only because He has a perfectly good reason. That lie slanders the very nature of God and will hamper your trust in Him. How can you trust someone who causes pain and suffering? It will also lead to passivity and prolonged sickness as you think, *God gave me this sickness, so I'll bear the burden until He decides to take it away. What will be will be.*

In rebuttal, you might cite the Old Testament, where God struck people down with plagues. It is true that before Jesus came, sickness was part of the curse and used as punishment for disobedience. But when Jesus became the curse for you (Gal. 3:13), you were brought out from under it and the penalty that came with it. God will not use sickness to punish you.

Hit Your Mark:

God heals, not hurts. You are blessed, not cursed. If you're dealing with something in your body today, tell God you know it wasn't from Him, that you trust in Him, and ask Him to show you the way through it. He didn't bring it, and He will get you past it.

June 18

The Target:

Therefore if any man be in Christ, he is a new creature: old things are passed away; behold, all things are become new.

2 Corinthians 5:17

Set Your Sights:

When you were born again, something passed away (died) and something became new. You know your old man was crucified (died) with Christ when you believed (Rom. 6:6), but what was made new? You didn't instantly get a glorified body, and your mind didn't suddenly know everything, so there's only one part left that could have been created brand new: your spirit.

Your old spirit didn't just get a thorough overhaul. Rather, it was removed and replaced by a new spirit that is righteous, holy, perfect, and complete (Eph. 4:24, Heb. 12:23, Col. 2:10). It is flawless and overflowing with all the promises of God. Your spirit, the real you, is healed and whole, which is why you can say, "I am healed," even when symptoms are raging in your body. That isn't denying the symptoms, but speaking the truth from God's Word.

Hit Your Mark:

Spend today thinking about these verses and accept them as the real you. Renew your mind to them and speak what God says about you ("I am healed!") with confidence and authority, knowing that it is the truth in your spirit man. When you believe that above all else, what is true in your spirit can become a reality in your body.

June 19

The Target:

For "who has known the mind of the Lord that he may instruct Him?" But we have the mind of Christ.

1 Corinthians 2:16

Set Your Sights:

The fact is, you don't know all things in your mind. The truth, however, is you do know all things (1 John 2:20). You have the answers to all questions and the solutions to all problems. The wisdom of God is at your fingertips. You're thinking, *If I really have His wisdom, where is it and how do I access it?* The answer is tied to yesterday's devotion.

When you were born again, your spirit was created in absolute wisdom according to the likeness of God (Col. 3:10). This simply means the mind of Christ is in your spirit, not your brain. You access His perfect wisdom by studying and meditating on the Word (Rom. 12:2). As you do, it will begin to dominate your old way of thinking and give you a new perspective: His.

Hit Your Mark:

Having the mind of Christ is like having a friend who knows everything. If you have a problem, they have the answer. If you need something fixed, they can fix it. In essence, that is precisely what you have inside you: An all-knowing friend who is always right and always there for you. Start telling yourself you do have the mind of Christ and start pursuing His wisdom today.

June 20

The Target:

The thief does not come except to steal, and to kill, and to destroy. I have come that they may have life, and that they may have it more abundantly.

John 10:10

Set Your Sights:

There are thieves in this world, but safeguards are available to protect people and their homes, such as safes for irreplaceable items, security alarms, and weapons for self-defense. When a thief breaks into a home that's prepared, the alarm goes off, the possessions are secure, and if someone is home, they have a weapon to defend themselves, armed with a fierce determination to protect what belongs to them.

In the spirit world, the thief is Satan and he has one purpose: steal from, kill, and destroy you. For now, your body is your home. Sadly, many people are ill-prepared to fend off his attacks and lack the resoluteness to protect them. They let him right in the front door through ignorance because they don't know how to effectively use the primary weapon in their hand, the Word, to drive him out of their house.

Hit Your Mark:

See what you are standing against for what it truly is: an intruder, a thief invading your house. It wants to kill you. Get mad. Get protective of your body. Pick up your weapon, the Word of God, and beat that thing over the head until it retreats in defeat and hightails it for the door. It doesn't belong there. Tell it that and don't allow it to stay.

The Target:

Then Peter arose and went with them. When he had come, they brought him to the upper room. And all the widows stood by him weeping, showing the tunics and garments which Dorcas had made while she was with them. But Peter put them all out, and knelt down and prayed. And turning to the body he said, "Tabitha, arise." And she opened her eyes, and when she saw Peter she sat up.

Acts 9:39–40

Set Your Sights:

Here's the scene: Peter is summoned to the home of Dorcas, a deeply loved woman in the Joppa community who became sick and died. He is standing by her body, surrounded by weeping women mourning her death and lamenting over all the beautiful things she has done. They tell him how much she'll be missed and how terribly grieved they are over the loss.

The room is thick with despair, so the first thing Peter does is clear the room. In doing that, he removes the grief, a notable distractor of faith, from his sight. The second thing he does is humble himself before God and pray so he can hear His direction. Only then does he speak and raise Dorcas from the dead.

Hit Your Mark:

Set Peter's route to results into your personal navigation system. First, remove the distractions that cause your faith to waver. Second, turn your attention to God in prayer and listen for His guidance. Third, do what He tells you to do. Do it. Speak to your mountain, go to the doctor, or stand on a particular verse. Then repeat the route until you see the victory!

June 22 – Part I

The Target:

Therefore I say to you, whatever things you ask when you pray, believe that you receive them, and you will have them.

Mark 11:24

Set Your Sights:

This verse identifies two critical points in time: In the present, you pray and believe, and in the future, you have it. Many become discouraged when they pray and don't see immediate results, thinking it didn't work. Their belief is based on whether they see it, but that's backward. Seeing it is based on whether you believe.

When the "you will have them" comes to pass is different for everyone. It may come right away or take a while. The key is believing before you actually see it, just as 2 Corinthians 5:7 says: "For we walk by faith, not by sight." So when you pray, if you believe you received and then continue believing in the absence of any outward change, you will see what you're believing for become a reality. Asking in prayer, first. Believing, second. Having it, third.

Hit Your Mark:

Continuing to believe is the hardest thing to do on your journey until you genuinely believe you have what you prayed for. There is no more waiting when you believe you have received your healing. No more monitoring for change. No more wondering when it will happen. You know you will have it when you truly believe it's a done deal.

June 23 – Part II

The Target:

Therefore I say to you, whatever things you ask when you pray, believe that you receive them, and you will have them.

Mark 11:24

Set Your Sights:

Believing without seeing may seem impossible in the natural, but you actually do it every day. You turn on the television, believing electromagnetic waves will bring you a picture. You believe you have a brain, but you've never seen it.

Imagine this: You're admiring the stars in the sky and notice the moon is just a sliver. If someone came along, could they convince you that part of it disappeared or broke off? Of course not, because even though you can't see the whole thing, you know it's all there.

Likewise, with your healing, just because you can't see it doesn't mean it's not all there. You may only see a sliver of healing in your body, or maybe it's a moonless night altogether, but believing says, "I may not be able to see it, but I know it's there. I know I'm healed."

Hit Your Mark:

Think about this moon analogy and how absolutely confident you are the moon is always wholly intact whether you see it or not. Apply that same thinking to your healing as you set in your mind that what you see doesn't change the established truth that you are healed.

June 24

The Target:

And He said to him, "Go, wash in the pool of Siloam"
(which is translated, Sent). So he went and washed,
and came back seeing.

John 9:7

Set Your Sights:

To heal this blind man, Jesus spit in the dirt to make mud, plastered it on his eyes, and told him to wash it off in a distant pool. This assignment was not easy for the blind man who had to find someone willing to take him or feel his way there. But instead of looking at the difficulty of the designated task, he believed in Jesus and acted in faith.

He "washed and came back seeing" doesn't pinpoint when he actually saw. Was it when he washed or as he came back? If the latter is the case, imagine washing the mud away, opening your eyes in anticipation and seeing … nothing. He could have stopped believing then but continued to walk in faith and return to Jesus, receiving his healing as he went.

Hit Your Mark:

The moral of the story: Don't stop believing! After becoming convinced you are healed, the enemy will sometimes come in with a full-frontal assault and you'll actually get worse. It's his last-ditch effort to steal your confidence and get you to back away from what you know. Don't be discouraged if it happens. See it as confirmation that you are headed in the right direction and victory is close at hand!

June 25

The Target:

We know that whoever is born of God does not sin; but he who has been born of God keeps himself, and the wicked one does not touch him.

1 John 5:18

Set Your Sights:

This verse doesn't mean if you sin you aren't born again. If that were the case, no one would be saved because everyone sins (Rom. 3:23). The part of you that is "born of God" is your born-again spirit, and it does not sin and cannot be touched by the enemy. When you believed, the Holy Spirit sealed your spirit, rendering the enemy incapable of corrupting it or stealing from within it (Eph. 1:13).

This is important to know because God gave you everything you need for life and godliness and made it available within your spirit man (2 Peter 1:3). It is the ultimate big-box store where every item is free and in mass supply, with the Holy Spirit as the impenetrable security system. If you need joy, peace, or healing, it's in there. The enemy cannot steal what God has freely given you.

Hit Your Mark:

As part of your inheritance, healing is irrevocable and perpetually available, something the enemy can never strip from you. Recognize that healing is within you. It's not somewhere in a galaxy far, far away, having to traverse the cosmos to get to you. It is right there. You're not waiting on healing; it's part of you. Think about that today.

The Target:

Then Jesus answered and said to her, "O woman, great is your faith! Let it be to you as you desire." And her daughter was healed from that very hour.

Matthew 15:28

Set Your Sights:

This desperate Syrophenician woman came to Jesus for help because her daughter was being tormented by a demon. However, because she was not an Israelite, she was not part of their covenant with God and had no right to ask Jesus for anything. Despite this, she humbled herself and laid her complete dependence bare before Him.

Her dependence on Jesus earned her the title of "great faith" and was the reason her daughter was healed. A woman who wasn't even in covenant with God received the benefit of healing by faith. How much more so you, who has a covenant with God? She received this by putting her faith in what Jesus could do. You receive by putting your faith in what Jesus already did.

Hit Your Mark:

There wasn't anything she could do in the natural to receive healing for her daughter. She didn't deserve it and she couldn't earn it. All she did was believe in Jesus and humble herself before Him. You can also do nothing to be more or less deserving of healing. It can't be earned. God wants you well, and just like the Syrophenician woman, all you have to do is believe in Jesus and depend on Him.

June 27 – Part I

The Target:

Now a certain woman had a flow of blood for twelve years, and had suffered many things from many physicians. She had spent all that she had and was no better, but rather grew worse.

Mark 5:25–26

Set Your Sights:

We will look closely at this decisive, tenacious woman over the next several days. She had tried the world's medicines and methods and remained sick, tired, and eventually broke. She had enough. After hearing about Jesus, she believed in Him, set her face like a flint, and went hard after Him.

When it comes to healing, determination and perseverance are your friends as you go against the flow of what most people believe about sickness. They will tell you it's hopeless and that you're crazy to think God can, will, or even wants to heal you. Everything around you will tempt you to quit, but let God's word trump those deceitful voices. If you continue to put it first, you will have the tenacity, like this woman, to see it through to the end.

Hit Your Mark:

Access your inner bulldog today and get determined to walk in God's best. Stir yourself up by speaking the Word out loud, praying in the Spirit, and rebuking the enemy attacking your body. Feel Christ's authority rise in you as you speak words of life over yourself. Do a little shouting if you have to, but be resolute in your belief that nothing will keep you from your healing!

June 28 – Part II

The Target:

*When she heard about Jesus, she came behind Him
in the crowd and touched His garment.*

Mark 5:27

Set Your Sights:

This sentence speaks volumes about this woman's determination
and courage. Under Jewish law, she was considered "unclean"
because of her issue of blood. She wasn't supposed to be out in
public because whomever she touched would become unclean. If
she was caught, the punishment was death by stoning. Adding that
Jesus was walking with Jairus, a ruler of the synagogue who had
the authority to approve her stoning, amplifies the extent of her
courage.

She had a lot of obstacles to overcome (fear of being stoned,
unbelief due to prolonged sickness, and the massive crowd). Still,
she pressed through them all and touched the hem of Jesus's
garment. To touch the hem, she had to be on the ground. Imagine
her, with dogged determination, crawling on her hands and knees
through dirt and a sea of sandals and robes to receive what she was
believing for.

Hit Your Mark:

Make a decision today that you will stand on His word and not be
moved by the circumstances or what other people say. Shut out the
fear that says you'll always deal with this problem and never live a
normal life. They are all lies meant to keep you from taking another
step forward toward receiving your healing. You will receive if you
don't quit!

June 29 – Part III

The Target:

For she said, "If only I may touch His clothes, I shall be made well." Immediately the fountain of her blood was dried up, and she felt in her body that she was healed of the affliction.

Mark 5:28–29

Set Your Sights:

In yesterday's devotion, the woman with the issue of blood made her way through the crowd, likely on hands and knees, intending to touch the hem of Jesus's garment. That probably sounded strange until you read today's verses and learned that touching His garment was where she set her faith to be healed. Once set, nothing was going to deter her.

Her touch stopped Jesus in His tracks. Think about the scene: The people are packed around Him, pressing in from every side. Everyone is touching Him, but He recognizes a different kind of touch—the touch of faith that draws healing power from Him. He smiles as He realizes someone believed in Him and took hold of their healing with an act of faith.

Hit Your Mark:

The woman received her healing by touching Jesus, which continues to be how you receive it today. The great news is that you don't have to fight through a crowd to touch Him. He lives inside you (Gal. 4:6) and is ready to touch you every moment of every day. To release His healing touch into your body, set your faith in Him alone, act on what you believe, and let nothing stand in your way of receiving!

June 30 – Part IV

The Target:

And Jesus, immediately knowing in Himself that power had gone out of Him, turned around in the crowd and said, "Who touched My clothes?"

And He said to her, "Daughter, your faith has made you well. Go in peace, and be healed of your affliction."

Mark 5:30, 34

Set Your Sights:

We're wrapping up our time on the account of the woman with the issue of blood today and bringing it all together, putting it into one neat little package of how to receive healing. First, the woman heard about Jesus and His healing power. Second, she believed what she heard. Third, she set her faith and got determined to receive. And fourth, she acted on what she believed.

There is no difference between how she received it and how you will. First, you hear the truth that God wants everyone healed and sent Jesus to ensure it. Second, believe it above all else. Third, set your faith and be relentless in receiving. And fourth, step out in faith by acting on your beliefs. Then, in a matter of time, the manifestation of your healing will come.

Hit Your Mark:

When you apply steps one through four, even if there's no change in your body, press on, knowing your healing is guaranteed. Don't back down for one second. Your faith releases the healing power of God as you are persistent in your beliefs and consistent in your words and actions. Healing is in you, and activated by faith, is on its way from the inside out!

set your sights

JULY

July 1

The Target:

The Lord also will be a refuge for the oppressed,
A refuge in times of trouble.

Psalm 9:9

Set Your Sights:

Not all sickness comes in the form of a cold or cancer. Mental disorders also fall under the category of "sickness" and are prevalent today. In God's eyes, there is no difference between a sickness of the body and one of the mind. They are all evil works of the enemy that were defeated through the blood of Jesus Christ.

God promises to be a refuge for those who suffer from mental illness. A place where anyone who feels crushed by the anguish or distress surrounding them can hide. The Word is your refuge, and as you hide in it, those things which cause fear, anxiety, and depression will be unable to reach you. In the refuge of the Word, you will find peace and comfort, there will be light and not darkness, and your mind will be healed.

Hit Your Mark:

If you are struggling with mental illness today, run to the refuge of God's word. Focus on the fact God sent Jesus so you could live free from the bondage of a mental prison. You don't have to be tortured and bound in your mind. When evil thoughts come, read this verse and envision yourself hiding in God's refuge. Find peace there as you focus on His words. You are free.

July 2 – Part I

The Target:

But He answered and said, "It is not good to take the
children's bread and throw it to the little dogs."

Matthew 15:26

Set Your Sights:

In talking to this Gentile woman seeking healing for her daughter, Jesus refers to healing as "bread." In the beginning, this bread of healing was exclusively promised to the designated children of God, the Israelites, but the passion of Jesus made it possible for anyone who believes in Him to become His child and, therefore, an authorized heir of His bread (John 1:12).

David says in Psalm 37:25 that he has never seen the children of the righteous begging for bread. As His child, you don't have to beg for the bread of healing nor settle for the scraps. You are seated at His table with a bottomless basket of hot, fresh bread within reach. It is part of your redemption, covenant, and inheritance in Christ and nothing can take it away from you.

Hit Your Mark:

Think about what it means to be a child of God. It means you aren't a slave doing the work of your master but a child who is deeply cared for and loved by your Father. The bread of life, Jesus (John 6:35), was freely given to you, and He will never make you beg for it. Don't let the enemy deceive you into thinking otherwise. Choose to believe it is yours … because you are His.

The Target:

Then Jesus answered and said unto her, "O woman, great is thy faith: be it unto thee even as thou wilt." And her daughter was made whole from that very hour.

Matthew 15:28 (KJV)

Set Your Sights:

This is a continuation of the account of the Gentile woman pursuing healing for her daughter. Jesus said it would be to her as she "wilt," which means as she resolved and purposed in her heart. Her resolve was Jesus healing her daughter, and even when it looked as if healing was denied, she didn't back down until she got it.

Receiving healing is a daily, sometimes minute-by-minute choice to maintain a bold stance of faith, holding on to the Word as if it were a matter of life and death. For some, that may be the case. Keeping the Word squarely in front of you enables you to resist the temptation to divert your eyes to the negative reports around you. Starve the negative of your attention until it shrivels up and dies, leaving nothing but the glorious word of God that will grow into a harvest of healing in your body.

Hit Your Mark:

This can never be said enough: Don't give up. Don't listen to the lies of the enemy trying to convince you that healing isn't yours. Take a firm stance, stay focused on the Word, and it will give you the strength to continue. Do these things, and just like this woman, you'll receive what you're believing for. Don't. Give. Up.

July 4

The Target:

There shall not any man be able to stand before thee all the days of thy life: as I was with Moses, so I will be with thee: I will not fail thee, nor forsake thee.

Joshua 1:5 (KJV)

Set Your Sights:

When God says no man will be able to stand against you, He means nothing has the power to get in your way and prevent you from receiving what He has promised you. For example, God promised Moses He would deliver the Israelites out of bondage to Egypt, and that's exactly what He did, despite Pharaoh being "in the face" of Moses most of the time.

God also promises to never fail you, which includes never abandoning you, losing His grip on you, or letting you fall. In a nutshell, God will never let you down. His word is truth and will knock down every obstacle the enemy puts in front of you. It doesn't matter if that obstacle is a thought or a person; His word goes with you so you can go through it.

Hit Your Mark:

Think about all the obstacles Moses faced on his way to seeing God's promise fulfilled and how God had a solution for every one of them. As you walk your journey, stuff will get in your face (bad reports, negative comments from people, symptoms), but God knows how you'll overcome it. Ask Him to show you His solution, act on it, and then watch as those obstacles fall one by one.

July 5

The Target:

And you will seek Me and find Me, when you search for Me with all your heart.

Jeremiah 29:13

Set Your Sights:

Electromagnetic radio waves always transmit sounds, but hearing them depends entirely on turning on your radio, which is a receiver. A receiver converts the waves into sounds you can hear, which become clear when you turn the converter on and find the right frequency.

Like radio waves, God always transmits sounds (speaks). To hear Him, you turn on your receivers (your spiritual ears) and tune them to the right frequency. God broadcasts on an unlimited number of frequencies to ensure you hear Him. These frequencies consist of songs, verses, beautiful sunsets, or random acts of kindness by strangers. When you search for Him with your whole heart, you will find the right frequency every time.

Hit Your Mark:

Hearing God is an essential component of a successful healing journey. His instructions and revelations are pivotal as you navigate unknown paths. Ask the Spirit to sharpen your receivers and then intentionally listen for His voice throughout the day. Don't just listen in the usual places, but also where you'd least expect it. As you consistently seek Him, fine-tuning your receivers, you will hear Him more and more and grow in confidence in what you hear. This will lead to faith. And faith will always lead to healing.

July 6 – Part I

The Target:

Be anxious for nothing, but in everything by prayer and supplication, with thanksgiving, let your requests be made known to God; and the peace of God, which surpasses all understanding, will guard your hearts and minds through Christ Jesus.

Philippians 4:6–7

Set Your Sights:

In no uncertain terms God is saying, "[Insert your name here], don't be anxious about anything." He would be unjust to instruct you to do something you couldn't do, so as impossible as it may sound, living an anxiety-free life is achievable. God has equipped you with several means to rid yourself of all sickness-producing anxiety: prayer, supplication, and thanksgiving.

Prayer is simply your conversation with God. Supplication is asking God for help on a particular matter instead of a generalized prayer. An example might be when you know you're healed but don't see it yet, so you ask God to show you if something is hindering your healing. Along with prayer and supplication, giving thanks is a great way to banish anxiety because a thankful heart and anxiety can't coexist.

Hit Your Mark:

Being anxious about nothing certainly isn't easy. It takes perseverance to remain in an attitude of prayer (mind fixed on Him), to ask for help on your journey, and to give Him thanks in the middle of the struggle. These three acts will drive out anxiety, leaving only the peace of God that passes all understanding. Start expelling anxiety today by receiving this Word and acting on it.

July 7 – Part II

The Target:

Finally, brethren, whatever things are true, whatever things are noble, whatever things are just, whatever things are pure, whatever things are lovely, whatever things are of good report, if there is any virtue and if there is anything praiseworthy—meditate on these things.

Philippians 4:8

Set Your Sights:

Anxiety is a flaming arrow of the enemy that can only be extinguished by God's peace. Yesterday's devotion was all about the actions which quench anxiety: prayer, supplication, and giving thanks. Today is all about your thoughts because the actual battle between peace and anxiety is won and lost in your mind.

Whether peace wins or loses is dependent upon your thoughts. God sets clear parameters for your thinking to ensure victory goes to peace. The first and most important parameter is to think about whatever things are true. God's word is truth (John 17:17), and every thought you have should submit to that truth. You will face anxiety-producing facts, but God's peace-giving truth will always triumph over them.

Hit Your Mark:

Every day you are bombarded with thoughts, good and bad, and you decide which of those thoughts you'll entertain. This verse gives you guidelines to follow that will lead you to peace. Whenever you're wrestling with a thought, read this verse. If it fits within the parameters, consider it further. If it doesn't, trash it, replace it with God's truth and peace will prevail.

July 8

The Target:

The Lord thy God in the midst of thee is mighty; he will save, he will rejoice over thee with joy; he will rest in his love, he will joy over thee with singing.

Zephaniah 3:17 (KJV)

Set Your Sights:

The entire book of Zephaniah is a declaration of the judgments Israel would suffer for their rebellion until the very end when God promises that one day His mercy would be poured out on all of humanity. You are living in that "one day," and this verse paints a beautiful picture of God's extravagant love for you.

No longer past tense, but for the here and now, this verse states God has saved you and is rejoicing over you. He is resting in His love for you, unable to love you any more than He does right now. It continues with, "He will joy over thee with singing," expressing how God is dancing over you, spinning around with violent emotion! You were created for His pleasure (Rev. 4:11), and He is pleased with you!

Hit Your Mark:

Knowing that you are right with God is one thing, but knowing He loves you to the point of dancing with violent emotion over you is another. Keep your thoughts on just one thing today: God is so pleased and in love with you that He is dancing over you. So pick a favorite song, see Him dancing, and then glue that image in your mind until it sticks.

The Target:

Cause me to hear Your lovingkindness in the morning,
For in You do I trust;

Cause me to know the way in which I should walk,
For I lift up my soul to You.

Psalm 143:8

Set Your Sights:

David didn't beg God to show him love, kindness, and favor. He asked to "hear" it, to understand it, knowing there was something more concrete than the physical evidence of God's love. When you can see His love, believing it and feeling safe is easy. But when things are crumbling around you, believing in His love is tough, and understanding it is what will get you through.

David also didn't beg God to reveal His will and plan for his life, knowing he was firmly held in His mighty right hand (Ps. 139:10). He trusted God knew the way and would show him through any trial he faced. You don't have to beg God for help and direction either. To walk in His love and leading as David did, there is only one thing for you to do: Lift up your soul to God.

Hit Your Mark:

In the every day, lifting up your soul looks like surrendering your mind, will, and emotions to Him. You readily cast all thoughts that don't line up with His word at His feet. You allow Him to expose wrong motives and destructive emotions and swiftly change them. Lift up your soul! And take the next step on your journey.

July 10

The Target:

And we know that God causes everything to work together for the good of those who love God and are called according to his purpose for them.

Romans 8:28

Set Your Sights:

This promise is used to wrongly teach that whatever happens, good or bad, is from God and for your good. If that were true, Jesus would have caused both good and bad to happen to the people He encountered. Personal experience also makes the fallacy clear as you observe people whose lives have been ruined by sickness. Where is the good in that?

The true meaning of this promise is God can take anything terrible the devil throws at you and turn it into something good. As one who loves God, walking in this promise depends on your cooperation with the Holy Spirit. As you pray in the Spirit, listen for His wisdom and direction, and act on what you hear, God will put His hands to work and transform what was ugly into something beautiful.

Hit Your Mark:

You will face bad things in your life because the devil is evil, but God can turn them all around when you submit to Him. Instead of turning to the situation, turn to Him. Instead of contemplating the facts and circumstances, think about His Word instead. When you do these things, He can and will turn it around for your good.

July 11 – Part I

The Target:

But when Jesus saw her, He called her to Him and said to her, "Woman, you are loosed from your infirmity."

Luke 13:12

Set Your Sights:

Jesus spoke "you are loosed" using the perfect tense, meaning the action of releasing had already been completed. He was telling this woman, who was bowed over at the waist and staring at His feet, that she was already healed. He didn't see the outward prison of her crippled body but the truth that, as a child of God (v. 16), she was free.

Focusing on the natural is like a prisoner who receives a pardon but is so focused on the four walls around them they don't realize their shackles are gone and the prison door is wide open. If that were you, wouldn't you run as fast as you could out of bondage, rejoicing and praising God the whole way? Sadly, many believers don't realize they've been loosed and remain in bondage even though they are totally free.

Hit Your Mark:

Don't continue to be held captive when Jesus issued you a full pardon and set you free (John 8:36). He opened the prison door and cleared the way for you to walk out unhindered. See the shackles of your sickness unlocking and feel the weight of them falling away. See the light shining through the open door to freedom. The first step to freedom is knowing you are free.

July 12 – Part II

The Target:

Now He was teaching in one of the synagogues on the Sabbath. And behold, there was a woman who had a spirit of infirmity eighteen years, and was bent over and could in no way raise herself up. But when Jesus saw her, He called her to Him and said to her, "Woman, you are loosed from your infirmity." And He laid His hands on her, and immediately she was made straight, and glorified God.

Luke 13:10-13

Set Your Sights:

It was challenging for this disabled woman to get to the synagogue, considering she was basically bent in half, but if she hadn't gone, she would not have been healed. Faith is rarely easy or convenient, but it is always worth the effort. On that day, Jesus was teaching, and hearing His words produced faith that compelled her into action (Rom. 10:17).

Her first opportunity to act was when Jesus called her to Him. She could have said, "I'm disabled and can't come to you," remaining in bondage to her condition, but she made her way to Him instead. Her second opportunity came after He touched her. She could have remained bent over but stood up and claimed her freedom instead. Straight and tall.

Hit Your Mark:

The first step to freedom is recognizing you're already free. The second step is to act on what you know. Ask God to tell you how to act on what you believe. Hearing Him will produce faith and lead you to action. Maybe it's getting out of bed. Perhaps it's going for a walk. Whatever it is, do it. When you act in faith, you will confidently head to the open prison door, knowing Satan can't hold you there anymore.

July 13

The Target:

If you diligently heed the voice of the Lord your God and do what is right in His sight, give ear to His commandments and keep all His statutes, I will put none of the diseases on you which I have brought on the Egyptians. For I am the Lord who heals you.

Exodus 15:26

Set Your Sights:

This was God's first healing covenant with His people before He brought them out of Egypt, resulting in not a single sick person being among them as they left (Ps. 105:37). Everyone who would "give ear" to His commands would walk in health, creating a link between hearing and healing that still applies today. When you hear the Word and believe, healing is a natural byproduct.

The last sentence of this verse holds a powerful truth not to be missed. God didn't say, "I will be" or "I was" the Lord who heals you, but "I am the Lord who heals you." God does not change (James 1:17), and since His promise covered everyone then, it covers everyone now. Especially you.

Hit Your Mark:

It can be easy to be deceived into thinking that if you don't do everything perfectly, you won't receive. But God made a covenant of healing with you, and there is nothing you have to do to receive it except to hear the Word and believe it. Stop jumping through hoops and think about the fact that He's given you healing, you are healed, and nothing can change that. His covenant of healing with you is unbreakable.

July 14

The Target:

Beloved, I pray that you may prosper in all things and be in health, just as your soul prospers.

3 John 1:2

Set Your Sights:

The word "prosper" is rich with meaning. In addition to referring to money, it means to help on the road and lead by a direct and easy way. The word "health" encompasses more than being healed and whole, but also that your doctrine is uncorrupted; in other words, you have correct thinking. So health pertains to both your body and your mind.

Let's flip the verse around and fill in the meanings: As your soul is helped by the Holy Spirit and He leads you down the most direct and easy path, you will be healed and whole in your body and sound in your mind. You will avoid the long and treacherous road, successfully reaching your intended destination. That's God's promise to you.

Hit Your Mark:

There will be ups and downs on your journey, but you will have many more ups than downs when you listen for the voice of the Holy Spirit and follow it. He will show you the way, the easy way, right through the middle of any circumstance you may face. That is the key to prospering in your mind, will, and emotions ... step by step, being led by Him.

July 15

The Target:

Surely he hath borne our griefs, and carried our sorrows: yet we did esteem him stricken, smitten of God, and afflicted.

Isaiah 53:4 (KJV)

Set Your Sights:

Hundreds of years before Jesus became flesh, Isaiah prophesied about the type of death He would die and the reason for it. This part of the prophecy specifically addresses what He would do with sickness and pain.

It would be easy to read this verse and say griefs and sorrows have nothing to do with sickness, but if you look at the original Hebrew text, they obviously have everything to do with it. In Hebrew, "griefs" is translated as sickness and "sorrows" as anguish and pain.

Jesus lifted up and took away sickness and carried away mental and physical pain. He literally took every disorder and associated pain, named and unnamed (Deut. 28:61), into His own body, causing it to be deformed beyond recognition as a human (Isa. 52:14). He did that for you. He took it and there wasn't a single thing He missed.

Hit Your Mark:

See this truth that will heal you today. Jesus took what you're dealing with so you wouldn't have to. He took it into His own body and carried it far, far away from you. Recognize that the sickness you're fighting doesn't belong to you because Jesus defeated it on the cross. Call it what it is: not yours and finished.

July 16

The Target:

But he was wounded for our transgressions, he was bruised for our iniquities: the chastisement of our peace was upon him; and with his stripes we are healed.

Isaiah 53:5 (KJV)

Set Your Sights:

Jesus's death made provision for your entire being. He was bruised for every sin you will commit, leaving you blameless in God's sight (Col. 1:22). Spirit, covered. His stripes paid for all sickness and pain. Body, covered. What about your soul?

It is readily accepted that mental illness is covered by Jesus's blood. Still, many believers are needlessly tormented by another sickness of the mind called guilt and condemnation. According to this verse, Jesus took the punishment you deserved in exchange for your peace. Because He took the punishment, you don't have to hurt yourself with guilt and condemnation. There is no penance to be paid. Even guilt was covered, leaving peace in its place. Soul, covered.

Hit Your Mark:

Your mental peace is secure. To walk in that peace, take every thought captive and make it obedient to the truth (2 Cor. 10:5). When guilt and condemnation try to rob you of peace, rebuke them and set your sights on the Word. Remind yourself God has forgiven you of all your sins and He's not the one condemning you for them. Tell the devil what he can do with his condemnation. Then turn to Father and expect peace to flow up like a river, drowning out everything else. Peace is yours.

July 17

The Target:

For as in Adam all die, even so in Christ all shall be made alive.

1 Corinthians 15:22

Set Your Sights:

When Adam and Eve sinned in the garden, they ushered in an era of destruction, giving Satan authority to wreak havoc on the earth. With his rule came sickness, disease, and everything evil. The world continues to suffer from the effects of their fall, but the good news is you don't have to join them. You may have been born in Adam, but you live in Christ.

With your new life in Christ comes the promise of being made alive in Him. The word "alive" is the same Greek word used in Romans 8:11 when it says the Spirit will "quicken" your physical body. In other words, through the power of the Holy Spirit, your physical body can be brought back to life, invigorated, and revitalized. Death and sickness arrived by Adam, but life and health are available through Christ.

Hit Your Mark:

You are already fixed in Christ, so you can expect the Holy Spirit to impact your physical body. This will happen more and more as the Word becomes your only foundation, source, counselor, and guide. When faced with doubt, run to it for assurance. As the Word becomes rooted in your soul, your body will be made alive. That's guaranteed because it's His promise.

July 18

The Target:

For our light affliction, which is but for a moment, is working for us a far more exceeding and eternal weight of glory ...

2 Corinthians 4:17

Set Your Sights:

Affliction is pressure in the form of anguish, burdens, persecutions, tribulations, or trouble. Anyone who has suffered from illness can tell you it can be all those things at one point or another, and sometimes it's all at once. Some will use this verse to persuade you an affliction is something God gives you for some glorified purpose.

It is true glory can come out of sickness: Glory to God when your healing comes and you testify. Glory as the power of faith is displayed. Future glory in heaven for your faithful stand. The only reason good can come out of affliction is because God makes all things work out for the good of those who love Him (Rom. 8:28). But remember, just because He can make it good doesn't mean He made it happen.

Hit Your Mark:

If you think God gave you an affliction to lead you into some future glory for you or Him, scrutinize that philosophy under the microscope of the nature and character of a loving God. You will see it could not have come from Him when you do. See it for what it is: An attack from a cowardly enemy, not a blessing from a loving God.

July 19

The Target:

Now may the God of peace Himself sanctify you completely; and may your whole spirit, soul, and body be preserved blameless at the coming of our Lord Jesus Christ.

1 Thessalonians 5:23

Set Your Sights:

This verse contains the vital truth that you are a three-part being, made in the image of God (Gen. 1:26). Just as God is three parts (Father, Son, and Holy Spirit), so are you. You are a spirit, have a soul, and live in a body.

The spirit is the real you and is perfect, whole and complete (Col. 1:22). The soul is your personality and makes you unique from everyone else. The body is where you live, your earth suit, and you need it to engage with the world around you.

Knowing this truth will set you free as it changes your perspective of sickness. It becomes a trespasser on holy ground, causing you to separate yourself from it and actively resist it. No longer is it inevitable and insurmountable, but a temporary problem on its way to defeat.

Hit Your Mark:

Make an effort to distinguish your three parts. Your body is easy, but how about your spirit and soul? Here are a few good hints: Your spirit man only speaks truth and life, so if your statement starts with "I feel," most likely that is your soul. If a thought doesn't line up with the truth, it's definitely your soul. Get started making this truth your truth today!

July 20

The Target:

Therefore, if anyone is in Christ, he is a new creation; old things have passed away; behold, all things have become new.

2 Corinthians 5:17

Set Your Sights:

When you were born again, your old sinful nature died. In its place, a novel and unprecedented spirit was created in perfection. It was then sealed with the Holy Spirit (Eph. 1:13), assuring its contents would be there forever and in ample supply, never to be depleted or corrupted.

What does your spirit contain? First and foremost, Jesus's spirit, making you complete in Him and lacking nothing (Gal. 4:6, Col. 2:10). It has everything necessary for a vibrant spiritual life and godliness (2 Peter 1:3). Regardless if you feel like it or not, everything you need is there and available, including healing, prosperity, and freedom from the bondage of sin.

Hit Your Mark:

You aren't waiting on God to heal you. He provided healing through Jesus's sacrifice, which you accepted when you believed in Him. Healing is as sure as your sins are forgiven. It is yours and available through the Holy Spirit who lives inside you. Allow these truths to change your thinking today from *I'm waiting for healing* to *Healing is mine!* The Spirit is in you, waiting for you to believe it is yours and to reach out and take it.

July 21

The Target:

Now may the God of peace Himself sanctify you completely; and may your whole spirit, soul, and body be preserved blameless at the coming of our Lord Jesus Christ.

1 Thessalonians 5:23

Set Your Sights:

This verse answers how you can confidently confess you're healed when you obviously aren't in the natural. The truth is, healing isn't something you get but something you already possess in your spirit. (See July 19 and 20 for more.)

When you don't really believe that, your confession will come from a place of denial. You'll repeatedly declare, "I'm healed," hoping that if you pretend the problem isn't there and state it frequently enough, it will magically happen. That is not the same as faith.

However, saying you're healed is not denial when you believe the truth. It's agreeing with what God says about you. It's professing you know you have it before you see it happen. It's calling those things that are not as though they are (Rom. 4:17). That is a confession that will see results.

Hit Your Mark:

Grab hold of this truth today. When you believe you are healed no matter what you feel or what the world sees, you are not a hypocrite for stating it emphatically. Turn what you believe into a proclamation, and declare it confidently in the face of every opposition. In the presence of those faith-filled words, no sickness can survive!

July 22

The Target:

Then He went up into the boat to them, and the wind ceased. And they were greatly amazed in themselves beyond measure, and marveled. For they had not understood about the loaves, because their heart was hardened.

Mark 6:51–52

Set Your Sights:

The disciples had just witnessed Jesus feed the five thousand with five loaves and two fish, yet their hearts were hardened. They were so fixated on the violent storm they neglected to consider the miracle they had seen, nor the promise Jesus made of getting to the other side (Mark 6:45). Their wayward focus made them callous and insensitive to the works and words of Jesus.

Hardness of heart is an issue that can fly under the radar, but once you're aware of it, it's easy to get rid of. It's a simple principle: Thinking about things that promote fear and doubt cause you to be sensitive to them and calloused to the Word, leading to a hardened heart. Whereas thinking about the things of God causes you to be sensitive to His promises and calloused to fear and doubt, leading you to a heart that is open to receive.

Hit Your Mark:

Your mission: Train your heart to be sensitive to God and calloused to fear and doubt by focusing on things that are true, pure, lovely, and of good report (Phil. 4:8). Refuse to be consumed by your circumstances and purpose to consider the work He has already done in your life and the promise you have of healing.

The Target:

But the ones that fell on the good ground are those who, having heard the word with a noble and good heart, keep it and bear fruit with patience.

Luke 8:15

Set Your Sights:

This is a parable about seeds, ground, and fruit. The seeds represent God's word, and the ground represents the condition of your heart. In both the natural and the spiritual, you can tell what kind of seeds were planted by the fruit they produce. Good or bad, you'll get exactly what you planted.

Growing a garden demands the hard work of tilling and fertilizing the ground, pulling the weeds so they don't choke the good seeds, and diligently watering it. You also won't plant seeds one day and see fruit the next. Reaping a harvest involves time and patience, and God's word is no different. It will grow when you plant it, pull out the weeds, and water it daily.

Hit Your Mark:

Healing is one of the seeds of the Word you plant in your heart. You care for it by focusing on the truth it represents, consistently pulling out every lie the enemy may try to choke it with, and watering it daily with reflection and prayer. When you protect the seed you've sown, it will do the rest. And with time and patience, you will see the harvest of healing in your life and body.

July 24 – Part I

The Target:

Peace I leave with you, My peace I give to you; not as the world gives do I give to you. Let not your heart be troubled, neither let it be afraid.

John 14:27

Set Your Sights:

Peace is the calm state of a soul assured of salvation which fears nothing from God and is perfectly content. It comes from knowing God loves you and has your back no matter what is happening. With an unshakeable understanding of this truth, you can walk through any turbulence life may throw at you unphased and full of peace.

Like forgiveness and healing, peace was freely given to you as part of the salvation package. God's way of giving is not like the world's, marked by changing its mind and violently snatching back what it has previously so generously given. God does not change His mind or regret His promises (Num. 23:19). Once He gives something, He doesn't take it back. He left you with peace, so it is available today, tomorrow, and forever.

Hit Your Mark:

Peace is yours right now as part of the promised fruit of the Spirit inside you (Gal. 5:22). Whether or not you experience that peace is totally up to you. Take your first step toward peace today by changing your thinking and professing, "I have the peace of God inside me no matter what I feel, and I'm going to walk in it today." Choose peace and walk in it.

July 25 – Part II

The Target:

Peace I leave with you, My peace I give to you; not as the world gives do I give to you. Let not your heart be troubled, neither let it be afraid.

John 14:27

Set Your Sights:

The second half of this verse holds the how-to for walking in peace. Notice it doesn't instruct you to ask God for peace. Because you already have it (Gal. 5:22). Whether or not you experience God's peace in your life comes down to one thing: choice. *Your* choice.

The implied subject of this sentence is "you." *You* do not let your heart be troubled and afraid, which is understandably hard to hear when you're bombarded with fear and anxiety night and day. Choosing peace in your current situation might sound impossible, but this verse tells you it's not.

No matter what you're up against, you have abundant peace inside you to carry you through. You choose that peace by getting your sights off of everything non-peace producing and focusing them on the peace you know is right there at your disposal.

Hit Your Mark:

After your initial thought, *This girl is crazy if she thinks I can have peace in the middle of this sickness*, take another look at this verse. Study it. Meditate on it. Let the truth sink in. God has given you peace and is telling you to walk in it. Don't let your circumstances steal your peace. It is yours. Fight for it.

July 26

The Target:

Come to Me, all you who labor and are heavy laden, and I will give you rest. Take My yoke upon you and learn from Me, for I am gentle and lowly in heart, and you will find rest for your souls.

Mathew 11:28–29

Set Your Sights:

Picture an ox pulling a cart ten times its weight up a mountain pass. Its muscles strain and quake as it struggles to take another step. The owner recognizes it needs help, so he yokes the struggling ox to his strongest and most experienced ox. Yoke in place, the strongest ox bears the brunt of the weight and the two easily make it up the mountain together.

A yoke is a symbol of submission. God is asking you to submit to Him and promises rest in return. But there's more. As you submit to the Word, you must also learn from it. Learning implies meditating on it, praying about it, and asking for the wisdom to apply it. Submitting and learning will lead to rest from the backbreaking load of racing thoughts and roller coaster emotions.

Hit Your Mark:

Your journey doesn't have to be a never-ending uphill climb with a 200-pound pack strapped to your back. If today is one of those days and you're barely making it, remind yourself of God's promise that you don't have to carry the load uphill, both ways, in the snow, alone. He will take the load as you submit to and learn from Him. You just walk by His side, up the mountain, together.

July 27

The Target:

With long life I will satisfy him, and show him My salvation.

Psalm 91:16

Set Your Sights:

God wants you to have a long and satisfying life. Long life means living out all the days He planned for you, not one day less. Being satisfied means living life to the fullest, not suffering daily from sickness. A life cut short and filled with pain is not His design. His design shows you the satisfying life which He guaranteed through salvation.

The word "salvation" means victorious and healthy, and "show" means to see or experience. When God shows you His salvation, He causes you to understand and experience the life it brings. The benefits of this promise hinge on two things: dwelling and abiding in the secret place of the Most High and saying so (Ps. 91:1–2). It is in that place you will experience everything salvation has to offer.

Hit Your Mark:

If sickness threatens to deprive you of the long life Jesus died for you to have, dig your heels into this promise from the Father of a long life free from sickness. Dwell and abide in His shadow by believing in the promise and refusing to accept what the doctors, lab reports, or statistics say is true. He promised you long life. That is the truth. Say so today.

July 28

The Target:

Your sandals shall be iron and bronze; as your days, so shall your strength be.

Deuteronomy 33:25

Set Your Sights:

The promise: You will have as much strength as you have days. That is quite the opposite of what the world says. It says as you age, your muscles will weaken, you'll lose bone mass, and energy levels will plummet. Science even confirms it. These are worldly facts that are far removed from the spiritual truth.

Moses is your example of the spiritual truth of aging: At 120 years old, his eyes were not dimmed, and his strength had not faded (Deut. 34:7). The ads on television advertising all the different medications you're going to need for this and that are not your example but lies the enemy plants claiming you can't live out your days healthy and robust. His lies are not meant to be part of your aging process.

Hit Your Mark:

Your challenge: When watching television, mute every medication commercial. Don't listen to that garbage or read the fine print of symptoms. That is what the world has to offer, not God. You can be strong even if you feel weak because God says so. Keep your sights set on Moses and do something to strengthen your body today. Move in that direction and God will fulfill His promise as you do.

The Target:

And He said unto him, "Arise, go thy way: thy faith hath made thee whole."

Luke 17:19 (KJV)

Set Your Sights:

Jesus healed ten lepers, but of the ten, only this one was made whole after returning to thank Him. It wasn't unusual for leprosy to eat away digits, ears, or noses, so maybe this leper, in addition to being healed, had fingers grow back or a nose reconstructed on his face. That is a possibility, but one thing is sure: Gratitude made him whole, something the other nine didn't experience.

Notice the progression: The leper had faith in Jesus, which caused him to follow His command to show himself to the priests. In the going, he was healed. Imagine his delight as the whiteness of his leprous skin was replaced with normal flesh, and though he wasn't yet whole, he didn't hold back his praise. Swept up in thanksgiving, he was made whole.

Hit Your Mark:

Don't be like the nine and wait for everything to be perfect in your body before you give Him praise. With every step toward healing—every change, improvement, and glimmer of hope—let the sound of thanksgiving and praise be on your lips. Gratitude is like a wave that will carry you up and over the next hurdle. Get swept up today and ride the wave all the way to wholeness!

July 30

The Target:

People do not despise a thief if he steals to satisfy himself when he is starving. Yet when he is found, he must restore sevenfold; he may have to give up all the substance of his house.

Proverbs 6:30–31

Set Your Sights:

Although this is about a thief who steals for good reasons, he is still taking something that doesn't belong to him and must pay back sevenfold what he took. "Sevenfold" doesn't just mean to literally replace what he took times seven, but represents full, complete, and perfect payback and compensation. The devil is not exempt from this truth.

Satan is the father of stealing and has no good reason to take from you other than he loves to (John 10:10). He steals whatever he can get his grubby little hands on, including your health. So whatever he has taken from you, he is required to restore fully, completely, and perfectly until his storehouses are empty. Once you discover this truth, payback must begin.

Hit Your Mark:

Your payback is coming. Restoration is coming. God says He will restore your health and heal your wounds (Jer. 30:17). Don't be content with two- or threefold. Expect a full, complete, and perfect recovery. Expect to walk without a limp and to pick up your kids and grandkids without pain. Expect strength to return. Throw off the limitations the doctor prescribed you and expect to be restored because it is the will and promise of God!

July 31

The Target:

And they overcame him by the blood of the Lamb and by the word of their testimony, and they did not love their lives to the death.

Revelation 12:11

Set Your Sights:

This verse specifically refers to the believers who held on to the gospel and overcame Satan's efforts to erase Christianity from the world through persecution, many of whom were martyred because of their stand. Passed down through the ages, the testimony they shared with courage and resolve of Jesus's blood justifying you from all sin and healing you of all diseases (Ps. 103:3) is the reason you have victory over Satan today.

Understanding that the blood of the Lamb, a symbol of victory, is the power that has covered every charge the enemy brings against you is the first step in walking this out. Next is overcoming by the word of your testimony. The Word you know, believe, and speak is quick and powerful, sharper than any two-edged sword, and will pull down any stronghold you may face (Heb. 4:12, 2 Cor. 10:4).

Hit Your Mark:

Testify to what you know. Declare that because of Jesus's blood, you have already won. That you have dominion over every attack of the enemy. That you are not the sick trying to get healed, but the healed reclaiming territory that is rightfully yours. Use the sword of the Spirit to expel the enemy from your body. Acknowledge the power of the blood and speak out the truth today!

AUGUST

August 1

The Target:

And Jesus answered and said to her, "Martha, Martha, you are worried and troubled about many things. But one thing is needed, and Mary has chosen that good part, which will not be taken away from her."

Luke 10:41–42

Set Your Sights:

Mary and Martha are the perfect example of what happens when you do and don't set your sights on Jesus. Notice how Martha initially sat at Jesus's feet with Mary but chose to get up and get busy (v. 39), while Mary chose to remain in His presence and hear His word.

When Martha left Jesus and put her hands to work, she became worried and troubled about everything. She focused on doing, serving, and being busy *for* Him and was no longer on Him. She thought she was doing what was right and was angry others weren't doing the same. You can fall into this trap very quickly, getting so busy doing that you forget His desire is for you to simply be with Him.

Hit Your Mark:

If you are worried and anxious, busy doing this and that trying to impress Jesus so you can receive your healing, stop it. Stop what you're doing, return to His feet, and be with Him. Return to Him by focusing on Him and what He has done for you. Focus on His love for you and your love for Him. Just sit at His feet and learn. Seek Him first and your healing will manifest (Matt. 6:33). It's a promise.

August 2

The Target:

And the Word became flesh and dwelt among us, and we beheld His glory, the glory as of the only begotten of the Father, full of grace and truth.

John 1:14

Set Your Sights:

In the target verse for today, the Word is identified as Jesus. That truth makes Psalm 107:20 come alive: "He sent His word and healed them, and delivered them from their destructions." God sent His Word and healed you. Since Jesus is the Word, you could say God sent *Jesus* and healed you. When He took the stripes and hung on the cross, He literally carried your sickness in His body, becoming sin and sickness for you (2 Cor. 5:21).

His sacrifice made the way for you to have an intimate relationship with God by covering all your sins and paving the way for you to live in health. As a believer, you are as free from sickness as you are from the bondage of sin and death. Jesus's sacrifice paid for it all.

Hit Your Mark:

When you accepted Jesus as Lord, you put your faith in what His death and resurrection accomplished for you. Today, once again, put your confidence in everything He did. You know all your sins are forgiven, but see the truth that all sickness was paid for too. Don't leave any part of what Jesus did for you untouched. Have faith that because of what He did, you are saved—forgiven, free, and healed.

The Target:

When evening had come, they brought to Him many who were demon-possessed. And He cast out the spirits with a word, and healed all who were sick, that it might be fulfilled which was spoken by Isaiah the prophet, saying: "He Himself took our infirmities and bore our sicknesses."

Matthew 8:16–17

Set Your Sights:

There is a prevalent teaching out there asserting that the healing Jesus secured for you was solely spiritual in nature and doesn't apply to physical healing at all. These verses disprove that false doctrine, revealing the beginning of the fulfillment of prophecy about how Jesus would die and the totality of what would be achieved through His sacrifice.

Under the inspiration of the Holy Spirit, Matthew quotes from the prophecy: "Surely he has borne our griefs and carried our sorrows" (Isa. 53:4). However, in place of "griefs" and "sorrows," he uses "infirmities" and "sicknesses." This substitution was not an error, but God making sure you would understand everything Jesus did for you. Your spirit man does not need healing because it is perfect and will remain perfect (Eph. 4:24). It is your body that needs healing, and Jesus covered that too.

Hit Your Mark:

Don't believe the lies Jesus's sacrifice doesn't apply to physical healing. Look to the Word for the truth. God wants you walking in health (3 John 2), and He made that possible through Jesus. Don't be deceived and miss out on the beautiful gift of healing God has given you. Your mark for the day is to think about this: Jesus provided healing for your physical body.

August 4

The Target:

But many were amazed when they saw him. His face was so disfigured he seemed hardly human, and from his appearance, one would scarcely know he was a man.

Isaiah 52:14 (NLT)

Set Your Sights:

This describes the condition of Jesus's body as He hung on the cross. His face and body were so disfigured He wasn't identifiable as a human to those who gazed upon Him. No amount of beating by the Roman soldiers, not even the most brutal with whips and scourges, could have inflicted that much damage.

There is only one explanation for the degree of disfigurement:

After taking the stripes, as Jesus hung on the cross, He literally took every sickness and disease into His body. He took cleft lips, gangrene, spinal deformities, leprosy, and elephantiasis. He took every evil thing, known and unknown (Deut. 28:61). There wasn't a single thing He missed or forgot. He took it all at once, and it destroyed His body.

Hit Your Mark:

Whatever you're facing today, know Jesus took it from you and carried it for you in His body on the cross. In your mind's eye, imagine Jesus hanging on the cross, and see what you're standing against leaving your body and being placed on Him. As you envision it, tell yourself that is exactly what happened: He took it from you and you are free.

August 5

The Target:

Then Jesus said to the centurion, "Go your way; and as you have believed, so let it be done for you." And his servant was healed that same hour.

Matthew 8:13

Set Your Sights:

This is the account of the centurion whose servant was sick and close to death. He first sent respected Jewish elders to ask Jesus to come to him but changed his mind as Jesus got closer. Thinking as an officer in a position of authority, he recognized Jesus also held a position of authority. He decided all Jesus needed to do was say the word and his servant would be healed.

The centurion believed that when Jesus spoke, sickness listened, and because of that his servant was healed. The same Jesus who healed this man's servant, raised the dead, and cast out demons lives inside you. When you speak following the truth of the Word, it is as if Jesus Himself is speaking. His words, spoken from your lips, hold His authority and will produce life.

Hit Your Mark:

Listen to your words carefully today and speak only what God says, filling your comments with the life-giving breath of the Word. Your circumstances may be butting heads with the truth, but that doesn't make it any less true or diminish its power. Speak the Word today, knowing it is backed by the authority of Jesus, and the full force of the Holy Spirit will see it to completion!

August 6

The Target:

And when they had come to the multitude, a man came to Him, kneeling down to Him and saying, "Lord, have mercy on my son, for he is an epileptic and suffers severely; for he often falls into the fire and often into the water. So I brought him to Your disciples, but they could not cure him."

Matthew 17:14–16

Set Your Sights:

The father of an epileptic boy brought his son to Jesus's disciples, who could not heal him. At this point the father could have said, "If the ones closest to Jesus couldn't heal my son, it must not be God's will to heal him." But instead, he brought him to the Man himself. He had faith that even though man couldn't heal him, the Son of Man could.

Many people have attended healing conferences and been prayed for by mighty men of God and still aren't healed. Like the father, they could say, "If God's generals couldn't heal me, it must not be His will." That is what putting your faith in man, not the Son of Man, looks like. It's running from this person to the next for healing instead of going to the source Himself, Jesus.

Hit Your Mark:

There is absolutely nothing wrong with healing conferences and being prayed for unless your faith doesn't reach beyond the event or person to heal you. Faith needs to start and end with the finished work of Jesus. Today, stop thinking of all the times it "didn't work" in the past, and focus your attention on Jesus through prayer and study of the Word. He works. Every time.

August 7

The Target:

There is no fear in love; but perfect love casts out fear, because fear involves torment. But he who fears has not been made perfect in love. We love Him because He first loved us.

1 John 4:18–19

Set Your Sights:

Fear is one of the biggest weapons in the enemy's arsenal, especially when you're on a healing journey. He'll use friends, family, lab reports, whatever he can, to firmly establish fear in your mind. If he can get you walking in fear, you'll stray from the path of faith and be led straight to doubt and unbelief. The good news is you have a sure-fire anti-fear weapon: God's love.

The even better news is you don't have to work to have this weapon at your disposal because His love is unconditional. You don't have to love Him first and then He loves you in response. In fact, He loved you so much that when you were a sinner, living life for yourself, He sacrificed Jesus so He could have an intimate relationship with you (Rom. 5:8). This is the love that casts out all fear.

Hit Your Mark:

Fear has no power over love. When you know God loves you no matter what, a confidence emerges that will drive out fear every time. Spend today with your sights focused on this verse along with Romans 5:8. As you purpose to do that, fear won't even be a thought in your mind. It can't be because His perfect love casts out all fear.

August 8

The Target:

Now it happened on another Sabbath, also, that He entered the synagogue and taught. And a man was there whose right hand was withered. … And when He had looked around at them all, He said to the man, "Stretch out your hand." And he did so, and his hand was restored as whole as the other.

Luke 6:6, 10

Set Your Sights:

This man's hand had shriveled and wasted away, its muscles atrophied and joints locked in place. But with the faith that is born from hearing the words of Jesus, he stretched out his hand and received a miracle. There can be confusion about the difference between healing and a miracle. What sets a miracle apart from healing is a miracle defies natural law and is usually instantaneous and complete.

The man who had been lame since birth and received instant strength in his feet and ankles was a miracle (Acts 3:1–8). Steel rods in someone's back being replaced by bone is a miracle. Nerves reconnected and a spine reconstructed so a paralyzed person walks again, a miracle. The blind being able to see, a miracle. A miracle can't be explained away by science or logic. It is supernatural.

Hit Your Mark:

Don't get hung up on your journey because you don't know if you need healing or a miracle. It really doesn't matter. No matter which it is, you can have confidence God knows exactly what you need and has already made provision for it in Jesus. So take your focus off the "what" and put it on the "who." Hear His word and faith will take what you need.

August 9

The Target:

And it shall come to pass that whoever calls on the name of the Lord shall be saved.

Acts 2:21

Set Your Sights:

Another aspect of the word "saved" is to restore to health. Health is the general state of someone or something. It may be helpful to think of "state" in terms of the State of the Union Address in which the President shares the overall condition, or general welfare, of the nation as a whole.

As one who calls on Him, restored health not only applies to your body but to every aspect of your life. Being physically healthy but sick in your finances is not His idea of you walking in health. He has so much more.

The health promised in salvation encompasses your overall well-being. To say the health Jesus provided on the cross only applies to your physical health is to deny a large portion of what He did for you. He wants you walking in health in every area, and He died and rose again to ensure you could.

Hit Your Mark:

Jesus overcame the world (John 16:33), all of it, so you could live free from physical sickness, but also so you could have a great marriage and relationship with your kids. He died so you could have healthy finances, with bread to eat and seed to sow (2 Cor. 9:10). He died for everything. Think about that today.

August 10

The Target:

These things I have spoken to you, that in Me you may have peace. In the world you will have tribulation; but be of good cheer, I have overcome the world.

John 16:33

Set Your Sights:

Yesterday's truth that God's health is not limited to your physical body is echoed today in the fact that Jesus defeated the world. He went head-to-head with the universe and came out triumphant. He stood against sickness and disease but also against anxiety, depression, poverty, and divorce. The blood He shed covered it all.

Life will not be perfect, and there will be trials, but you can have peace and walk in health despite it. You will have peace and health when you focus on His words, knowing and believing there is nothing He didn't overcome. He wants you healed, full of joy, and prosperous. He wants His beautiful covenant of marriage intact and cherished and health restored to parent-child relationships. He wants you to walk in divine health—the total health that is of and from God.

Hit Your Mark:

Whatever you're dealing with, God is encouraging you to keep your chin up because He has given you the victory. Whatever the situation, find out what He has said about it in His Word, and then tell the enemy that Jesus's blood paid whatever price he's demanding of you. Start walking in the total health that Jesus provided for you today.

August 11

The Target:

The thief does not come except to steal, and to kill, and to destroy. I have come that they may have life, and that they may have it more abundantly.

John 10:10

Set Your Sights:

The word "life" wholly represents the divine health Jesus died on the cross for you to have. It means having absolute fullness of life, a vibrant life that is devoted to God. It is a blessed life, not just in the sweet by-and-by, but in this present life. He didn't die so you could just eke by. He died so you could thrive.

Get this straight: You are not normal (John 17:16). You don't live by the standards the world sets. Jesus came so you could have an abundant life, an uncommon life, a life beyond anything you could dream of. Life should be like a cup running over, your paths dripping with abundance. God wants to lavish you with health, freedom, and prosperity. He wouldn't have sent Jesus to guarantee it if this weren't true.

Hit Your Mark:

Tell yourself today, "I am not normal. I am not of this world. I am something different and I expect something different. I expect abundance in every area of my life, and I won't settle for anything less!" Take that statement and make it yours. Declare to the enemy you are done eating the scraps he is feeding you. You are a child of the King and you're going to start living it!

August 12

The Target:

Now it came to pass in those days that He went out to the mountain to pray, and continued all night in prayer to God.

Luke 6:12

Set Your Sights:

Jesus was faced with the crucial task of choosing the twelve men who would be responsible for spreading His message around the world after He was gone. Notice what He did. He didn't say a quick prayer and then wing it, hoping for the best. He prayed until He had an answer, which took all night. He knew God would tell Him, and He was determined to be listening when He did.

Jesus frequently went up into the mountain, isolating Himself to pray. Several times the Bible records Him rising early in the morning or praying all night. He prayed in His most conflicted moment in the Garden of Gethsemane (Matt. 26:36–44). Jesus understood the gravity of prayer and demonstrated its significance frequently. He is your example to follow.

Hit Your Mark:

As you navigate your path, you need God to lead the way. There will be decisions to be made and questions that need answers. Prayer holds the answer and wisdom for every one of those questions and decisions, so do what Jesus did: separate yourself and pray. Then listen. Listen as long as it takes. He is always speaking, but sometimes it takes a while to shut everything else out so you can hear. Pray and listen.

August 13

The Target:

Who, contrary to hope, in hope believed, so that he became the father of many nations, according to what was spoken, "So shall your descendants be." And not being weak in faith, he did not consider his own body, already dead (since he was about a hundred years old), and the deadness of Sarah's womb.

Romans 4:18–19

Set Your Sights:

You can see in this passage there is a reference to both hope and faith, and that's because hope and faith are two different things. Hope is a positive expectation or desire to see a particular something happen. Faith knows that something is already done. Hope is the precursor to faith. It's where faith starts, and it is a powerful weapon that needs to be understood and implemented in your daily life.

Hope is the ability to see with your heart what you can't see with your eyes (Rom. 8:24–25). Hope is a positive image that comes from your innermost thoughts, what you focus on, and your understanding of the Word. Hope doesn't say, "Well, I'm going to try this and hope it works," or "I sure wish this would happen." It is far more powerful than that. Hope is founded on the promises in God's word (Rom. 4:20) and it expects to see results.

Hit Your Mark:

Recognize your imagination as the powerful weapon it is against the enemy. Put it to work by taking the promise of God you're standing on and seeing the results you're expecting. Imagine it. See yourself healed and whole, doing all the things you couldn't do before. Go on! Get your hopes up!

August 14

The Target:

And they come unto him, bringing one sick of the palsy, which was borne of four. And when they could not come nigh unto him for the press, they uncovered the roof where he was: and when they had broken it up, they let down the bed wherein the sick of the palsy lay.

Mark 2:3–4 (KJV)

Set Your Sights:

This lame man had four crazy, faith-filled friends. When they got to Jesus and saw it was too crowded to bring him in through the traditional route, they destroyed a portion of the roof and lowered him down through the ceiling. You need friends like that who will support you when everyone else says you're nuts. Friends who will tear the roof off to make sure you experience the healing power of Jesus.

The lame man was "sick of the palsy." This could mean he was sick with the palsy or sick of it. In other words, he was over it. He had enough. That attitude will cause you to act in faith and refuse to give up until you receive what you're believing for. His determination, coupled with the faith and resolve of his friends, was a powerful combination that led to his healing. It was faith in action.

Hit Your Mark:

Get sick of what you're dealing with today. Surround yourself with people who will believe with you, friends who will encourage and inspire you to never give up. Find those crazy four who will tear down walls to get you one step closer to victory. Today is the day to draw a line in the sand and say, "Enough is enough!"

August 15

The Target:

But that you may know that the Son of Man has power on earth to forgive sins—He said to the paralytic, "I say to you, arise, take up your bed, and go to your house."

Mark 2:10–11

Set Your Sights:

This is the same lame man who was lowered through the roof to be healed by Jesus, who then used the opportunity to prove the extent of His authority. He used what could be seen, physical healing of a body, to prove what couldn't be seen, forgiveness of sins. By demonstration, He made His authority over sin and sickness tangible.

Jesus's authority didn't stop there. In the end, Roman soldiers didn't overcome him, and they didn't take Him by surprise. No man could have taken His life without Him first willingly laying it down (John 10:18). It was in His power, and His power alone, to give up His life. Jesus went to the cross with authority, gave His life with authority, was raised with authority, and has now given His authority to you (Matt. 28:18-19).

Hit Your Mark:

Through His name, you have the same unquestionable authority over sin and sickness as Jesus. He is the source of all authority, and because He is always with you, authority is with you in abundant supply whenever you need it. Think on that today and recognize the authority you have in Him. Once you believe it, you will speak the Word with authority, and your situation will change!

August 16

The Target:

Jesus said to her, "I am the resurrection and the life. He who believes in Me, though he may die, he shall live."

John 11:25

Set Your Sights:

To die can mean to literally die or to perish. Think about the uneaten banana on your counter that turns from green to yellow, brown, and finally black. That is perishing. To live can refer to the literal act of breathing or to enjoying life, being full of vigor and strength. It is clear that the resurrection is not only for the future but also for the present.

The resurrection is not an event but a person: Jesus. He is the source of all things being raised to life again. The resurrection pertains to the dead in Christ being raised when He returns and to those perishing among the living because of physical and mental sickness. Jesus says you don't have to perish one more day. Through believing in Him, He can, and will, turn any perishing into life.

Hit Your Mark:

Have you seen a seemingly dead plant come back to life with a bit of water and sunshine? That is what Jesus does as your living water and light. So today, see the perishing area of your life as that dead plant. See yourself watering it and giving it the light it needs through the Word and prayer, then sit back and watch as it is resurrected back to life.

August 17

The Target:

So Jesus said to them, "Because of your unbelief; for assuredly, I say to you, if you have faith as a mustard seed, you will say to this mountain, 'Move from here to there,' and it will move; and nothing will be impossible for you."

Matthew 17:20

Set Your Sights:

Let's talk mustard seeds. They are usually only about 1 to 2 millimeters in diameter and germinate best in moist, rich soil. Under the right conditions, each seed has the explosive potential of growing to as tall as 9 feet high.

Your faith has the same potential. One tiny seed of faith contains all the power needed to overcome sickness in your body. With as little faith as a mustard seed, you can see every promise of God become a reality. And just like a natural seed, your faith will be most effective when planted in moist, fertile soil. That means a heart full of the wisdom of God that is ruled and led by the Holy Spirit.

Hit Your Mark:

Weeds choke seeds. Weeds can include adverse reports or symptoms in your body. It is important to recognize the weeds and immediately pluck them up. Don't allow them to stay long enough to take root in your heart, stealing precious nutrients from your faith that may hinder you from receiving. Your faith is enough, so protect it, water it, nourish it with the Word, pull up the weeds, and watch as your faith seed moves the mountain in front of you.

August 18

The Target:

Rejoice and be exceedingly glad, for great is your reward in heaven, for so they persecuted the prophets who were before you.

Matthew 5:12

Set Your Sights:

Rejoice and be exceedingly glad. Jesus said it and He meant it, which means it is absolutely possible to have joy in any situation. Even if the situation is grim, you can still rejoice. You can still have joy. Rejoicing in the midst of trouble can be a difficult subject to talk about, but it is an important message to receive and act on.

Joy, unlike happiness, is not based on circumstances. Happiness comes and goes like the wind, influenced by life's experiences, but joy is constant. Here is some great news about joy: One, it is an assured cure for whatever ails you (Prov. 17:22), and two, you already have it. Joy is a fruit of the Spirit you received the moment you were saved (Gal. 5:22). In your born-again spirit is an unlimited source of abundant joy!

Hit Your Mark:

Joy is a Bible-prescribed cure for your body and mind and is available every moment of every day. No matter what life throws your way, you can choose joy instead of sadness, anxiety, or fear. (You'll learn how tomorrow.) Think on the verses above and recognize the joy within you right now. That is your first step to walking in joy.

August 19

The Target:

For I consider that the sufferings of this present time are not worthy to be compared with the glory which shall be revealed in us.

Romans 8:18

Set Your Sights:

How do you walk in joy when the going is rough?

First, deal with the inside. You can't always control what happens on the outside, but you can control what happens inside by putting God's word above your thoughts, feelings, and experiences. You will bring out the joy from within by meditating on verses such as Nehemiah 8:10 and Psalm 103:1–5.

Next, deal with your perception of the outside. Paul experienced shipwrecks, beatings, and imprisonment. Despite these "light afflictions," he remained content in all situations by keeping everything in an eternal perspective (2 Cor. 11:24–27, 4:17; Phil. 4:11). He knew every experience would pale in comparison to eternity with Jesus. What you're going through is short-lived compared to what is to come. Keeping that in mind will make the outside a lot less important and joy a lot easier to tap into.

Hit Your Mark:

Don't let your circumstances determine your joy. Take control. Choose joy by keeping your sights set on the truth of God's word and by looking at your situation with an eternal perspective. This isn't said lightly: It may be rough now, but it's nothing in light of eternity. Think about these things and watch as the joy of the Lord becomes your strength.

August 20

The Target:

However, the report went around concerning Him all the more; and great multitudes came together to hear, and to be healed by Him of their infirmities.

Luke 5:15

Set Your Sights:

People came to Jesus to hear His message and be healed. They came to *hear* and be healed, not *talk* and be healed. Too often, people miss out on the power in a message because they're preoccupied with rehearsing the list of problems they don't want to forget to tell the prayer minister at the end. They're so busy talking in their minds they don't hear the message.

The power of healing was contained in the message Jesus spoke, and it is still contained in the gospel message today. To be healed, you have to hear. To hear, you have to stop talking. This means with your mouth but also with your mind. Stop running over the list of medications and diagnoses. Stop thinking about the lab reports and what the doctor said. Just stop it. Stop talking so you can hear.

Hit Your Mark:

There is power in hearing because hearing brings faith (Rom. 10:17), and faith enables you to receive the healing available to you. When you're listening to a message, stop the inner dialogue that tries to play on repeat. See yourself pushing the "Stop" button and opening your ears to the message that has the power to heal your body and mind. Hear and be healed.

The Target:

The nobleman said to Him, "Sir, come down before my child dies!" Jesus said to him, "Go your way; your son lives." So the man believed the word that Jesus spoke to him, and he went his way.

John 4:49–50

Set Your Sights:

This nobleman traveled a great distance to see Jesus, and by the time he found Him, his son was most certainly close to death. With urgency, he implored Jesus to come to his house. Jesus responded with, "Go back home. Your boy is healed." This was probably not the response the nobleman hoped for, so he had a choice to make. Should he keep trying to convince Jesus to come to his house or take Him at His word and head home?

He had nothing in the natural to stand on. He couldn't make a quick call to check on his son's status. All he had to base his faith on was the words of Jesus, and he decided that was enough. The minute he did and headed for home, his son began to recover (John 4:52–53).

Hit Your Mark:

You can put the full weight of your faith on the words of Jesus. Regardless of what you see or feel, even if you seem to get worse after you pray, choose to believe you are healed. Don't wait for goosebumps and a "feeling." Do what this nobleman did: Seek Jesus, hear His Word, then believe and act on it. That will always result in healing. Every time. Guaranteed.

August 22

The Target:

And what is the exceeding greatness of His power toward us who believe, according to the working of His mighty power which He worked in Christ when He raised Him from the dead.

Ephesians 1:19–20a

Set Your Sights:

Paul's prayer for you is that you get a revelation of the exceedingly great power that is in you. Despite how you feel, it is at your disposal when you need it. Though always present, this power is available only to those who believe. You must believe you have this power in order to receive it.

What kind of power is it? The phrase "according to" answers that question. It means the power you have is the same power God used to raise Christ from the dead. You don't have just a smidgen of power. He didn't water it down when He gave it to you. You have full-strength, raise-the-dead power, which is more than enough to overcome any evil work of the enemy.

Hit Your Mark:

God will not exhibit a grand act of power on your behalf because He gave you His power in the form of the Holy Spirit when you accepted Him as Lord and Savior. It's up to you to believe the truth and act on it. The first step to walking in power is to recognize you have it. You can begin by making the simple confession that you have all the power you need ... right there ... on the inside of you.

The Target:

And seated Him at His right hand in the heavenly places, far above all principality and power and might and dominion, and every name that is named, not only in this age but also in that which is to come. And He put all things under His feet, and gave Him to be head over all things to the church.

Ephesians 1:20b–22

Set Your Sights:

Authority makes power effective. If people speak the Word (the power) and it does not affect their bodies, they don't understand their authority. You can scream and shout all day long, but if you don't know your authority, the devil will tell you what he said to the seven sons of Sceva in Acts 19:15: "Jesus I know, and Paul I know; but who are you?"

After Jesus was resurrected, He was seated at the Father's right hand (the position of authority), far above every demonic force. You need to know that you were raised with Christ and are seated with Him (Eph. 2:5–6). This means you have the same authority Jesus has over every principality, power, might, and dominion. God not only gave you the power but the authority to back it up.

Hit Your Mark:

Even if you don't believe it yet, practice speaking with authority. Speak to your dog or to yourself in the mirror. Use different tones and volumes. Get used to what authoritative you sounds like, letting it resonate in your ears and mind. You have the power and authority. Now it's time to speak like you know it.

August 24

The Target:

For assuredly, I say to you, whoever says to this mountain, 'Be removed and be cast into the sea,' and does not doubt in his heart, but believes that those things he says will be done, he will have whatever he says.

Mark 11:23

Set Your Sights:

Over the last two days, you learned you have power and authority that you exercise through words. According to this verse, words should be carefully selected because what you say is what you get. Whether authority works for or against you is determined by the words you speak, either of life or death (Prov. 18:21).

A good indicator of what is truly in your heart is to listen to the words coming out of your mouth (Luke 6:45). What's important to understand is your words have power. Jesus casts out demons with words (Matt. 8:16), and gracious words bring healing to your bones (Prov. 16:24). With your mouth, confession is made unto salvation (Rom. 10:10). In other words, you can speak healing right into your body. Words have power.

Hit Your Mark:

Focus on your words today. Speak only about what you want to see. Resist the urge to complain and speak words of doubt because you will reap the harmful fruit they produce. In the words of my mother, "Think before you speak." Speak words that align with God's words, and you will have what you say. Even if you don't believe them at first, speak them anyway, and faith will be born (Rom. 10:17) that will move your mountain. Guaranteed.

August 25 – Part I

The Target:

But if ye have bitter envying and strife in your hearts, glory not, and lie not against the truth. This wisdom descendeth not from above, but is earthly, sensual, devilish. For where envying and strife is, there is confusion and every evil work.

James 3:14–16 (KJV)

Set Your Sights:

Over the next several days, we'll identify hindrances to healing, starting with strife. Strife comes as resentment, jealousy, quarreling, or bitterness. It can look like clashes with your spouse or kids and feel like an unshakable heaviness. Or like an offense you take that feels like a wave of slow-boil anger on the inside. Or a nagging, unsettling thought that picks at you until it creates an open wound in your soul.

Left unchecked, strife has one outcome: every evil work manifesting in your mind and body. It is important to recognize when strife rears its ugly head and not let it take root in your heart because the condition of your heart toward others is a major player in the health of your body. Your body was designed to live in peace, not strife. Because of that, you can't live in strife and expect to walk in health.

Hit Your Mark:

Take a look in your heart for any hint of strife. If you find some, confess your faults to one another and pray for each other so you can be healed (James 5:16). Getting rid of the strife in your life will bring healing, so don't hesitate to act. Don't let strife keep you from receiving your healing one more day!

August 26 – Part II

The Target:

No longer drink only water, but use a little wine for your stomach's sake and your frequent infirmities.

1 Timothy 5:23

Set Your Sights:

Strife was the first hindrance to healing identified yesterday, and today's culprit is food. According to Paul, Timothy was having frequent issues with his stomach. From the context, you can surmise his problems were caused by the water he was drinking, so Paul's solution was to simply stop drinking it.

This godly principle can also be applied to food. If it's making you sick, don't eat it. Many of the diseases running rampant today—diabetes, high cholesterol, skin issues—are caused by a poor diet high in bad fats and sugar. Sickness is spiritualized too often, blamed on a spirit of infirmity, when it has nothing to do with the spiritual at all but is a natural problem with a natural solution.

Hit Your Mark:

Don't be discouraged if you need to change your diet. Instead, be encouraged there is something you can do about the condition you're in. If you are suffering in your body because of the fuel you are putting in it, then change the fuel. Take responsibility and treat your body right by giving it the proper fuel. You will see a difference!

August 27 – Part III

The Target:

And behold, there was a woman who had a spirit of infirmity eighteen years, and was bent over and could in no way raise herself up.

Luke 13:11

Set Your Sights:

The third possible hindrance to healing is a spirit of infirmity. If this woman had gone to a doctor of this day and age, it is doubtful he would have said, "A spirit is causing the deformity in your spine." He would have run tests and taken x-rays that showed arthritis and scoliosis and then prescribed medication and treatment that wouldn't have helped her.

Some afflictions are natural and some are spiritual. In the instance of this woman, when Jesus recognized the spirit and cast it out, her back was immediately straightened (vv. 12–13). If x-rays and labs had been retaken, they would have shown no evidence of anything wrong with her body. That is what happens when the spirit of infirmity goes: restoration is quick and complete.

Hit Your Mark:

Not every hindrance to healing is a spirit of infirmity that needs to be cast out. Still, it is a possibility to consider, especially if you know you're healed, have been standing in faith for an extended period of time, and still aren't seeing any change in your body. Let the Lord show you if this is the case, and if it is, take your God-given authority and cast it out, expecting quick and complete results.

August 28 – Part IV

The Target:

Afterward Jesus found him in the temple, and said to him, "See, you have been made well. Sin no more, lest a worse thing come upon you."

John 5:14

Set Your Sights:

Personal sin is the next hindrance to healing. Jesus made it clear sin can lead to physical issues when He told this man He healed to stop sinning or something worse could come upon him.

Bad news first, then good news: Sin has consequences, some of which include sickness. For example, sexual sin can lead to STDs and AIDS, and gluttony can lead to obesity, joint problems, and diabetes. Those things are not punishments from God but natural consequences of poor choices.

The good news: When Jesus encountered the lame man, He healed him without even a mention of sin. He didn't say, "You caused it, so live with it." Sin didn't disqualify him from being healed. That is a lie the enemy will whisper in your ear. You are not disqualified and there is no consequence the blood of Jesus didn't cover.

Hit Your Mark:

If you are suffering from an affliction because of personal sin, eliminate that hindrance to your healing by recognizing it and repenting. This doesn't mean to grovel and beg God for forgiveness but to admit your error and turn from it. There is no penance to pay for your wrongdoings, including holding on to sickness. Stop living in and with the mistakes of the past.

August 29 – Part V

The Target:

And release those who through fear of death were all their lifetime subject to bondage.

Hebrews 2:15

Set Your Sights:

Fear can be a significant hindrance to healing because it leads to bondage, which often presents as sickness. Fear and faith are opposites, but they work the same in that they both come by hearing: Faith by hearing the Word and fear by hearing the world (past experience, bad reports, or prognoses).

The hindrance of fear is removed when you recognize and cast it out. A personal example: I suffered from alektorophobia (fear of chickens) for years because of a traumatic childhood incident. No joke. When I realized fear of those small yard birds had me in bondage, I took control by focusing on Genesis 1:26 and Psalm 8:6, which say I have dominion. Over time, I came to know my dominion and am totally free from that bondage.

Hit Your Mark:

You have a choice in what you hear, which means you decide whether to operate in fear or faith. It is not always an easy or quick process to eliminate fear, but you can do it by changing what you hear. Stop listening to the things that create fear and start listening to what produces faith. When you do that consistently, faith will come, fear will go, and sickness will go along with it.

August 30 – Part VI

The Target:

Because for the work of Christ he came close to death, not regarding his life, to supply what was lacking in your service toward me.

Philippians 2:30

Set Your Sights:

Ready for another hindrance? In verses 25–30 of this chapter, Paul talks about Epaphroditus, a fellow laborer in Christ who became deathly ill. Paul didn't say it was because he lacked faith or had the wrong confession but because he worked so hard, he almost killed himself. That is not the life God intended for you or expects from you.

You do have a call on your life, and He has the perfect plan to fulfill it, but amid all the "doing," you need to refresh and recharge yourself daily. You need to slow down and take a breath. If you constantly give, give, give, and never take time to fill yourself back up through prayer and study, you will eventually dry up and burn out. As your body becomes stressed, worn out, and compromised, that leaves a place for sickness to sneak in, just like it did with Epaphroditus.

Hit Your Mark:

Say this out loud: "I can't please everybody and I can't do everything. I will not give place to sickness in my body through busyness. I choose today to not spread myself too thin and to leave a space open in my day for rest." That's a great start. Now do it.

August 31 – Part VII

The Target:

Have mercy on me, O Lord, for I am in trouble; My eye wastes away with grief, Yes, my soul and my body! For my life is spent with grief, And my years with sighing; My strength fails because of my iniquity, And my bones waste away.

Psalm 31:9–10

Set Your Sights:

This is the final day of hindrances to healing. Trauma of any kind has the potential to impact your life. It could be the death of a loved one, a near-death experience, or a divorce. Trauma can leave an open door for sickness to enter if not dealt with. In today's verse, trauma takes the form of grief.

Grief is deep sorrow usually associated with losing a loved one, but it can also be experienced with divorce or regret over a past action or inaction. In this case, David was grieved over his sins, and he was so focused on the things causing the grief that his strength was failing and his bones were wasting away. Grief is a real threat to healing.

Hit Your Mark:

If you know there is some trauma in your past you've tried to bury in the ground and cover in concrete, that's not the way to deal with it. Not dealing with it may be precisely what's allowing sickness, pain, or digestive issues to plague your body. God loves you and is right there to help you through it. Grab the shovel or the jackhammer if there's concrete, and dig that seed of trauma out of your heart. Cast it at His feet and let Him heal that wound.

SEPTEMBER

September 1

The Target:

And He said to her, "Daughter, be of good cheer;
your faith has made you well. Go in peace."

Luke 8:48

Set Your Sights:

If you are unfamiliar with this account, what is important to know for this devotion is there was a woman with a medical issue who invested all she had in doctors and they couldn't cure her. She heard about Jesus and set her faith to be healed by Him. That's where we pick up.

When she touched Jesus, notice what He didn't say, "I can't believe you went to the doctor before coming to Me. I see where your priorities lie." He did not condemn her for going to the doctor and didn't withhold healing because of it.

Jesus wants you healed by whatever means necessary. The best way to be healed is to follow the leading of the Holy Spirit because He knows where your faith is. If you're fully persuaded you will be healed through Jesus and man's medicine, go to the doctor and expect Jesus to work healing through them.

Hit Your Mark:

Stop condemning yourself for going to the doctor, and don't let anyone else blame you either. It is possible to get to a place where you're fully persuaded that healing can come through Jesus alone, and that's the target you should aim for. But until then, do what is on your heart and Jesus will meet you there.

September 2

The Target:

Forbidding to marry, and commanding to abstain from foods which God created to be received with thanksgiving by those who believe and know the truth. For every creature of God is good, and nothing is to be refused if it is received with thanksgiving; for it is sanctified by the word of God and prayer.

1 Timothy 4:3–5

Set Your Sights:

This devotion is ammunition for those struggling on a digestive healing journey, especially those who have no explanation for why their bodies reject the food they eat. Food was created for your stomach, and your stomach was made for food (1 Cor. 6:13). They were divinely designed to work together to nourish your body.

You have two responsibilities when it comes to food: First, pray the Word over it, renewing your mind to the truth that God has sanctified (purified) it. Second, receive the food you've prayed over with thanksgiving, which means unto God as an act of worship. Eating food can be an act of worship. Eating in fear of impending symptoms is not receiving it with thanksgiving. The attitude with which you eat is often more important than what you eat.

Hit Your Mark:

If the enemy has convinced you that you are a prisoner to what you can and cannot eat, he has deceived you. You are in bondage to nothing, including food. Today is the day to change your thinking about what you eat. Recognize your food is purified by the word of God, pray over it, and then receive it with thanksgiving! That's what it was created for.

September 3

The Target:

For by grace you have been saved through faith, and that not of yourselves; it is the gift of God, not of works, lest anyone should boast.

Ephesians 2:8

Set Your Sights:

The enemy wants you to believe you have to perform flawlessly to receive healing, including never doubting, never having a fearful thought, never speaking a negative word, spending every waking moment meditating on the Word, and not listening to anything "non-Christian." Ever. And if you do mess up, it negates everything you've done up to that point and sends you back to the beginning. You can't slip up, not one time, or you won't receive.

The devil wants you to be occupied with those thoughts because it makes receiving healing all about you and what you're doing and not about what Jesus has already done. He wants you to think you'll never get it right, so you'll never be healed. This verse clearly says you are saved through faith, not through works, which also means you are healed through faith, not through works. Your faith. His works.

Hit Your Mark:

Healing is a gift, not something you have to work for. All the work required to secure healing for your body was done by Jesus. Your "work" is to believe it. In believing, your words and your actions will effortlessly line up with that truth. Rest, my friend, in that it is already finished. Not by your works, but by His.

September 4

The Target:

Grace and peace be multiplied to you in the knowledge of God and of Jesus our Lord, as His divine power has given to us all things that pertain to life and godliness, through the knowledge of Him who called us by glory and virtue.

2 Peter 1:2–3

Set Your Sights:

Having knowledge of God's word means recognizing and accepting its validity and understanding the truth revealed. Knowledge is necessary because it multiplies grace and peace in your life, and all things pertaining to life and godliness come through it.

The life promised is an abundant life. Not a scraping by, just plodding along in life, but a life saturated with the goodness of God. Since these elements come through knowledge of His Word, only the Word you know will bring you this life.

For example, suppose you don't know what God promises about healing. In that case, you'll have nothing to stand on in the face of sickness, and you won't experience that part of the abundant life. Through knowledge, you accept, understand, and walk in what is promised.

Hit Your Mark:

Listening to teachings and reading books is great, but gaining knowledge of God means getting in the Word for yourself and letting the Holy Spirit make it clear and real to you. As you study and gain knowledge of His Word, you will see the effects of it as grace, peace, and life are multiplied to you, in you, and through you. Be active in your pursuit of His Word today!

September 5

The Target:

By which have been given to us exceedingly great and precious promises, that through these you may be partakers of the divine nature, having escaped the corruption that is in the world through lust.

2 Peter 1:4

Set Your Sights:

Being a partaker means you take part in and experience something. For example, if you participate in a basketball game, you are in it, playing it, and experiencing it. When you know the exceedingly great and precious promises God has given you, you will be a partaker of the divine nature.

What does the divine nature look like? When Jesus was transfigured, His face shined like the sun and His clothes were white as light (Matt. 17:2). It was as if, for a brief moment, His veil of flesh was pulled back and His true nature, the divine nature, was revealed. As a child of God, you have the same divine nature inside you.

Through knowledge of God's promises, you will experience the benefits of the divine nature. God's nature is healing, which means your nature is healing. Through this knowledge, you will escape corruption (sickness, disease, bondage) as your divine nature is revealed and your mind and body are transformed.

Hit Your Mark:

Imagine Jesus on the Mount of Transfiguration, His face shining and clothes white as light. Now imagine yourself standing there, your face shining and clothes white as light. That is your true nature ... your divine nature. Sickness cannot stay in the presence of your true nature. It. Must. Go.

September 6

The Target:

That the sharing of your faith may become effective by the acknowledgment of every good thing which is in you in Christ Jesus.

Philemon 1:6

Set Your Sights:

The Word states that when you were born again, you were given everything you need for life, which would include healing (2 Peter 1:3). You weren't given the short end of the stick when God handed out healing, so you have more than you'll ever need. If you don't know healing is already yours and within you, you'll constantly be waiting for some outside source to give it to you.

When you acknowledge every good thing in you, sharing your faith will become effective. In context, this means your testimony to others will be fruitful. Conceptually, it can mean when you acknowledge the "good thing" of healing is already in you, your faith will become effective. When your faith becomes effective, it is released, and you will see the healing within you manifest in your physical body.

Hit Your Mark:

Imagine the healing inside of you as a bank account with an endless supply of funds where you can make a withdrawal at any time. To release those funds, you must first acknowledge and believe they're there, then all that's left to do is write out the withdrawal slip. The healing bank is always open. Acknowledge it. Believe it. And make a withdrawal today!

September 7

The Target:

Now faith is the assurance (the confirmation, the title deed) of the things [we] hope for, being the proof of things [we] do not see and the conviction of their reality [faith perceiving as real fact what is not revealed to the senses].

Hebrews 11:1 (AMPC)

Set Your Sights:

Faith is the confirmation of what you're hoping for. Hope is believing something is possible, whereas faith believes it is a reality. Hope is a positive expectation that something good will happen in the future, while faith knows it is already done. Hope is an optimistic attitude, but faith is unwavering confidence. Hope comes and goes, but faith remains steadfast.

Faith gives substance to hope and access to every good and precious gift of salvation. Those gifts exist right now but in spiritual form. It's important to understand faith doesn't create things, taking something nonexistent and making it real. It appropriates existing things that the senses can't perceive. For example, faith believes you are healed before you see it. It understands healing is a fact, a done deal, and can't be moved from that belief.

Hit Your Mark:

If you read the devotion on hope (August 13), you've imagined yourself healed and whole. As you continue that practice, faith will arise and give substance to your hope until you are convinced you are healed ... no matter what. That is faith. When that happens, the next step is seeing what you're believing for. It's just one step away. You're almost there. Don't quit.

September 8

The Target:

Blessed is she who believed, for there will be a fulfillment of those things which were told her from the Lord.

Luke 1:45

Set Your Sights:

The angel of the Lord told Mary she would be the mother of the Son of God. In the natural, there was no possible way she could be a mother. She was, after all, a virgin. Mary had a choice to either accept God's words to her as truth or reject them and move on.

As evidenced by her statement to the angel, "Be it unto me according to your word" (v. 38), she chose to believe that God's word would accomplish exactly what He said it would. For her, that trumped everything.

That is faith: Believing it because God said it. Period. When you believe the word of God above your natural circumstances, you will have the same result as Mary: You will see a fulfillment of that which was promised.

Hit Your Mark:

To have the same outcome as Mary, you first have to hear the word of God. Do you need to hear it's His will for you to be healed every time and of everything? Do you need to hear it doesn't matter what you've done, that you aren't disqualified from walking in health? Once you hear, choose to believe His promise above all else. Set your sights on the promise. Believe it. See the fulfillment of it.

September 9

The Target:

Then he said to me, "This is the word of the Lord to Zerubbabel: Not by might, nor by power, but by my Spirit, says the Lord of hosts. Who are you, O great mountain? Before Zerubbabel you shall become a plain. And he shall bring forward the top stone amid shouts of "Grace, grace to it!"

Zechariah 4:6–7 (ESV)

Set Your Sights:

This power-packed prophetic word tells you how God dealt with all your mountains. In context, the prophet Zechariah heard a word from the Lord for Zerubbabel that the mountain looming in front of him (rebuilding the temple) would become a plain by the power of the Holy Spirit. And when the top stone was placed, completing the temple, the people would shout to the Lord in praise.

In fulfilling this prophetic word, God crushed your mountains when He put the top stone in place. Jesus is the top stone (Ps. 118:22). Because of Him, it is not by your might or power but by His Spirit alone that sin and sickness are flattened before you. And when the people see what the Lord has done in you through His grace and power, all will give Him the glory and praise.

Hit Your Mark:

What is the name of the mountain looming before you? Is it cancer, arthritis, injury, or depression? Jesus, your top stone has come, and you can now speak to the mountain with faith-filled words and watch as the power of Jesus's finished work responds as a mountain-crushing bulldozer. Let grace do all the work and watch your mountain become plain.

September 10

The Target:

There is none to uphold your cause, no medicine for your wound, no healing for you. ... Therefore all who devour you shall be devoured, and all your foes, every one of them, shall go into captivity; those who plunder you shall be plundered, and all who prey on you I will make a prey. For I will restore health to you, and your wounds I will heal, declares the Lord.

Jeremiah 30:13, 16–17a (ESV)

Set Your Sights:

This is a beautiful picture of redemption. The Israelites were in a desperate state. All their allies and friends left them, making them easy prey for their enemies. No one could save them and they couldn't save themselves. They were without hope until God revealed His love for them through Jeremiah, saying, "I will do it. I will step in and annihilate your enemies and restore you to health."

You were in their shoes once, without God, having no one to save you or heal your brokenness. But God, in His unrelenting love for you, said, "I will do it. I will step in and annihilate your enemies and restore you to health." But you first had to see that no one, including yourself, could save you. No one, including yourself, could heal you. You had no one to stand up for you ... until God sent Jesus.

Hit Your Mark:

Jesus stood up for you, disarming and putting your enemies to shame, then sending them out as prey (Col. 2:15). They tremble when they see you because they see Jesus inside you. Defeating your enemy and being restored to health is not, and has never been, about you standing up for yourself. Think on this today and let it transform you, inside and out.

September 11

The Target:

That you do not become sluggish, but imitate those who through faith and patience inherit the promises.

Hebrews 6:12

Set Your Sights:

Patience is faith that withstands the test of time. It's faith that remains despite the circumstances that have seemed to drag on forever. It stares persistent symptoms in the face, saying, "You will never get me to believe I am not healed. I will not be moved, you lying symptoms." It knows the promises and diligently pursues them.

Just as in the natural, a lack of exercising faith and patience results in becoming sluggish (that is, lazy and foolish). Those who are determined and focused, not sluggish, will experience their inheritance. In practice, this means standing firm on what you believe, even when presented with facts to the contrary. Patience added to your faith will lead to what you're believing for being made manifest in your body.

Hit Your Mark:

Here's your good news for the day: You have all the faith and patience you need to see the inheritance of healing you've believed for. You were given them both the moment you accepted Christ (Eph. 2:8, Gal. 5:22). You've already got them, and when you put them to use effectively, you will inherit the promises.

September 12 – Part I

The Target:

And the prayer of faith will save the sick, and the Lord will raise him up.

James 5:15a

Set Your Sights:

In the previous verse, sick believers are instructed to go to the church's elders for prayer and anointing with oil. Prayer and oil, in and of themselves, have no power to heal. This verse makes it clear that faith mixed with prayer and oil is what makes them effective.

This is why prayers spoken in unbelief (For example, "If it's Your will, please heal me.") and prayers repeated over and over to get God to do something have no power to heal. They are wish-filled, not faith-filled prayers.

But when you mix faith with your prayer, God promises it will save and raise you up. A conviction and profession of the truth will heal you, make you whole, and cause you to rise out of sickness and death.

Hit Your Mark:

A prayer of faith sounds like this: "I thank you I am healed in Jesus's name despite what I feel. I know Jesus died for my sickness and pain, and I reject and resist every single thing the enemy is trying to get me to accept. I choose to believe God's word over Satan's lies. Body, you are healed and that's that. It's a done deal." Proclaim it and then stick to it!

September 13 – Part II

The Target:

And if he has committed sins, he will be forgiven. Confess your trespasses to one another, and pray for one another, that you may be healed.

James 5:15b–16a

Set Your Sights:

Adding on to yesterday's devotion, the prayer of faith is linked to the forgiveness of sins, and the forgiveness of sins to the healing of the body. Sin can be an inroad of sickness (by way of consequences, not punishment from God), and verse 16 reveals how to disconnect yourself from sin-induced sickness: Confess your trespasses to one another.

This is not talking about confessing to a priest, who will then absolve you of your sins. You only need one priest, Jesus Christ (Heb. 4:14), and your confession is before God. Still, there's something to be said about humbling yourself before a trusted friend and bringing what you've done into the light. It's not always easy, but the promised benefit is great.

Hit Your Mark:

Not all sickness is caused by sin, but in cases where it is, you have the solution: Humble yourself and admit you've done wrong. Eating a bite of humble pie is worth it if it tears down a barrier to your healing. If you've done wrong and you know it, cut off a slice of that pie. With a heart willing to change, take a bite and thank Him for the forgiveness and healing that are sure to follow.

September 14

The Target:

The effective, fervent prayer of a righteous man avails much.

James 5:16b

Set Your Sights:

The prayer of faith hinges on three key words: righteous, fervent, and effective. First, you need to know you are, in fact, a righteous man and this verse pertains to you. (See 2 Cor. 5:21 for proof.) Check one.

Second, fervent prayer is filled with passionate intensity and is purposeful and single-minded. It is determined, not wavering, and confident in the outcome. Fervency comes from knowing God's word and, more specifically, what it says about your situation. Check two.

Lastly, an effective prayer will put forth power and go to work for you. You'll see the effects of your prayer, whether in your body or in your mind. It may first come in the form of confidence and boldness rising up within you and will surely be followed by a manifestation of the Word in your body. A faith-filled, fervent prayer *will* be effective. Check three.

Hit Your Mark:

When you pray the prayer of faith, you can expect it to contain all the power it needs to give you victory over any sickness trying to invade your body. That's what "avails much" means. Your prayer has the potential to overcome anything. Like a hot knife passing through butter, nothing can stand in its way. Victory is in your fervent, effective prayer.

September 15

The Target:

So he cried out to the Lord, and the Lord showed him a tree. When he cast it into the waters, the waters were made sweet.

Exodus 15:25a

Set Your Sights:

The backstory: Three days earlier, God delivered the Israelites through the Red Sea on dry land (Ex. 14:22). Since then, they had been wandering in the wilderness without water until they reached Marah. Unfortunately, Marah's water was bitter.

Without water, they would die, and there was nothing they could do. They needed a savior. Moses turned to the Lord, who told him to throw a specific tree into the water. When he did, it healed the water and it became sweet.

Their situation was a prophetic picture. The tree was symbolic of the cross; and the water, the nations of the world, including you. Just like the Israelites, you were dying and in need of a savior. And as the tree was to the water, the cross is to you. The tree healed the water and the cross healed you.

Hit Your Mark:

Envision this scene in your mind: See Marah's murky waters and imagine its foul stench. See Moses throwing the tree into it and it becomes crystal clear as the muck disappears. Breathe in the sweet smell of it. That's what happened when you believed. The cross touched your life and everything bitter was made sweet. Everything sick was made well. You. Were. Healed.

September 16

The Target:

Abide in Me, and I in you. As the branch cannot bear fruit of itself, unless it abides in the vine, neither can you, unless you abide in Me. I am the vine, you are the branches. He who abides in Me, and I in him, bears much fruit; for without Me you can do nothing.

John 15:4–5

Set Your Sights:

The fruit you bear in your body can be good or bad. If you believe your eyesight will diminish as you age, because that's just what happens, it will. Bad fruit. If you believe your crooked spine will become straight because Jesus healed you, it will. Good fruit. If you don't see the results you want, this verse makes it clear how to change that.

The type of fruit you see is determined by where you spend your time (abide) and what you focus on. You can abide in scientific research, the social media that constantly vies for your attention, or what the doctors say over you. You can just as easily abide in the vine, which means staying put in the Word. That is where you will produce the good fruit you're believing for.

Hit Your Mark:

The fruit you bear is all about location, location, location, so evaluate where you're spending your time. When you recognize you are camped in the wrong place, pack up your tent, and move to the only place that will result in much good fruit—the Word. Once you're there, drive a stake in the ground, take up permanent residency, and don't be moved again.

September 17

The Target:

And Abraham called the name of that place Jehovahjireh: as it is said to this day, In the mount of the Lord it shall be seen.

Genesis 22:14 (KJV)

Set Your Sights:

When God instructed Abraham to go to a specific mount in the land of Moriah to sacrifice his son, Isaac (v. 2), he heard the word of the Lord and responded by acting in faith. He packed up everything he needed to build an altar and headed for Moriah with Isaac in tow. When Isaac asked him where the lamb for the sacrifice was, Abraham responded that God would provide it (v. 8).

You know the rest. God provided and Abraham called the place Jehovah-Jireh, which means God will see to it. God saw to it Abraham had everything he needed. He upholds that name today by continuing to provide. He saw to it that you would have everything you'd need to live a victorious life by offering up one final sacrifice: His one and only son, Jesus Christ.

Hit Your Mark:

God's name was, is, and forever will be Jehovah-Jireh. His nature is to provide and He can be no other way. He knew before the foundation of the world what you would need and when you would need it, and that's why He placed healing inside of you for easy access the moment you were born again. Healing was provided by the grace of Jehovah-Jireh. He saw to it.

September 18

The Target:

And throwing aside his garment, he rose and came to Jesus.

Mark 10:50

Set Your Sights:

In this account, blind Bartimaeus heard Jesus was close by and started crying out for him. He must have created quite a disturbance because the people shushed him, which made him holler even more. He didn't care what anyone thought and was determined to be healed by Jesus.

(Beware: There will always be people who are offended by radical faith, and they are usually the ones who would prefer to stay untouched by Jesus rather than draw attention to themselves for fear of what others will think.)

Bartimaeus's faith stopped Jesus in His tracks (v. 49). Notice the first thing he did: He took off the old garment that labeled him as a beggar. Before he could even see, he threw off the old identity, saying, "I'm not a blind beggar anymore. I don't need this old garment!" That was an act of faith, and his faith made him whole (v. 52).

Hit Your Mark:

What is your identity? Are you the sick trying to get well, or are you the healed resisting sickness? How you think of yourself and your situation is very important. Stop Jesus in His tracks by casting off the old identity of "the sick" and putting on the new identity of "the healed"!

September 19

The Target:

But He said, "The things which are impossible with men are possible with God."

Luke 18:27

Set Your Sights:

Sometimes it feels as if your situation is simply impossible and you'll never be healed. Maybe no doctor or treatment has been able to help. Perhaps "incurable" has been spoken over you, and the doctors have said there's nothing more they can do. If you're not careful, focusing on those things will lead to a hardness of heart in the area of healing.

A hard heart develops when you are more tuned in to the natural, seemingly impossible situation than on the immeasurable power of the almighty God. It comes from focusing on the list of diagnoses and medications instead of on the blood Jesus shed for you that covers every item on that list. Hardness of heart is unbelief that will hinder your faith and should be guarded against with all diligence.

Hit Your Mark:

If you struggle with believing healing is even a possibility, guard against a hard heart by writing this verse down and keeping it with you. The moment you think, *This is impossible* or *This is never going to happen*, read it. Speak it out loud. Remind yourself that even though it is impossible for man, it is not impossible for God because the blood of Jesus trumps every impossible situation.

September 20

The Target:

For there is no partiality with God.

Romans 2:11

Set Your Sights:

Was there ever a time you needed healing and heard about a new believer who was instantly healed? How about a time you prayed for someone with the same issue as you, and they were healed while you remained unchanged?

The resulting questions—"What about me? Why did they get healed and I didn't?"—are often accompanied by the temptation to get offended at God, as if it's His fault you aren't healed, or He's holding back something from you that He freely gave to another.

At the heart of those questions is a lack of understanding that God does not show favoritism or prefer one person over another based on performance. Everyone receives healing on the same intrinsic merit, the merit of faith, which He has given to all in equal measure (Rom. 12:3).

Hit Your Mark:

What God did through Jesus belongs to every believer equally. He isn't saying, "You don't measure up to John, so you aren't going to be healed," or "I have more compassion for Suzy, so I'll heal her but not you." What Jesus did, He did for all. God's word works for everyone when it is received by faith. It worked for me, and it will work for you. Let this verse settle that for you today.

September 21

The Target:

This is the message which we have heard from Him and declare to you, that God is light and in Him is no darkness at all.

1 John 1:5

Set Your Sights:

The word "heard" goes beyond the physical act of hearing what was spoken. It means what was said was listened to and understood. It was considered and accepted. What you hear is ultimately what you'll come to believe (2 Cor. 4:13), which is why guarding the gateway to your ears is so important.

What truth was declared and heard here? God is light. It seems like such a trivial statement, yet it has the power to free you from and eradicate the darkness that has unlawfully taken up residency in your body.

If you are standing in a room filled with light, darkness cannot enter. However, the slightest spark will light up a room filled with pitch-black darkness. That is what God does wherever He goes. He bursts through the darkness. God is in you. Light is in you. Darkness cannot exist in the presence of the light.

Hit Your Mark:

See what you're standing against today as a dark spot inside you. Now see the light of God pierce that dark spot and imagine it bursting into a million pieces, blown into nothingness. Light violently and without mercy overcomes the darkness. Every time.

September 22

The Target:

For the wages of sin is death, but the gift of God is eternal life in Christ Jesus our Lord.

Romans 6:23

Set Your Sights:

To state it differently, the paycheck of your old sinful nature is death and all the drawbacks that come with it, including sickness, bondage, poverty, condemnation, guilt, and shame. But as a child of God, your old sinful nature is dead and gone (Rom. 6:6). Instead of wages of death, you started receiving the salary of eternal life in the blink of an eye when you believed in Jesus.

Eternal life is a gift from God that will never be rescinded and never come to an end. It is an abundant life, a full life, a life overflowing with health, prosperity, and freedom. When you believe you should be experiencing the wages of an abundant life, not drawing paychecks from death, you will begin to clearly see the difference between the two, rejecting the drawbacks and accepting the benefits.

Hit Your Mark:

Start seeing yourself for who you really are (a child of God whose nature is eternal life) and the sickness in your body for what it really is (the odd man out, the nature of death that no longer belongs). Sickness is not a reflection of your new nature. Health is your nature now. Expect nothing less.

September 23

The Target:

The Spirit Himself bears witness with our spirit that we are children of God.

Romans 8:16

Set Your Sights:

Don't miss this: The Spirit bears witness with, not to, your spirit. The difference between "with" and "to" is enormous. In a court of law, if you bear witness to someone, you tell them something they don't know. When you bear witness with someone, you tell the same story they do, and your testimonies agree.

Applying that understanding to this verse, the Spirit confirms the truth your spirit already knows, not telling it something it doesn't. In fact, your spirit knows all truth because it has the mind of Christ (1 Cor. 2:16).

So who has the Spirit and your spirit partnered up to bear witness to? The ultimate jury, your very own decision-maker: your mind. As you renew it to the truths your spirit already holds, revelation comes and change happens (Rom. 12:2).

Hit Your Mark:

Your spirit knows all it needs to know about healing, which means you aren't waiting on God for revelation, and He isn't withholding it from you. Understanding this truth will give you confidence that revelation is yours, causing you to break out of passivity and aggressively pursue what's inside you. Revelation is for you. Revelation is in you. Renew your mind to that truth today and expect to receive it.

September 24

The Target:

And so it was, when Moses held up his hand, that Israel prevailed; and when he let down his hand, Amalek prevailed. But Moses' hands became heavy; so they took a stone and put it under him, and he sat on it. And Aaron and Hur supported his hands, one on one side, and the other on the other side; and his hands were steady until the going down of the sun. So Joshua defeated Amalek and his people with the edge of the sword.

Exodus 17:11–13

Set Your Sights:

Moses, the man who parted the Red Sea, needed help from his friends as fatigue overtook him in the middle of a battle. When his hands were raised, Israel was winning. When he couldn't hold them up any longer, Israel began to lose. He couldn't have done it alone, but with the help of Aaron and Hur, he persevered until the hard-fought battle was won.

You don't have to fight your battle alone. There is nothing wrong with asking for help when you get weary. Asking a friend to pray with or for you does not indicate a lack of faith. The enemy will use that lie in an attempt to bring condemnation and isolate you. He knows that just as a lamb separated from the flock, you are easier prey when you stand alone.

Hit Your Mark:

It's okay to admit you're weary and ask others to stand with you in the fight. Any believer would be happy to lock their shield of faith with yours, encourage you, and agree that you are the healed of the Lord. If you're tired today, reach out to a friend who will declare what God says about you: You are healed. Don't give up!

279

September 25

The Target:

Therefore comfort each other and edify one another,
just as you also are doing.

1 Thessalonians 5:11

Set Your Sights:

You can get so wrapped up in your own healing you become blind to those struggling beside you. Many people won't ask for help, even when they obviously need it. This verse urges you to recognize and comfort them, call them to your side, even as you walk out your own healing.

You have the tools to comfort someone. Through the Word (Acts 20:32), encouraging them to focus on the truth. Through the gifts of the Spirit, such as prophecy or a word of wisdom (1 Cor. 12:7). Through gentle and gracious words, which are health to the bones (Prov. 16:24).

A powerful way to comfort is to share what God has done for you and encourage them to see their own victory in your story. Assure them as the Word worked for you, it will work for them (Rom. 2:11), and they will overcome (Rev. 12:11). That's what comfort does … it helps them overcome.

Hit Your Mark:

You won't see others in need until you lift your eyes up from your path and look around. Do that today. Keep your eyes peeled and your ears tuned. If you recognize someone in need, take the initiative and reach out to them. You have the tools to edify them. Put them to use.

September 26

The Target:

Jesus saith unto him, Go thy way; thy son liveth. And the man believed the word that Jesus had spoken unto him, and he went his way. And as he was now going down, his servants met him, and told him, saying, Thy son liveth. Then enquired he of them the hour when he began to amend. And they said unto him, Yesterday at the seventh hour the fever left him.

John 4:50–52 (KJV)

Set Your Sights:

Focus your attention on verse 52. Notice the man asked his servants the exact time his son began to get better. He understood the progressive nature of the healing that took place. This is a sticking point where many people miss the mark and fail to receive their healing, not realizing healing can be supernaturally instant or supernaturally progressive. Either way, it is supernatural.

Many people believe if there is no instant change, they didn't receive. They pray in faith but then immediately check if they feel better. When there is no outward change, the firestorm of faith they were using to receive is quenched by a tsunami of unbelief. The truth is, the healing process began the moment they prayed and believed. See it or not. Feel it or not.

Hit Your Mark:

Draw a line in the sand and determine you will not be moved by what you see or feel. When you speak health over your body and command it to line up with the healing promised in the Word, don't be moved from the truth that healing began at that moment. Whether it takes one minute, one week, or one year, keep believing, knowing it is in the process of coming to pass.

September 27

The Target:

My soul, wait silently for God alone, For my expectation is from Him. He only is my rock and my salvation; He is my defense; I shall not be moved.

Psalm 62:5–6

Set Your Sights:

You can never be encouraged too much on the topic of not being moved from what you're believing, and David demonstrated the daily necessity of it when he wrote this passage. Notice who he's talking to: his soul. He's commanding it to wait on God and not be moved. His soul (mind, will, and emotions) needed a reminder to remain steadfast and focused.

Just like David, it is your soul that wavers. It can be tempted to be swayed by circumstances, words, and daily interactions with the world. It needs constant reminding, *from you*, that the Word is your rock and your salvation. Where it is focused will determine where your expectation lies (for good or for evil) and, ultimately, whether or not the enemy can uproot your belief in the Word.

Hit Your Mark:

"Set Your Sights" isn't just a catchy title. It's an instruction on how to receive every single promise that is yes and amen in Christ (2 Cor. 1:20). When you set your sights on the Word by keeping your soul laser-focused on what He says, nothing is impossible. No obstacle is too high or wide. No diagnosis is too terminal. No pain is too great. Command your soul today, just like David, to not be moved.

September 28

The Target:

But unto you that fear my name shall the Sun of righteousness arise with healing in his wings; and ye shall go forth, and grow up as calves of the stall.

Malachi 4:2 (KJV)

Set Your Sights:

This promise to those with deep respect and the highest esteem for God is two-fold. First, they will grow up as calves of the stall. A stall-raised calf wanted for nothing, with all its needs supplied in abundance. It didn't have to forage through the fields for food or fear the dangers of the lion and bear because it was tucked safely away in a stall.

Second was a promise of healing. The Sun of righteousness rising was a foreshadowing of Jesus's resurrection. The power of healing wasn't in His crucifixion or death but in His rising from the grave as He defeated death. If He hadn't risen, you would still be operating under the law, where the only healing depended on your futile works. But Jesus is no longer in the grave, and divine health is yours because of it.

Hit Your Mark:

To become that fat and happy calf, elevate His Word above all else. Give up the worry and care about your situation because you know He has healed you. Give up your fear of the lion and bear seeking to devour you because you know He is watching over you. There is nothing to fear: Jesus is risen and healing is yours.

September 29

The Target:

Set a guard over my mouth, Lord; keep watch over the door of my lips.

Psalm 141:3 (NIV)

Set Your Sights:

From the beginning, words have held the power to create things. God spoke and created heaven and earth, light and dark, land and sea. Since you were made in His image, your words hold the same creative power. They hold life and death (Prov. 18:21) and can be a fountain of life or a path leading to destruction (Prov. 10:11, 13:3).

Your lips are a doorway for the good and bad, which is why it's so important to guard what you say. You can speak what you see and feel, operating purely out of the realm of your flesh, or you can speak Spirit and life (John 6:63). Your words can hinder you from, or expedite you toward, receiving what you're believing. It's not always natural or easy to speak truth over the reality of your circumstances, but that's precisely what makes it a choice.

Hit Your Mark:

Jesus said what you say is what you get (Mark 11:23), so listen closely to the words you're speaking. Does what you're speaking reflect what you're believing for? Are you speaking what you want to see? Most importantly, is it what the Word says about your situation? Set a guard over your mouth today by purposefully lining up your words with His.

September 30

The Target:

And this is eternal life, that they may know You, the only true God, and Jesus Christ whom You have sent.

John 17:3

Set Your Sights:

There is more to eternal life than living forever in heaven after death. Many believe that once they accept Jesus, their ticket is punched, and one day they'll live happily ever after in heaven. While that is true, they'll have missed out on the eternal life God has for them in the here and now.

Jesus said eternal life is to know Him and the only true God. As He used it, the word "know" has the same meaning as Adam "knew" Eve and she conceived. That's close. He wasn't talking about after death, but right now, in your physical body on this earth.

God chose that specific word because He wants you to know He longs for an intimate relationship with you. He wants to talk with you and be involved in your day. He knows everything about you and wants you to know everything about Him.

Hit Your Mark:

The relationship aspect of eternal life is the most crucial element of your healing journey. Even though your body may shout otherwise, it isn't healing you need most, but a relationship with the Healer. Pursue a relationship with Him through prayer, reading, and sitting quietly in His presence. While you are pursuing Him, remember that He is passionately pursuing you because He is smitten with you.

OCTOBER

October 1

The Target:

And when he brings out his own sheep, he goes before them; and the sheep follow him, for they know his voice.

John 10:4

Set Your Sights:

A relationship cannot exist without communication. If you meet someone new and neither of you speaks, or if you speak to them and they don't speak to you, how would you get to know each other? You get to know someone when you talk to them and they talk to you. The same principle applies to a relationship with God.

Some think God only talks to the super-dupers, but Jesus exposed that lie when He said His sheep know His voice. Sheep couldn't know His voice if He didn't speak to them. He also wouldn't have said the Spirit would bring back to your memory everything He said to you if He hasn't said anything to you (John 14:26). If you don't know God is always speaking, you won't be listening. And if you aren't listening, you won't hear.

Hit Your Mark:

If you don't know the God of the universe is talking to *you*, I am delighted to be the bearer of such fantastic news. And now that you know, the best way to jumpstart your hearing is with your confession. Start each day by declaring, "Thank you, God, for wanting a relationship with me and speaking to me today!" Then listen. And expect to hear. Expectation is the start of hearing.

October 2

The Target:

My sheep hear My voice, and I know them, and they follow Me.

John 10:27

Set Your Sights:

Many believers wrongly confess, "I can't hear Him, so either He's not talking or something is wrong with me." Yesterday's devotion revealed God is always speaking to you, so let's address the "I can't hear Him" part. Thinking you can't hear Him is the enemy's deception to keep you from an intimate relationship with your Father.

Jesus very plainly says, "My sheep hear My voice." He didn't say that some of His sheep will hear and some of them won't. If you are His sheep, you hear His voice. Period. Some things can keep you from hearing—such as lack of knowledge, busyness, and where you focus your attention—but that doesn't change the truth that you can hear Him.

Hit Your Mark:

First, relax. Straining to hear and stressing over not hearing are common earplugs for spiritual ears. Second, add to your confession from yesterday: "Thank you, God, for wanting a relationship with me and speaking to me. I declare that I do hear your voice because I have ears to hear." Your speaking, belief, and understanding of that confession, just like a Q-tip, will clean the junk out of your ears so you can hear.

October 3

The Target:

Yet they will by no means follow a stranger, but will flee from him, for they do not know the voice of strangers.

John 10:5

Set Your Sights:

A sheep will follow the voice it knows best. That is the nature of the sheep, and it is your nature as well. The voice you are most familiar with is the voice you will hear and ultimately follow. The enemy constantly speaks, knowing if he can get you to listen to and become familiar with his voice, he can lead you away from the true Shepherd.

His voice is the voice of science, medical research, statistics showing the prognosis isn't good, and Internet sites that keep you in fear that your symptoms mean you have this or that. Each one of those voices serves the purpose of distracting you from the voice of the Shepherd that is guaranteed to lead you to lush green pastures and rest.

Hit Your Mark:

You can determine whose voice you're following by identifying your dominant emotion. If it's fear or anxiety, the enemy's voice is what you hear most. You can start changing that today by making the decision to block out the voice of the world every time you hear it. Reject its lies and focus on the voice of your Shepherd, who will speak only truth and life and lead you to peace and healing.

October 4

The Target:

The spirit of a man is the lamp of the Lord, searching all the inner depths of his heart.

Proverbs 20:27

Set Your Sights:

A lamp can be used to light up a dark room or keep a traveler from stumbling over obstacles in their path. It provides safety and surety of step. In the same way, your spirit is God's lamp. Through it, He speaks His wisdom and understanding and leads the way as you navigate your path. God is a spirit, and because of that, He communicates with you through your spirit (John 4:24).

When God speaks to your spirit, it relays what was said to your mind through thoughts and impressions. It may sound something like, "I think I need to study about God's love for me." Or maybe a verse will suddenly pop into your head, and when you look it up, out of the 31,102 verses in the Bible, it is the exact one you need to hear. That is God using your spirit as a lamp to guide you.

Hit Your Mark:

God wants to get you to your destination as quickly as possible, and He is lighting the way to ensure it. From the previous days' devotions, you know He is speaking and you can hear Him, and now you know He is lighting your path. See that well-lit path before you today, and know you cannot fail because He is leading the way.

October 5

The Target:

The Lord will perfect that which concerns me.

Psalm 138:8

Set Your Sights:

God wants to fellowship with you all day long about everything, not just when there's a problem. Maybe you think, *I don't want to bother Him with this, I can probably figure it out on my own*, or *He doesn't want to hear about that.* But He does want to hear about it, and this verse says so.

The things which concern you are the things you're interested in and are important to you. He wants to hear about your hobbies and talk about the things you love. He wants to help you solve the problem of getting that stain out of your new shirt or help you find the keys that have mysteriously disappeared … again. He is there for you always, not just when things are rough, because He cares about every aspect of your life.

Hit Your Mark:

Using your imagination is a great way to start a conversation with Father. On your drive to work, see Him next to you, fastened in and happy to keep you company. See Him next to you on a walk, hanging out and enjoying the fresh air. Wherever you are, imagine Him with you and just talk to Him. He is right there, a constant companion. Always.

October 6

The Target:

The grace of the Lord Jesus Christ, and the love of God, and the communion of the Holy Spirit be with you all. Amen.

2 Corinthians 13:14

Set Your Sights:

A big deception of the enemy to keep people from fellowship with God is that He can't, or won't, speak to them because of their sins. They envision their sin as a great chasm between them that His voice cannot traverse. That is a lie, and here are some examples from the Word to refute it:

Number one: Immediately after Cain murdered his brother, Abel, God spoke to him (Gen. 4:9). Number two: In his letters to the Corinthian church, Paul addressed grievous sins, such as a man sleeping with his father's wife and churchgoers getting drunk during communion, and yet he told them the grace, love, and fellowship of the Father was still available to them. Nothing they did (and nothing you do) could chase God away. He is always in pursuit.

Hit Your Mark:

More than ever, God wants to speak to you in the middle of your mess because He has the way out. Don't let the sin-silences-God lie of the enemy keep you from hearing His voice one moment longer. Once and for all, settle this issue today. Nothing, not even your own pieces of stupid, will separate you from God's love and prevent Him from speaking. He will not be silent. No matter what.

October 7

The Target:

Then He said, "Go out, and stand on the mountain before the Lord." And behold, the Lord passed by, and a great and strong wind tore into the mountains and broke the rocks in pieces before the Lord, but the Lord was not in the wind; and after the wind an earthquake, but the Lord was not in the earthquake; and after the earthquake a fire, but the Lord was not in the fire; and after the fire a still small voice.

1 Kings 19:11–12

Set Your Sights:

This passage holds an important truth about hearing God that could make all the difference in whether you hear Him or not. It says God passed by and a mighty wind came, then an earthquake, and finally a raging fire; however, He was not in those thunderous, spectacular displays of power, but in a still small voice.

Many people miss the still small voice because they are fixated on hearing an audible voice or seeing a burning bush. God can speak in those ways, but He most often speaks through less extreme means such as verses, an inner voice, your "gut," songs, or other people. The ways He can communicate are endless, but if you are intent on hearing Him in one particular way, you may miss Him entirely.

Hit Your Mark:

Take off your limits and expectations on how God will speak to you. Open your ears and listen for Him in everything around you. You'll know when He speaks because something will stand out to you: a verse you're reading or something a friend said that penetrates your very core. Recognize those things as God speaking, and don't let it end there. Talk back and keep the conversation going!

October 8

The Target:

"Did he not say to me, 'She is my sister'? And she, even she herself said, 'He is my brother.' In the integrity of my heart and innocence of my hands I have done this."

Genesis 20:5

Set Your Sights:

Many times after hearing God, unsure if it was Him or not, the fear of missing it leads to paralysis as the hearer waits and waits until the word they heard becomes stagnant. Let today's target set your mind at ease and give you the confidence to act on what you hear.

Cutting to the chase of the verse, Abimelech did something God found worthy of death. Abimelech was mortified and told Him his intentions and actions were pure. When God looked in his heart and saw it was true, He spared Abimelech's life.

What's that got to do with hearing God? Simple. If you are seeking God and act on what you believe He said, even if you're wrong, He will either bless the work of your hands or put a "check" in your spirit to let you know you've missed it. Either way, He's right there with you.

Hit Your Mark:

If you've been seeking God and believe He spoke to you, act on what you heard. (NOTE: What He speaks will always line up with the written Word.) Step out in faith and say, "God, I believe this is You, so I'm going to act on what I heard." Don't be afraid to miss it. He's pleased you're listening and won't let you fail.

October 9

The Target:

There remains therefore a rest for the people of God. For he who has entered His rest has himself also ceased from his works as God did from His. Let us therefore be diligent to enter that rest, lest anyone fall according to the same example of disobedience.

Hebrews 4:9–11

Set Your Sights:

Though rest is available as a believer travels from sickness to health, many are exhausted and frustrated instead. The exhaustion comes from the checklist of things you assign to yourself that have to be done perfectly every single day so you can be healed. It's an exchange of works for healing, inevitably leading to burnout.

If you aren't resting, some level of unbelief dominates your mind, causing you to overwork (Heb. 3:19). Maybe it comes from symptoms or a lack of understanding of Jesus's finished work. Whatever the cause, you can choose rest by tearing up your checklist and focusing on Him. Quitting your works and putting your faith in His is not easy, which is why it says you must labor to enter His rest.

Hit Your Mark:

Put away your to-do list and believe He'll tell you if you need to do something. Until then, any time a you-should-be-doing-more thought comes to mind, reject it and say, "I don't have to do anything but believe in Him, so I choose to believe instead of wearing myself out." Then think about the work Jesus did for you. He did all the heavy lifting so you could rest in knowing the work is finished.

October 10

The Target:

My people are destroyed for lack of knowledge.

Hosea 4:6

Set Your Sights:

Destruction is the direct opposite of life, health, and freedom, and knowledge of God's word is how you avoid it. Knowledge, as used in this verse, goes beyond simply knowing the facts and includes understanding and knowing how to apply them.

Here's how that looks: Basic knowledge is knowing what eggs, flour, butter, milk, and sugar are; understanding is knowing those ingredients can be combined to create a cake; and wisdom is knowing how to put them together correctly to make something moist and delicious.

Those are the three crucial ingredients of a health-filled life: knowledge, understanding, and wisdom. If you don't know what the Word says (knowledge), you can't understand it. If you don't understand it, you can't know how to apply it practically, which makes all the difference between remaining unchanged and receiving the promises of God.

Hit Your Mark:

If you are experiencing destruction, an ingredient is missing, so start from the beginning. First, get knowledge by searching the Word for what God says about your situation. Second, gain an understanding of that Word through prayer, meditation, and study. Third, once you have an understanding, the wisdom of how to apply it will come. Then all that's left to do is to act as He leads and receive!

October 11

The Target:

We have also a more sure word of prophecy; whereunto ye do well that ye take heed, as unto a light that shineth in a dark place, until the day dawn, and the day star arise in your hearts. Knowing this first, that no prophecy of the scripture is of any private interpretation.

2 Peter 1:19–20 (KJV)

Set Your Sights:

Peter walked closely with Jesus during His earthly ministry. He heard Jesus's voice, saw His works, and witnessed His resurrection from the dead. Yet he says, "Even though I have seen firsthand what I testify about, there is something with even more authority than personal experience: scripture." Peter had a revelation that having the written word of God was even more sure than being with Jesus in the flesh.

You have the advantage over those who walked with Jesus because you have the written word of God, through which you can know the character and nature of God in a way they couldn't. You can know with absolute certainty it is His will to heal you and stand firm on it. You can know you have authority over sickness and disease and act on it. You can know the Word and the Word will set you free (John 8:32).

Hit Your Mark:

Let this truth sink in today. Think about it. Meditate on it. You are truly blessed to have and hold the written word of God in your hands. Let that thought penetrate your mind and fill your heart with gratitude. You will hold in the highest esteem what you are grateful for, so take the time and thank Him for His precious Word.

October 12

The Target:

Be sober, be vigilant; because your adversary the devil walks about like a roaring lion, seeking whom he may devour.

1 Peter 5:8

Set Your Sights:

The devil will make a lot of noise and cast a big shadow to convince you he is a lion, but in reality, he is a toothless nothing. One day you will even look down on him and ask, "*He* made the earth tremble?" (Isa. 14:16) The only power he has is by deception. If he can get you thinking he's a dangerous lion, he stands a better chance of devouring you.

How do you avoid the deception and the devouring? By being sober and vigilant, meaning on your guard with eyes wide open for his lies. You are calm when he approaches, knowing greater is He who is in you than he that is in the world (1 John 4:4). When he roars, you laugh. When he postures, you yawn. He can't touch you, and he knows it.

Hit Your Mark:

How you view the devil is an integral part of how you deal with him. If you see him as a giant, muscled, sharp-toothed lion, then that's the power he'll have. But if you see him for what he is (a squished bug on the bottom of your shoe), you strip him of the deception he needs to do his work. Go ahead. Laugh. Yawn. Put him in his place.

October 13

The Target:

For who has despised the day of small things? For these seven rejoice to see the plumb line in the hand of Zerubbabel. They are the eyes of the Lord, which scan to and fro throughout the whole earth.

Zechariah 4:10

Set Your Sights:

This verse is part of a prophecy Zechariah gave Zerubbabel concerning rebuilding the temple. The "day of small things" referred to the new foundation that had been laid, which those who had seen the majesty of the first temple were looking at with disdain and loathing.

They were so focused on the work to be done they couldn't see the improvements taking place nor remember the promise God spoke through Haggai that the second temple would be greater than the first (Hag. 2:9), which caused them to doubt and become ungrateful.

Healing is often approached in the same way, becoming so focused on how far there is to go that little improvements are overlooked and God's promises are forgotten, leading to discouragement and unbelief.

Hit Your Mark:

When you recognize the small things, write them down and be grateful. See them as tangible proof that God's word is at work and as a guarantee that He will complete it in your body. Use them to squash unbelief and fuel your faith that healing is right around the corner. No matter how small, an improvement is a step in the right direction. Don't miss the opportunity to be thankful and rejoice over the small things today!

October 14

The Target:

There is therefore now no condemnation to those who are in Christ Jesus, who do not walk according to the flesh, but according to the Spirit.

Romans 8:1

Set Your Sights:

Condemnation is a guilty verdict rendered against someone that carries the heavy sentence of shame and self-loathing. There is a doctrine that says the Spirit was sent to the believer to condemn them when they sin. On the contrary, He was sent to convince them they are the righteousness of God in Christ (John 16:10), their record is clean, and that God remembers their sins no more (Ps. 103:12, Heb. 8:12). Not once. Not ever.

The accuser of the brethren (Rev. 12:10) wants you focused on your sins. You may feel ashamed or think you deserve to suffer the consequences, but how you feel doesn't change the fact God's love for you covered them all through the sacrifice of His son (1 John 2:2). He paid for your sin and its consequences so you could live without a consciousness of sins and walk in the health and freedom that mindset brings (Heb. 10:2).

Hit Your Mark:

Not forgiving yourself is a bitter root that will eat at your soul and body. There is no sin and no consequence that He hasn't already forgiven, so stop holding on to the sins of the past. God forgave you the moment you accepted His son, and now it's time to forgive yourself. Do that today.

October 15

The Target:

It is the spirit that quickeneth; the flesh profiteth nothing: the words that I speak unto you, they are spirit, and they are life.

John 6:63 (KJV)

Set Your Sights:

If your spirit left your body, it would fall over dead because it is the spirit that gives life (James 2:26). Your spirit is the real you, and your body is the suit you wear to navigate this world. It's worth noting this doesn't mean you focus only on spiritual growth and neglect your body. As God's temple, you should take care of it so you can run your race successfully and to completion.

Jesus stresses that the things of the spirit are more important than the things of the flesh, and then He labels His words as spirit. In other words, they are more important than anything the flesh has to say. The symptoms in your body and unrenewed thoughts in your mind will have plenty to say, but He gave you His words so you could focus on them and experience life.

Hit Your Mark:

Every day can be a battle of where you place your focus. You may do good one day and fall flat on your face the next day with a meltdown. That's okay. It doesn't change the fact that the Word is still there and the Word is still true. His Word is life. And it is eternal. Focus on that truth today.

October 16

The Target:

They are not of the world, just as I am not of the world. Sanctify them by Your truth. Your word is truth. As You sent Me into the world, I also have sent them into the world.

John 17:16–18

Set Your Sights:

Jesus is talking about a group of people whose citizenship is not on this earth. As a believer, your passport might say the United States or India, but your true nation of origin is heaven. You live on planet Earth for a short time and for one purpose: to be an ambassador of Christ (2 Cor. 5:20).

An ambassador has absolute authority to represent his home nation, so when he makes decisions, it is as if the head of state himself has spoken and is exercising power. A few of their tasks include explaining foreign policy and evacuating refugees from hostile environments.

As an ambassador of Jesus, your tasks are the same: preach the gospel (foreign policy) and evacuate refugees from the hostile environment of life without God by drawing them to Christ. Everything you do in line with your heavenly home is backed by the full power and authority of the name of Jesus.

Hit Your Mark:

You may not feel like it, but you are Christ's ambassador, full of power and equipped with the authority you need to dominate in this life and represent Him well. See yourself as His ambassador and feel the confidence that comes from knowing your official position. The start of victory is acknowledging the authority you have.

October 17

The Target:

Behold, I give you the authority to trample on serpents and scorpions, and over all the power of the enemy, and nothing shall by any means hurt you.

Luke 10:19

Set Your Sights:

As an ambassador of Christ, in addition to your authority through His name, you have also been given the power to back it up. There's a difference. A police officer has the authority to arrest you, but the power to enforce that authority is carried in the weapon in his side holster or a quick radio call resulting in a show of force by the entire police department.

The power you have backing you far outweighs any carnal weapons of steel and strength (2 Cor. 10:4). Your power annihilates serpents, scorpions, and any evil thing the enemy may throw at you. This power is contained in the word of God and is activated by faith. And when His Word is spoken by one who knows their authority, it releases the Holy Spirit, who will wield His sword and cut down the enemy.

Hit Your Mark:

You have authority and power. Cancer, arthritis, depression, and bipolar disorder are all snakes and scorpions that are powerless against you when you know your authority and use it to release the power inside you. As you solidify in your mind today that you are not defenseless but full of His authority and power, you will move one step closer to victory.

October 18

The Target:

And as you go, preach, saying, 'The kingdom of heaven is at hand.' Heal the sick, cleanse the lepers, raise the dead, cast out demons. Freely you have received, freely give.

Matthew 10:7-8

Set Your Sights:

Jesus commanded you to heal the sick because God gave you the authority and placed the power within you to do it. Understand: It isn't you who does the healing, but the Healer who lives within you. Jesus made it very clear that the Father inside does the work (John 14:10). You are simply the conduit through which His healing power flows.

Jesus demonstrated how to heal the sick by rebuking the fever, commanding life back into Lazarus, and ordering blind eyes and deaf ears to be opened. Peter displayed this authority when he healed the lame man looking for money at the gate called Beautiful. Peter didn't have any money, so he gave him what he knew he had (Acts 3:6): the healing power of God flowing within.

Hit Your Mark:

You aren't waiting for God to heal you because He has given you absolute authority and ample power to defeat anything attacking your body. Think about that truth until it is so real that no one can convince you otherwise. Then act, armed with the revelation that it doesn't matter if the sickness is in you or your neighbor, you have authority over it, and it must flee. Through you, He will overcome.

October 19

The Target:

You will keep him in perfect peace, whose mind is stayed on You, because he trusts in You.

Isaiah 26:3

Set Your Sights:

One of the translations of the word "mind" is imagination. God didn't create the imagination solely for children to fill their days with endless adventure. As a believer, it is a building block of faith. As you engage your imagination, images are created in your mind, good or bad. You choose whether you envision the best or worst possible outcome.

Envisioning the best is what the New Testament refers to as hope. Hope is more than "I sure hope this happens." That's a wish, not a hope. Hope is deep-rooted in your imagination as it sees the unseen (Rom. 8:24). Hope produces expectancy and confidence and leads to an activation of your faith, which is the substance of the things you hope for (Heb. 11:1). Faith turns what you see into reality, but the seeing must come first.

Hit Your Mark:

What you see is what you get. It's not a cliché but a biblical truth. So identify what you believe and engage your imagination to see it. See yourself doing the things sickness has prevented you from doing. See yourself healed and whole. See what you want and faith will take care of the rest. Go ahead. Close your eyes and see it.

October 20

The Target:

For though we walk in the flesh, we do not war according to the flesh. For the weapons of our warfare are not carnal but mighty in God for pulling down strongholds, casting down arguments and every high thing that exalts itself against the knowledge of God, bringing every thought into captivity to the obedience of Christ.

2 Corinthians 10:3–5

Set Your Sights:

The opposite of hope is worry. With hope, you imagine and expect the best. With worry, you imagine and expect the worst. Every day, a spiritual war rages in your mind that determines whether you go down the road of hope or worry. The enemy will place obstacles in your way in an effort to reroute you from Hope Road to Worry Lane, but embracing this verse will keep you on track.

The truth of the Word will clear away any obstacle blocking the path of hope that would cause you to detour to worry. For example, if you begin to imagine yourself getting sick and dying, before you get detoured to Worry Lane, the Word will take that imagination captive and remove it with the truth that you will live and not die (Ps. 118:17), keeping Hope Road clear before you.

Hit Your Mark:

When you see the obstacle and detour sign fast approaching, it's time to speak the truth. The Word you know will eliminate the obstacle, blow up the road to worry, and freshly pave the road of hope. Avoid the detours by thinking on the truth and speaking it out. When you do, glance in your rear-view mirror and watch Worry Lane disappear behind you.

October 21

The Target:

*For as often as you eat this bread and drink this cup,
you proclaim the Lord's death till He comes.*

1 Corinthians 11:26

Set Your Sights:

Paul addresses the unworthy manner in which some members of the Corinthian church took communion, specifically, getting drunk and eating to excess. His correction came in admonishing them to go back to why they were taking communion in the first place: to bring to remembrance and declare their faith in the tremendous price Jesus paid for them on the cross.

Communion serves the same purpose today and is a powerful contact point for healing. As you take the bread and wine, it focuses your thoughts on Jesus, confirms your belief in Him, and receives His sacrifice into your physical body.

The power of healing is in the faith stirring within you, not the elements themselves, as you remember His body was broken for your healing and the new covenant was ushered in through the shedding of His blood. The power is not in the ritual, but in the remembering.

Hit Your Mark:

You can take communion wherever you are and as often as you'd like. The type of juice or bread isn't important, but what you think about is. Using Matthew 26:26-28 as a guide, this simple act of remembrance will promote the manifestation of healing in your body. Starting today, make communion a regular practice in your life.

October 22

The Target:

Beware lest anyone cheat you through philosophy and empty deceit, according to the tradition of men, according to the basic principles of the world, and not according to Christ. For in Him dwells all the fullness of the Godhead bodily; and you are complete in Him, who is the head of all principality and power.

Colossians 2:8–10

Set Your Sights:

Philosophy is a particular way of thinking. For instance, the world's philosophy on aging is that everyone's eyesight diminishes and everyone loses strength. A religious philosophy on healing may be that God gives you sickness to teach you something. Both are meant to deceive you and deprive you of something very valuable: God's kind of health.

Paul warns you to be on the lookout for those deceptions and gives you a safeguard against them: the knowledge that you are complete in Christ. To be complete in Christ means you are crammed full to overflowing with everything you need for victory in life. It also means that since Christ is above all principality and power, so are you. Once you understand those truths, you will not be deceived into accepting anything less than what God has promised you.

Hit Your Mark:

Knowing the Word from front to back is the best way to not be deceived by the world's way of thinking and thereby led away from God's promises. The better you know it, the less you will be deceived. Here's an excellent place to start: Though the world says otherwise, you are complete in Him, nothing lacking, and that's the truth. Stick to it.

October 23

The Target:

By this we know love, because He laid down His life for us. And we also ought to lay down our lives for the brethren.

1 John 3:16

Set Your Sights:

Knowing God's love is the foundation for receiving His promises. Yet despite the countless verses professing His unconditional love, many people struggle to accept He could love them in their current state of undoneness. Desperate, they ask God to reveal His love for them, which is like asking for a gift they already hold. According to His Word, He showed His love through one defining act: He sent His only son to die for you (1 John 4:9, Rom. 5:8).

Stop right there. Don't miss the depth of that statement's meaning. Could there be any more tremendous sacrifice than laying down the life of your only child for people who may reject and hate you, all so they can know you intimately and live an abundant life? Is there any other act that could show His unconditional love for humanity? There isn't.

Hit Your Mark:

God did what He did because He is madly in love with you and wants you to live a life steeped in divine health. Today, think about the sacrifice He made and why He made it. You don't need God to show you His love in a tangible way. You have something more sure. You can see it, if you choose, in what He has already done for you.

October 24

The Target:

Now this is the confidence that we have in Him, that if we ask anything according to His will, He hears us. And if we know that He hears us, whatever we ask, we know that we have the petitions that we have asked of Him.

1 John 5:14–15

Set Your Sights:

For prayer to be effective, it doesn't have to be perfect, but it must line up with God's will. In other words, He won't ignore your prayer because you prayed the prayer of faith instead of the prayer of agreement. He's in the qualifying, not disqualifying, business.

Lining up with His will is what's most important, so how can you know if you are praying in conjunction with His will or not? The answer is simple and concrete: If it says it in the Word, it is His will.

If your prayers mirror what the Word says, you can have confidence you're in line with Him and that He hears you. And according to verse 15, because He hears you, you can know you'll have what you prayed for.

Hit Your Mark:

Your prayers should always resonate with the truth that you aren't a sinner begging for scraps but a child of God who has His ever-inclined ear. To pray His perfect will over your situation, you need to know what His Word says about it. Where the will of God is known, faith is activated. Get in there. Find out what God is saying. Pray that. And watch your faith work.

October 25

The Target:

But at midnight Paul and Silas were praying and singing hymns to God, and the prisoners were listening to them. Suddenly there was a great earthquake, so that the foundations of the prison were shaken; and immediately all the doors were opened and everyone's chains were loosed.

Acts 16:25–26

Set Your Sights:

This passage is remarkable because Paul and Silas weren't just in prison; they were in the inner prison, a veritable dungeon with no light or fresh air. There they sat, backs bleeding from the lashes they'd received and secured painfully in stocks. Stocks were wooden torture devices with slots for the head and arms, and leg holes spaced agonizingly wide apart.

If anyone was justified in grumbling and giving up, it was Paul and Silas. But at midnight, with no earthly reason to pray and sing hymns, not knowing whether they would be delivered or beheaded, they chose to praise God instead of complain. Their physical condition and location did not hinder their faith in God, and this one act of praise ushered in their miracle.

Hit Your Mark:

Your breakthrough, healing, or miracle may very well be contained in your ability to praise Him by faith. No matter how bad it may look on the surface, praise Him for no other reason than He is God and He is good. It may feel unnatural and contrived initially, but if you stick with it, it will morph into something heartfelt and intentional, a place where anything can happen.

October 26

The Target:

All Scripture is given by inspiration of God, and is profitable for doctrine, for reproof, for correction, for instruction in righteousness, that the man of God may be complete, thoroughly equipped for every good work.

2 Timothy 3:16–17

Set Your Sights:

A dangerous false doctrine being taught is that God gives you sickness to train you and equip you for what's ahead. If you've ever been sick, you know it doesn't teach you anything except that it really stinks to be sick and doesn't equip you for anything but the couch.

This verse clearly debunks that lie by revealing what He does use: Scripture. He uses it to teach you (doctrine), to give you a conviction of what the truth is (reproof), to straighten you out (correction), and to educate you as to who you are as a believer in Christ (instruction in righteousness).

Sickness hinders, not equips, and it makes you ineffective. The Kingdom of God does not benefit if you are sick, but it does if you are thoroughly outfitted for every good work with the life-changing truth of the Word.

Hit Your Mark:

Sickness is not how God works, but He can use it for your good. If you will turn to the Word in the midst of it, learning can take place, and learning will lead to a revelation of the truth and a change in your situation. The Word teaches you, not the sickness. Settle that truth in your heart today.

The Target:

And lest I should be exalted above measure by the abundance of the revelations, a thorn in the flesh was given to me, a messenger of Satan to buffet me, lest I be exalted above measure.

2 Corinthians 12:7

Set Your Sights:

Many people have accepted sickness in their bodies because of a misinterpretation of this verse. Namely, to keep Paul from getting a big head over his revelations, God gave him a terrible affliction to keep him humble.

Notice that the thorn was delivered by a messenger of Satan, not of God. Satan did this. Why? Paul was so admired (Godly exaltation) that Satan beat him repeatedly (buffeted him) in a desperate attempt to make the gospel less attractive to those who heard it. Satan was losing people by the droves and had to do something about it.

This verse in no way, shape, or form says that God gives sickness to keep you humble but that Satan will persecute you in any way he can, including sickness, to hinder you from spreading the message that has changed your life.

Hit Your Mark:

If you believe the sickness you're dealing with is a thorn in the flesh God gave you, Satan can keep you in bondage to it. Read this passage about Paul in a new light today, and let the Holy Spirit open your eyes to the truth that sickness is not from God. Once you see it, tell Satan you've got his number and eject his sickness from your body.

October 28

The Target:

Now to Him who is able to do exceedingly abundantly above all that we ask or think, according to the power that works in us.

Ephesians 3:20

Set Your Sights:

God having more grand plans than they could think or ask is often the only truth recognized in this verse. However, stopping there leaves out an essential part of it actually coming to pass. The amazing things He has for you are all appropriated by the power that works *in you*. Not God working as some outside source, but you utilizing the miracle-working power inside you, which comes from the indwelling presence of the Holy Spirit (Acts 1:8).

You put the Spirit to work by agreeing with what God says about you and acting on it. He says you have authority over the enemy, so you speak (Luke 10:19). He says you have raise-the-dead faith, so you act (2 Peter 1:1, Acts 9:40). He says you have His love in your heart, so you choose to use it (Rom. 5:5). You act and the Spirit does the heavy lifting.

Hit Your Mark:

You aren't waiting on God to release His power over you. He's waiting on you to unleash it from within. Now that you know what that looks like, set your sights on the Word, esteem it far above everything else, and then speak and act on what you are fully persuaded of. Guaranteed, the power within will flow!

October 29

The Target:

And the Lord said, If ye had faith as a grain of mustard seed, ye might say unto this sycamine tree, Be thou plucked up by the root, and be thou planted in the sea; and it should obey you.

Luke 17:6 (KJV)

Set Your Sights:

A characteristic of the sycamine tree is its expansive and deep root structure, which makes it virtually impossible to uproot. In context, Jesus was referring to bitterness and unforgiveness, but it can just as appropriately be applied to any stubborn obstacle standing in the way of healing.

If the sycamine tree represents an incessant obstacle, logical thinking reasons if it takes a lot to move it in the natural, it will take equal effort to move it in the spiritual. The bigger the obstacle, the more required of you to move it. But not so.

Jesus is saying that what looks impossible on the surface is easily accomplished with a tiny amount of faith. All you do is speak and the obstacle must obey you. Notice that no work is involved on your part. When you speak to it, it uproots itself and does as you command.

Hit Your Mark:

When you utter faith-filled words, there is no obstacle too big or deep-rooted that a tiny bit of faith won't absolutely demolish. Speak to that thing in your way. Speak to those symptoms. Speak to that disease. Then imagine it pulling itself up by the roots and running until it disappears into the sea.

October 30

The Target:

Now he who received seed among the thorns is he who hears the word, and the cares of this world and the deceitfulness of riches choke the word, and he becomes unfruitful.

Matthew 13:22

Set Your Sights:

Let's talk about setbacks. You know, when you are absolutely convinced you're healed, and then the symptoms get worse or the doctor calls with a bad report. When you take one step forward and immediately get thrown three steps back. What's that all about? That's the enemy wanting to steal your confidence in the Word (Heb. 10:32). He sees you gaining ground and will not give up without a fight.

Setbacks are thorns. The enemy sees the Word seed that's taken root and the shoot coming up out of the ground. He sends setbacks to choke that seed and your faith along with it. He does not want you to stand firm because he knows victory is right around the corner, and he will fight tooth and nail to keep you from seeing it. Don't let that lie of a symptom choke out the truth you know.

Hit Your Mark:

Change your perspective on setbacks today. See them as the futile attempt of an already-defeated foe desperately trying to get you to drop your shield of faith. See them as evidence you are getting closer to the promise of healing becoming a harvest in your body. Don't let them be evidence that you are not healed, but a confirmation that you are!

October 31

The Target:

Cast not away therefore your confidence, which hath great recompence of reward. For ye have need of patience, that, after ye have done the will of God, ye might receive the promise.

Hebrews 10:35–36 (KJV)

Set Your Sights:

Yesterday was about setbacks, and today is an exhortation to not let go because of them. It says you will be compensated tremendously if you do not abandon your confidence despite any harm you suffer. And if you hold on with patience, being steadfast in what you know, not being moved by your senses and bold in the face of adversity, you will receive the promise of healing.

Patience, which is faith exerted over time, is something you have in endless supply (Gal. 5:22). So how do you tap into this patience and exercise it in the face of a setback? Romans 15:4 says that patience comes through the Scriptures, so by focusing on the Word, confidence will reign over doubt, patience will be exercised, and what you're believing for will come to pass.

Hit Your Mark:

Nobody likes to talk about patience when it comes to healing because it means they didn't see it instantaneously. But if it doesn't happen instantly, you need to know that if you will not lose confidence in His Word, His promise of healing is yours, whether it happens in the next minute or the next year. Patience is a powerful weapon in your arsenal, and deploying it ensures victory!

NOVEMBER

November 1

The Target:

His mother said to the servants, "Whatever He says to you, do it."

John 2:5

Set Your Sights:

The simple command of a mother echoed through the ages and resonating through the church today. So simple. So profound. So overlooked. It's a directive that has been lost in a sea of political correctness, the desire to please men, and the laziness to pursue the promises that can heal the body and mind: do what Jesus says.

Jesus told the servants to fill the waterpots with water. When they listened and obeyed, the impossible happened: water became wine. It sounded ridiculous, but faith made it possible. Mary says to you, "Do what Jesus, the Word, says to do." Believing in and acting on the Word will turn your water into wine, your sickness into health. It may sound ridiculous to the world, but your faith will make it so.

Hit Your Mark:

Read the entire account and imagine yourself as one of the servants (John 2:1–10). Hear Jesus's command and imagine the anticipation as you fill your waterpot. Feel the butterflies as you walk up to the governor, dip your ladle into the pot, and pour deep, red wine into his cup. That same miracle-working power flows through you today when you hear the Word of the Lord and do what He tells you to do. Don't hesitate. Just do it.

November 2

The Target:

*But lift up your rod, and stretch out your hand over
the sea and divide it. And the children of Israel shall
go on dry ground through the midst of the sea.*

Exodus 14:16

Set Your Sights:

Moses and the children of Israel stood with their toes touching the
water of the Red Sea, the vast expanse looming ominously before
them. Behind them, the sound of thunder grew as the Egyptian
army approached. Every second brings them one breath closer to
annihilation. Moses gave them a rousing speech but then promptly
turned and cried out to God for help.

But God said, "Why are you crying to me?" There are times that
response is appropriate, but this wasn't one of them because God
had already placed all authority in the hand of Moses. The rod he
clutched contained the power of God (Ex. 4:20). He needed to
recognize what he had and use it. The moment he quit asking God,
acted in faith and employed the authority he had, the waters parted
and the people passed over on dry land.

Hit Your Mark:

Jesus put the rod, the authority and power of His name, in your hand
when He commanded you to heal the sick and gave you authority
over all the power of the enemy (Luke 10:19). You have the power
and it's time to use it. Speak to what is attacking you and watch it
part like the Red Sea before you. Go on. Walk on the dry land.

November 3

The Target:

And let them say continually, "Let the Lord be magnified, Who has pleasure in the prosperity of His servant."

Psalm 35:27b

Set Your Sights:

This prosperity covers so much more than finances. It means to prosper in your health and have favor, rest, safety, and peace ruling your walk with Him. It is an all-inclusive prosperity that impacts every facet of your life.

Contrary to popular belief, God doesn't enjoy watching you suffer. He isn't sitting in heaven saying to Jesus, "They deserve it, so let's sit back and watch them learn their lesson." That does not describe your loving heavenly Father.

He experiences joy when you prosper and smiles when you walk in health. He rejoices when you receive healing and beams when you experience peace in your soul. He takes pleasure when you succeed, not when you fail. He is for you and not against you.

Hit Your Mark:

Today's verse aims to put a smile on your face by setting your sights on the truth that God takes pleasure in your prosperity. He is on your side in this journey. He is right beside you to cheer you on, to celebrate the victories, and to pick you up when you suffer a defeat. That sounds like a pretty good reason to love Him even more today than you did yesterday. Take the time to think about that and smile.

November 4

The Target:

Then he said to me, "Do not fear, Daniel, for from the first day that you set your heart to understand, and to humble yourself before your God, your words were heard; and I have come because of your words. But the prince of the kingdom of Persia withstood me twenty-one days.

Daniel 10:12–13a

Set Your Sights:

From a purely human point of view, it took God three weeks to answer Daniel's prayer. Behind the scenes, however, you see that the moment Daniel prayed, God heard him and sent the answer into the spirit realm, where a battle commenced between the messenger of God and the prince of Persia, a demonic power. Though God's response was immediate, on the surface it could have appeared to Daniel that He was silent and unresponsive.

When waiting for an answer to prayer, three weeks seems like a lifetime and can tempt you to question God's love and willingness to help. Remembering this account of Daniel will help you see that God answered you the moment you prayed and that it's your enemy doing his best to keep you from receiving it. Don't get angry at God. Get mad at the devil for standing in the way.

Hit Your Mark:

You can remove the enemy from the path to your answer by acknowledging that the moment you prayed, God answered, whether you see it or not. Knowing the answer is there and on its way will give you the confidence to rebuke the enemy who is preventing it from reaching you. When you do, he will retreat and your answer will come.

November 5

The Target:

And if you are Christ's, then you are Abraham's seed,
and heirs according to the promise.

Galatians 3:29

Set Your Sights:

An heir is a person who inherits possessions or rank from a parent or predecessor, and you have inherited both. Because of what Jesus did, and your subsequent belief in Him and acceptance of Him as Lord, you were promoted from the rank of a child of darkness to a child of God in the blink of an eye (John 1:12). As His child, you have a legal right to the possessions contained in the promise given to Abraham.

God promised to bless and multiply Abraham so he could bless the nations (Gen. 22:17–18). Your possession is being blessed going in and coming out. It's being healthy and free, prosperous and full of life. To be a blessing to the nations, you have to be blessed yourself. The entire inheritance is yours because you are His child, and as His child, an heir to the promise.

Hit Your Mark:

The enemy has no inheritance, so he wants to make sure you don't take possession of yours. If you aren't walking in health, freedom, and prosperity, that's exactly what he's doing. Recognize the inheritance that is rightfully yours. See yourself reclaiming what he has taken from you today. Tell him, "Hands off, devil!" The promise is yours, and he can't touch it.

November 6

The Target:

Then I heard a loud voice saying in heaven, "Now salvation, and strength, and the kingdom of our God, and the power of His Christ have come, for the accuser of our brethren, who accused them before our God day and night, has been cast down."

Revelation 12:10

Set Your Sights:

This isn't a verse to be fulfilled in the future. It is a now verse and holds powerful truths for the believer today. It states that salvation, strength, God's kingdom and power have already come and that Satan has already been defeated.

This means forgiveness of sins and health have come—salvation. It means miracle-working power has come—strength. And that delegated authority to use the name of Jesus to possess what has freely been given has come—power.

Satan was conquered by Jesus's death, burial, and resurrection (v. 11). Power was stripped from him and he was cast down. Since he no longer has an audience with God to point out your faults, his only recourse is to convince you that you *don't* have what you *do* have, which is salvation, strength, and power. It is no coincidence he holds the title of Father of Lies (John 8:44) because deception is the only power he has left.

Hit Your Mark:

When you hear Satan's lies saying you aren't healed, free, and forgiven, just remember he was demoted and you were promoted. He was stripped of everything he had and you were given everything you need. Most importantly, he has no power because you were given it all!

The Target:

You shall dispossess the inhabitants of the land and dwell in it, for I have given you the land to possess.

Numbers 33:53

Set Your Sights:

Speaking to the children of Israel about the promised land, God told them *they* had to go in and dispossess its inhabitants. They had to take the land. They could rest in His promise that the land was theirs, the battle was won, and He was on their side, but there was still an effort to be made and a dispossessing to take place.

You have a promised land named "Healing," and if you're not living on that land, there may be inhabitants you need to dispossess, such as fear, doubt, or unbelief. God has stripped them of power (Num. 14:9), but you must drive them out. There is a battle to be fought, but you can rest in knowing the land is yours, He has ensured your victory, and He is by your side every step of the way.

Hit Your Mark:

You get rid of unwanted inhabitants trespassing on your promised land by evicting them with the truth of the Word. If one digs in its heels and refuses to go, tell it God promised you healing and it belongs to you, so you are taking possession of it. Don't allow it to squat on your land one more second. Step into your position as the landowner and evict that lying inhabitant.

November 8

The Target:

And Jesus said to them, "Yes. Have you never read, 'Out of the mouth of babes and nursing infants You have perfected praise'?"

Matthew 21:16

Set Your Sights:

For the full impact of Jesus's remark, put it alongside Psalm 8:2, the verse He quoted. It says, "Out of the mouth of babes and nursing infants You have ordained strength, because of Your enemies, that You may silence the enemy and the avenger." When you compare the two verses, you see that Jesus replaced "strength" with "praise," creating an unbreakable link between them. Praise leads to strength.

Psalm 8:2 goes on to say the purpose of praise is to silence your enemy. Praise is more than just an opportunity to sing a beautiful melody; it is intended for spiritual warfare. As one of your fiercest battle weapons, it will stop, silence, and decimate your enemy. When you sing praises to God, especially in the middle of a fierce battle, you will be renewed with strength and the enemy will be scattered (2 Chron. 20:22–23).

Hit Your Mark:

If you are weary and weak today, now is the ideal time to lift up your voice in praise. The devil hates it when you praise God because he wants your worship. He doesn't even want to be in earshot of your voice, so raise it up loud. Open up your mouth and praise the enemy right out of your life!

November 9

The Target:

And by this we know that we are of the truth, and shall assure our hearts before Him.

1 John 3:19

Set Your Sights:

In context, this verse says your outward love for others is an assurance, or proof, for your heart that you are saved. This means your heart is not automatically convinced you are righteous and redeemed at the moment of salvation. It needs to be reassured that no matter how you feel, or how many times you mess up, you are a child of God.

The same is true with healing. Many believe if they were healed, they would know it automatically and there would be zero doubt. For a few, that's the case, but others will have to assure their hearts of the truth.

You may believe in healing and not have a single doubt it can happen, but you still lack confidence and peace in your heart that it belongs to you. Your heart needs reassurance that no matter how you feel, you are healed.

Hit Your Mark:

"Assuring your heart" is another way of saying "renewing your mind." As you renew your mind with God's word, your heart will become fully persuaded that what it says about you is true, and nothing your body tells you will convince you otherwise. So when symptoms come knocking at your door, reassure your heart by stating the truth that healing is already yours.

November 10

The Target:

So He took the blind man by the hand and led him out of the town. And when He had spit on his eyes and put His hands on him, He asked him if he saw anything. And he looked up and said, "I see men like trees, walking." Then He put His hands on his eyes again and made him look up. And he was restored and saw everyone clearly.

Mark 8:23–25

Set Your Sights:

If this man was going to be healed, Jesus had to lead him out of Bethsaida, a town He harshly rebuked for their unbelief (Matt. 11:21). Unbelief can hinder healing, but that's not the focus today.

After touching him, Jesus asked if he saw anything. Why did He ask that? Jesus wasn't questioning the will of God or double-checking if God had heard Him. Asking the man what he saw focused his eyes on the improvement, not the deficit.

One small step toward healing—he saw men walking as trees—enabled his faith to overcome the blindness. And as Jesus released a second dose of God's power through His touch, healing came, demonstrating that when healing is not instantaneous, the enemy can be overcome by continuing to resist him.

Hit Your Mark:

After Jesus's first touch, the blind man could easily have said, "It didn't work." Instead, he focused on what he could see, not what he couldn't. Stand firm by looking to the progress, continuing to pray, believe, and thank God for the victory. The enemy aims to wear you down by reminding you how far you have to go, but you wear him down by reminding him of the good God has already done.

November 11

The Target:

Do not sorrow, for the joy of the Lord is your strength.

Nehemiah 8:10

Set Your Sights:

You can look at this verse from two different angles. One way is that the joy inside you, placed there by the Spirit when you were born again (Gal. 5:22), is a source of strength, which is absolutely true. It's very hard to feel joyful and weak simultaneously. If you don't believe me, on a day when you feel deficient in strength, tap into the well of joy on the inside and get a good belly laugh going. Just see what that does for you!

The second way you can look at it is this: God's joy is your strength. God never runs out of joy, which means that no matter your situation, there is a never-ending supply of strength at your disposal. There is always strength available because He is always full of joy. God never runs out of joy, so you will never run out of strength.

Hit Your Mark:

If you are facing a challenging situation or you're weary in battle, imagine Father sitting up in heaven, head thrown back, laughing at the enemy because he has already been defeated and he knows it. See the absolute joy on His face as He looks down at you and sees complete victory. Let His joy give you strength today.

November 12

The Target:

Indeed the hour is coming, yes, has now come, that you will be scattered, each to his own, and will leave Me alone. And yet I am not alone, because the Father is with Me.

John 16:32

Set Your Sights:

Think about what Jesus was going through when He uttered these powerful words, and let the magnitude of them sink in. Judas Iscariot, whom He loved and walked with, would soon betray Him. When the soldiers came to arrest Him, His disciples would abandon Him. And Peter, the bold and fearless one, would deny Him outright in the face of persecution.

Jesus gave these men all He had and was about to suffer unimaginably for them … and us. He would face His accusers alone. He would be beaten and bruised alone. He would be nailed to the cross alone. He would hang on the cross alone. He would die alone. Or so it may seem. But He was not alone. The Father was with Him to the end … and into a new beginning for you and me.

Hit Your Mark:

Let Jesus's words resonate in your heart today that Father is right there with you no matter what you're going through, who leaves or forsakes you, or how painful your journey may be. Don't let the enemy convince you that nobody understands and you're the only one in the world going through what you're going through. It is a lie. Father is with you every step of the way. You are not alone.

November 13

The Target:

He heals the brokenhearted and binds up their
wounds.

Psalm 147:3

Set Your Sights:

There are many types of wounds. Physical wounds are easy to recognize and treat with a good scrub, antibiotic ointment, and bandage. Healing occurs as the wound scabs over, and as long as you don't pull the scab off, healing will continue until finished. If you pick at it, however, the healing process will be interrupted and most likely leave a scar.

Soulical wounds, which affect your mind and emotions, can be caused by people, tragedies, divorce, etc. Jesus was sent to heal the broken heart as well as the body (Luke 4:18). He did so when He carried your sorrows on the cross (Isa. 53:4). These sorrows include all forms of pain, physical and mental. Jesus, the Word, provided healing for your broken heart.

Hit Your Mark:

The Word is the ultimate first-aid kit for your broken heart. It is the cleansing scrub, ointment, and bandage for every wound. Your heart will heal by recognizing and believing in what Jesus accomplished on the cross and applying a fresh dose of the Word to the wound daily. Focusing on the source of the wound would be like ripping off the scab, so stay focused on the Word until the wound is completely healed. No scar to remain.

November 14

The Target:

Or how can one enter a strong man's house and plunder his goods, unless he first binds the strong man? And then he will plunder his house.

Matthew 12:29

Set Your Sights:

This verse holds one key to your power and authority over Satan. But first, a few terms need to be defined. The "strong man" is the devil, and "his goods" are everything he took possession of when Adam sinned—health, prosperity, and freedom. To "bind" means to secure with chains. When something is bound, it is stripped of its power and no longer a threat.

By the time Jesus came on the scene, the devil's house was full of goods that belonged to the children of God, so he needed to be bound and his goods seized. Since sin originally gave him the authority and goods, only the sinless, righteous life of Christ could restrain him. Once bound, Jesus plundered his goods by healing the sick, casting out demons and setting people free. He was no longer a threat.

Hit Your Mark:

Righteousness incapacitates the enemy. Jesus's sacrifice made you righteous when you believed in Him (2 Cor. 5:21), giving you the same authority to bind the enemy and take back your goods. You are righteous, so he is bound. See the enemy wrapped tightly in chains and your healing sitting at his feet. Walk right up to him, pick it up, and walk away. He can keep it no longer.

The Target:

That you may walk worthy of the Lord, fully pleasing Him, being fruitful in every good work and increasing in the knowledge of God; strengthened with all might, according to His glorious power, for all patience and longsuffering with joy.

Colossians 1:10–11

Set Your Sights:

Have you ever been cruising along in life when out of nowhere, like a forceful wind in your face that takes your breath away, comes an unexpected diagnosis or startling new symptom? How you respond to that wind, whether you put your head down and press onward or stop dead in your tracks, is determined by endurance. Endurance enables you to stay the course and charge into the wind like a warrior (Joel 2:7).

Patience, a.k.a. endurance, comes through increasing in the knowledge of God, which you do by spending time in His Word and prayer and meditating on and putting into practice what you know. This will strengthen you with the power of the Holy Spirit ("all might"), leading to the development of endurance. With each wind you face head-on, endurance is built as you refuse to deviate course from the Word.

Hit Your Mark:

The wind will come and go, but God's word does not change, nor does its power fade away. Because the Word inside you is permanent, and the wind only temporary, you can outlast any wind you face. Put your head down and press in by leaning into the Word, allowing Him to strengthen you with His might until the wind fades and you're moving forward with ease once again.

November 16

The Target:

*For God has not given us a spirit of fear, but of power
and of love and of a sound mind.*

2 Timothy 1:7

Set Your Sights:

Sometimes you let fear in, and sometimes it sneaks in and takes control before you know what hit you. Either way, you can do something about it because fear is a direct byproduct of your thoughts. It comes from meditating on the wrong things, such as the symptoms that match perfectly with that medical website, lab reports, prognoses, and the multiple rabbit trails of negative imaginations you have ventured down.

Paul encouraged Timothy not to fear by reminding him of what he had inside: power, love, and a sound mind. The power you have is the miracle-working power of the Holy Spirit, the love you've been given is God's kind of love, and a sound mind means you have been given the ability to discipline and control the thoughts that lead to fear. Employing just one of those three gifts from God will enable you to overcome fear every time.

Hit Your Mark:

Your thoughts control whether you walk through life with or without fear. Today, center your thoughts on the powerful weapons you possess on the inside—power, love, a sound mind—and keep your focus there. As you think on what you have, fear will find no place and have no hold on your mind. It. Will. Leave.

November 17

The Target:

Now thanks be to God who always leads us in triumph in Christ, and through us diffuses the fragrance of His knowledge in every place.

2 Corinthians 2:14

Set Your Sights:

The word "triumph" encompasses two things: 1) to conquer completely and 2) to cheer or shout loudly in a procession. It's what would happen when a Roman general triumphed over a rival king. He would march his captives down the street (usually naked) and proudly display his spoils with thunderous fanfare. His total victory was cause for a celebratory parade. Triumph.

The only other time this word is used is in Colossians 2:15, where Jesus triumphed over principalities and powers, disarming and making a public spectacle of them. Jesus whipped the devil and threw a victorious procession. Triumph.

Because of His victory, and the fact that you are in Christ as a child of God, the devil is also devoid of any power or authority over you. You have absolute victory and should be participating in the parade with shouts of joy and expressions of praise. Triumph.

Hit Your Mark:

Take time to meditate on this today: The devil is defeated, which includes victory over all his evil works, including sickness and disease. You aren't waiting to triumph. You have already triumphed. The moment you accepted Christ, the devil was put under your feet, stripped naked, and put on display for all to see. Now shout it out and don't miss the parade!

November 18

The Target:

Forever, O Lord, Your word is settled in heaven.

Psalm 119:89

Set Your Sights:

This is important: If God said it, He meant it. He doesn't make mistakes or take back what He said. His words never become obsolete or politically incorrect. It doesn't matter how much the world changes; His Word still applies and is settled forever in heaven.

In heaven, everything is as God wills, which means no sickness, poverty, or bondage. That is His will for heaven, but also His will for your life on earth. As you pray according to His will (1 John 5:14–15), all the benefits of heaven are yours to the degree you believe and receive them.

Here's what that looks like: If you suffer from depression, knowing God will wipe away all your tears in heaven (Rev. 21:4), you can pray and believe to receive that promise now as you fix your eyes on Him. It is settled in heaven and available to you right now.

Hit Your Mark:

Imagine what heaven will be like. Imagine being free from sickness and pain, cancer, or depression. Imagine the joy and freedom. Imagine the thankfulness that will overwhelm you. Realize that what you imagine can be your reality. You don't have to wait for heaven to experience those things. As it is settled in heaven, it can be settled for you today.

November 19

The Target:

But when Jesus heard it, He answered him, saying, "Do not be afraid; only believe, and she will be made well."

Luke 8:50

Set Your Sights:

Jesus was on His way to Jairus's house to heal his daughter when they were told that his daughter was dead. Before Jairus even had a second to process the news, Jesus "answered." Nobody had asked a question, so what was Jesus answering? The unspoken questions in the mind of Jairus: *Will my daughter live again or will death triumph? Will I believe in Jesus or the supposed finality of death?*

Jesus answered: "Do not be afraid; only believe." The outcome of this encounter would come down to the faith of Jairus. His choice of fear or belief was the difference between life and death. He believed in Jesus before the report, and he now had to decide if he would continue to believe in Him after it. He chose to believe and his daughter was healed.

Hit Your Mark:

You may be in a similar situation today. You believe you are healed and you're walking next to Jesus toward receiving it. Still, the reports aren't confirming it and neither is your body. Just like Jairus, you have the choice to fear or believe. These are the times to turn your back on fear, take Jesus's hand, squeeze it a little harder, and keep moving forward. Do not fear. Only believe. And you *will* be made well.

November 20

The Target:

If anyone does not stumble in what he says [never saying the wrong thing], he is a perfect man [fully developed in character, without serious flaws], able to bridle his whole body and rein in his entire nature [taming his human faults and weaknesses].

James 3:2 (AMP)

Set Your Sights:

James chapter 3 talks about the power of the tongue, mainly about the damage it can do. Verse 4 likens it to a small rudder that effortlessly turns a massive ship whenever the captain chooses. Verses 5 and 6 call it a fire, able to start a raging inferno with the tiniest spark. Verse 8 says it is "an unruly evil, full of deadly poison."

Today's verse is the good news about your tongue. If you control it, you can rule your body and rein in your soul because they respond to your words. If you speak damning words, they will respond in a negative way. If you speak words of spirit and life (John 6:63), they will respond with life. Speaking what you believe, good or bad, will drive the outcome in your body and mind.

Hit Your Mark:

Think about the power contained in your words. Imagine them as a raging fire destroying everything in its path. Then imagine them as rivers of living water flowing through your mind and body, washing away every imperfection. Every word you speak is either fire or water. One will leave you charred and damaged; the other, clean and refreshed. Let those images leave a lasting impression in your mind today of the power of your words.

November 21

The Target:

This Book of the Law shall not depart from your mouth, but you shall meditate in it day and night, that you may observe to do according to all that is written in it. For then you will make your way prosperous, and then you will have good success.

Joshua 1:8

Set Your Sights:

Most people think of being prosperous and having success only in the context of financial prosperity, but that limits the scope of truth communicated in this verse. Being prosperous involves so much more than money and status.

Fully defined, prosperous means pushing forward, going over or through, attacking, and finishing well. Meditate not only means to contemplate, but also to roar, like the growl of a lion over its prey. The Word turns you into a warrior, giving you the strength to hover over your enemy like a hungry lion and overcome any resistance from it.

As you contemplate God's word day and night, letting its truth permeate every fiber of your being, the warrior in you will rise up and push through any challenge in your way. You'll attack and go right through it, finishing well as you see what you're believing for come to pass.

Hit Your Mark:

Meditate. Prosper. Succeed. That's the order of things. You won't succeed without first prospering, and you won't prosper without first meditating. So, first things first. Take the verse you're standing on and think on it day and night. This will give you the strength you need to charge ahead like a lion and overcome the enemy opposing you. Then … success!

November 22

The Target:

For who is this uncircumcised Philistine, that he should defy the armies of the living God?"

1 Samuel 17:26

Set Your Sights:

Goliath stood 9 feet 9 inches tall, with a mouth as big as his body, but his stature and trash-talk didn't deter David. Seeing this as an attack against God Himself, he went out with courage and boldness, knowing God was with him.

David wasn't looking at the giant but at the faithfulness of the one who stood beside him. Compared to God, Goliath was nothing more than a pesky gnat to be squished. Hear the confidence in his voice as he responded to Goliath's taunts (1 Sam. 17:45–46a):

"You come to me with a sword, with a spear, and with a javelin. But I come to you in the name of the Lord of hosts … This day the Lord will deliver you into my hand, and I will strike you and take your head from you."

Hit Your Mark:

The world sees sickness as a giant, but you can see it as the uncircumcised Philistine that has come to defy the living God who has declared you healed by the blood of Jesus. Go out with the confidence of knowing you will strike down the giant with a single rock, just like David. The Word is your rock. Pick it up and use it against the enemy today.

The Target:

And do not be conformed to this world, but be transformed by the renewing of your mind, that you may prove what is that good and acceptable and perfect will of God.

Romans 12:2

Set Your Sights:

This verse holds the master key to unlocking every promise in God's word. But just as with a physical key, if you don't put it in the keyhole and turn it, the door you're trying to open will remain locked. Access denied. The key you hold will have no effect if you don't use it.

The key is this: renew your mind. Without this key, every door remains locked. But with it, the doors to healing, freedom, and prosperity swing wide open. No instruction manual is required to use this key. Simply insert, turn, and open the door.

Knowing what the Word says about your situation puts the key in your hand. Regarding the Word above all else is tantamount to putting the key in the keyhole. Consistency turns the key and opens the door, putting you just one step away from crossing the threshold and seeing what you're believing for become a reality.

Hit Your Mark:

Envision a locked door in front of you. Now envision pulling a master key from your pocket and using it on the door. Hear the click as it unlocks. See the door open and yourself stepping inside. Envision the transformation that suddenly happens. The master key you hold is guaranteed to open that door and lead to change.

November 24

The Target:

And He was transfigured before them. His face shone like the sun, and His clothes became as white as the light.

Matthew 17:2

Set Your Sights:

Most believers know who they are in Christ. They know they are a child of God, righteous, and complete in Him (1 John 3:1, 2 Cor. 5:21, Col. 2:10). While crucial to know, there is another aspect of relationship with Him just as important to know and understand: who Christ is in you.

Today's verse reveals the true nature of Christ. It is who He was, is, and now is in you. Peter, James, and John witnessed this event as the veil of Jesus's flesh was pulled back and the glory inside was fully revealed.

His true nature, the Holy Spirit within, caused His face to shine like the sun and His clothes to be as white as light. The same Spirit resides in you, and you are filled with the same glory. That is your true nature as a child of God, and that is who He is in you.

Hit Your Mark:

Let that sink in today. Imagine if your flesh could be unzipped like a coat. As you unzip it, see a light burst forth that pierces everything around you. You are filled with such light, and no darkness can exist in the presence of its radiance. No work of the devil can stand as the glory of Christ is revealed in you.

November 25

The Target:

Now you are the body of Christ, and members individually.

1 Corinthians 12:27

Set Your Sights:

The physical body of Christ was the vehicle that brought redemption and healing to the earth. Through His body, He demonstrated the will of God to save and heal by healing all who encountered Him. However, the purpose of His body wasn't to heal only the few He could physically touch.

On the cross, He made healing available to everyone by taking every sickness, pain, and heartache into His body (Isa. 53:4–5), causing disfigurement to the point of not being recognizable as human (Isa. 52:14). That was the ultimate purpose for the physical body of Christ.

The church, and you as its member, are now the body of Christ (this verse, Col. 1:24), which means you are the vehicle that carries His healing power. He brought it then and brings it through you now. That power is there for you to personally receive, but it is also intended to impact the hurting world around you.

Hit Your Mark:

You are His body, meaning you can walk as He walked and do what He did. You are intended to reach out your hand and heal and to speak and see life restored. You are a carrier of healing. It's time to not only receive, but to give away what you have.

November 26

The Target:

For as the rain comes down, and the snow from heaven, and do not return there, but water the earth, and make it bring forth and bud, that it may give seed to the sower and bread to the eater, so shall My word be that goes forth from My mouth; it shall not return to Me void, but it shall accomplish what I please, and it shall prosper in the thing for which I sent it.

Isaiah 55:10–11

Set Your Sights:

In the natural, if it rained and the rain was sucked back up into the sky, it would have no effect on the soil, leaving it in the same condition it was when it fell: dry. Instead, the earth becomes saturated when rain falls, creating an environment where seeds can grow. That is its purpose, and nothing can change or stop that.

This is a powerful analogy between precipitation and God's word. Just as rain falls and accomplishes its purpose, so does the Word. And as surely as the rain doesn't return to the sky, neither does God's word return void. When spoken, it saturates the situation it was sent into and prospers. The rain is a constant reminder of the definiteness of God's word.

Hit Your Mark:

As you speak His Word, imagine it leaving your lips and watering the dry area of your life. See the seeds of healing you planted being watered and their roots reaching deep. Watch as the seeds sprout and the stems break the soil's surface, grow quickly into hearty plants, and produce the life-giving fruit of healing. See it and believe the Word will do what it says it will do. That is its purpose, and nothing can change or stop that.

The Target:

They gave Moses this account: "We went into the land to which you sent us, and it does flow with milk and honey! Here is its fruit. But … "

Numbers 13:27–28a (NIV)

Set Your Sights:

Moses sent a scouting party into the promised land to spy it out and report back. When they returned, the group confirmed the land was even more than they had imagined and hoped for, with clusters of grapes so big they had to be carried by two people.

However, after declaring the good news of the inheritance awaiting them, they followed it with a "but," which revealed their doubt and what they truly believed. Their "but" didn't change the fact the promised land was theirs for the taking, but it did keep them from possessing it (Num. 14:23).

You have a promised land, an inheritance full of health, prosperity, and freedom. Don't let a "but" keep you from claiming what is rightfully yours. Your "but" doesn't change the fact healing is yours, but it can keep you from walking in it.

Hit Your Mark:

"But" is a small, powerful word that reveals what you are putting your faith in. A "but" used in unbelief says, "I know I'm healed, but I still have this pain." This "but" has placed its faith in the pain. A "but" used in faith says, "I may have this pain, but I know I'm healed because God says so." Use the power of the properly placed "but" to your advantage today!

November 28

The Target:

By the mouth of two or three witnesses every word shall be established.

2 Corinthians 13:1b

Set Your Sights:

This verse is a quote from Deuteronomy 19:15, and in context is specifically referring to a tool that was implemented to prevent an innocent person from being falsely accused by another. It set the precedence that for the testimony of a witness to be accepted and established as fact, at least two people had to agree to the same story.

In concept, this principle is also at work in your everyday life. With every situation you face, two witnesses will present opposing sides. One side is presented by the devil, the other by God's word. When you choose a side, a majority vote results and establishes as fact whatever you agree to. You choose which witness you agree with and, ultimately, the outcome you experience.

Hit Your Mark:

Of the two witnesses, one speaks the truth and the other lies. One brings you peace and the other anxiety. One brings life and the other death. Reject the witness who brings lies, anxiety, and death, and get in agreement with the one who brings only truth, peace, and life. Choose to agree with the witness of the Word today, and every day, and its truth will set you free in your mind and body.

November 29

The Target:

And as it is appointed for men to die once, but after this the judgment.

Hebrews 9:27

Set Your Sights:

This verse does not mean you have no control over when and how you die. Those who interpret it like that believe when their time runs out, that's it, and there's nothing they can do about it. Whatever will be, will be. That is an incorrect interpretation and leaves a door open for the enemy to snuff their lives out prematurely. The life of Paul demonstrates that you can decide when you leave this earth.

When Paul was in prison awaiting execution, he said he hadn't decided whether to stay or go be with Jesus (Phil. 1:22–24). He ultimately chose to live because his work was unfinished. Then some time later, he said he had finished his race and his "time of departure" was soon approaching (2 Tim. 4:6–7). He lived until he was good and ready to go, knowing he had finished his work.

Hit Your Mark:

Don't let the enemy determine your exit strategy. You have the same authority as Paul to determine when and how you depart from this life. Believe God for a long, satisfying life (Ps. 91:16) and determine in your heart to not leave this earth until you have accomplished all He has appointed you to do. And not one moment sooner.

November 30

The Target:

With long life I will satisfy him, and show him My salvation.

Psalm 91:16

Set Your Sights:

Some say God has promised believers 120 years of life and others say 70 or 80 (Gen. 6:3, Ps. 90:10). It's interesting to note that both of those verses were written by the same man, Moses, and that after each verse was written, people consistently lived beyond the 70 and 120 years. This indicates the numbers were minimums, not maximums. A case in point is that even after writing Psalm 90:10, Moses lived to be 120 years old (Deut. 34:7).

All numbers aside, God has promised to satisfy you with long life. So no matter how many years "long" is to you, you can expect those years to be full of His grace, mercy, and abundance. You can expect to be satisfied.

Hit Your Mark:

More important than the quantity of your days is the quality of them. In the grand scheme of things, is how long you have on earth really important if you are completely satisfied with your life in the end? On the flip side, if you come to a day you think is the end and you're not satisfied with your life or know there is more work to do, it is not the end. That is a word you can stand on.

DECEMBER

December 1

The Target:

And since we have the same spirit of faith, according to what is written, "I believed and therefore I spoke," we also believe and therefore speak.

2 Corinthians 4:13

Set Your Sights:

Paul said he spoke what he believed, so what did he believe and speak about healing? He didn't say much about it, but he did demonstrate what he believed, and sometimes actions speak louder than words.

Paul "spoke" his belief in healing for others as he healed the crippled man at Lystra and cast a demon out of a young girl (Acts 14:10, 16:18). He "spoke" his belief in healing for himself as he shook off the poisonous snake that bit him without fear (Acts 28:3–5).

Your words and actions reflect your beliefs, and so does your countenance. Your face sometimes gives a clearer picture of your beliefs than your words. If your face is full of fear and worry, that's an indicator of what you truly believe—the facts of your circumstances over the truth of the Word.

Hit Your Mark:

Don't be discouraged if that's you because you can change that. Put your focus on the Word, on the truth that healing is yours, and watch your countenance and attitude change. As you consistently focus on God's promises, you will begin to believe what it says above your circumstances. Your forehead will unfurrow and you will find a smile forming on your lips. It is inevitable.

December 2

The Target:

Pray without ceasing.

1 Thessalonians 5:17

Set Your Sights:

Three words so important they stand alone. The instruction isn't "Pray when you have time or when you think about it," but pray continuously. With life to live and obligations to meet, how is that possible? How can you pray all the time? The ability to successfully do what is instructed comes down to one thing: how you define prayer.

If you define prayer as secluding yourself in a room, hands folded, each prayer starting with "Our Father, who art in heaven" and ending with "Amen," then not a single person on the planet could do that without ceasing.

However, if you define prayer as an open-ended conversation with God, you can do that all day long. It isn't about the prayer closet but about staying in an attitude of prayer with your ears open and sharing your heart with Him throughout the day.

Hit Your Mark:

Whenever you have a random thought about something utterly trivial today, take that as an opportunity to start a conversation with Father. Even if it's a simple, "Hi. I'm listening if you have anything to say," or "It's been a rough day. I'm so glad I'm not alone and you're watching over me." Don't make it complicated. Praying without ceasing is really that simple.

December 3

The Target:

Do you not believe that I am in the Father, and the Father in Me? The words that I speak to you I do not speak on My own authority; but the Father who dwells in Me does the works.

John 14:10

Set Your Sights:

Jesus was stating a truth about the works He did. He wanted everyone to know that He didn't heal the blind, deaf, and lame or raise the dead and calm the sea. Because even though He is the Son of God, He stripped off all His divine power to become flesh and blood (Phil. 2:6–7). Just like you. Jesus knew He could do nothing in and of Himself, that He wasn't the source of healing power, but it was the Spirit within Him.

A stick of dynamite consists of two things: a cardboard cylinder shell (the carrier) and nitroglycerin, sorbents, and stabilizers (the explosive element). Jesus was the carrier and the Holy Spirit was the explosive element. That same Spirit of explosive, miracle-working power lives in you. And just as He healed every single person Jesus touched from the outside in, He is present within you to heal you from the inside out.

Hit Your Mark:

Meditate on this analogy and see yourself and the Spirit coming together to form a stick of dynamite. You are the carrier of explosive power, and that power is present to heal you and those around you. Believe it for yourself, and act on it for someone else today.

December 4

The Target:

But the Helper, the Holy Spirit, whom the Father will send in My name, He will teach you all things, and bring to your remembrance all things that I said to you.

John 14:26

Set Your Sights:

When it comes to healing, you need a teacher, and the Holy Spirit is the best teacher in the universe. He knows the ins and outs, the ups and downs. He is the S.M.E. (subject matter expert).

Not only does He know healing, but He knows you. Ins and outs. Ups and downs. He knows every glitch in your belief system and what hinders you from receiving. He knows exactly what you need to know to receive.

As a kid, do you remember school days when you would sit at your desk and daydream, the bell would ring, and you wouldn't have any idea what the teacher taught? Your mind was elsewhere and you missed it. For the Spirit to teach you, you must pay attention and purpose to listen. Being taught by the Spirit is not accidental, but intentional.

Hit Your Mark:

The more you think on this verse and listen, the more aware you'll become of Him speaking. The more aware you are of His voice, the more He can teach you. The more He teaches you, the more you'll know. The more you know, the more you'll believe. The more you believe, the more you'll speak. The more you speak, the more you'll receive. From listening … to receiving.

December 5

The Target:

He who dwells in the secret place of the Most High shall abide under the shadow of the Almighty. I will say of the Lord, "He is my refuge and my fortress; my God, in Him I will trust."

Psalm 91:1–2

Set Your Sights:

God's secret place is a place of shelter and hope (refuge) that cannot be breached by the enemy (fortress). Envision a castle on top of a high hill, surrounded by a towering stone wall with well-trained armed guards intently watching for danger. As you enter the front gates and they close behind you, you know you are safe in the hands of the Most High.

You gain entrance to His refuge through dwelling, abiding, and saying. Dwelling and abiding mean you make your home there. You don't keep running in and out by focusing on His Word one minute and then spending the next ten concentrating on the problem. So fix your thoughts on the Word and then say what you believe, releasing that Word into the atmosphere to do its work.

Hit Your Mark:

If you are experiencing fear and worry over a situation today, envision God's refuge just up ahead. Imagine walking up to the impenetrable front gates and seeing an "Admission is Free" sign. When you turn your thoughts to Him, the gates swing open, you step inside, and breathe out a long sigh. The gate closes behind you, shutting out the fear and worry harassing you. Now stay there. Don't leave. Don't look back. Keep your sights fixed on Him.

December 6

The Target:

Now it came to pass, as He was praying in a certain place, when He ceased, that one of His disciples said to Him, "Lord, teach us to pray, as John also taught his disciples."

Luke 11:1

Set Your Sights:

The disciples witnessed the power of Jesus's prayers and asked Him to teach them how to pray. His response, known as the Lord's Prayer, wasn't meant to be memorized and recited but a model of what prayer should look like. That's why He said to pray "in this manner" (Matt. 6:9).

The prayer (as recorded in Matthew 6:9–13) addresses God as "Father" and starts with praise, reminding you He is your Father and worthy of your praise. Verse 10 admonishes you to pray in agreement with the Word and reminds you that whatever is done in heaven can be done in your life right now.

Verses 11 and 12 emphasize a lifestyle of dependence and the importance of keeping your heart soft before Him. Verse 13 is a request for guidance and a reminder of the divine protection He promised you (Ps. 91:1–6). And just as the prayer starts, it ends … with praise.

Hit Your Mark:

Prayer is a conversation between you and God. It is fluid. It is changing. You can use the Lord's Prayer as a template for effective prayer, but each prayer will be different as you face new challenges from one day to the next. Take Jesus's prayer and make it your own today … and every day.

December 7

The Target:

But let your 'Yes' be 'Yes,' and your 'No,' 'No.' For whatever is more than these is from the evil one.

Matthew 5:37

Set Your Sights:

This verse encourages you to be a person of your word. When you say something, mean it. When you say you'll be somewhere at a specific time, be there at that time. When you say you'll do something, do it. Don't lie and don't make promises you know you can't keep. Let those around you know that your "Yes" is "Yes" and your "No" is "No."

Speaking with integrity is not only important in relationships with other people, but it is also a factor in the ability of your body to receive healing. If you consistently speak untruths and don't stand by the words you speak, then when you speak the truth and say, "Body, you are healed by the stripes of Jesus," it won't know whether to believe you or not, and faith won't be activated to heal it.

Hit Your Mark:

When your words come from a place of integrity, they have power. When they have power, your body will respond when you speak to it. Fill your everyday conversations, with others and yourself, with grace and truth. Think on that today, act on it, and expect your body to respond to your truth-saturated, integrity-backed, faith-filled words.

December 8

The Target:

Where can I go from your Spirit? Where can I flee from your presence? If I go up to the heavens, you are there; if I make my bed in the depths, you are there. If I rise on the wings of the dawn, if I settle on the far side of the sea, even there your hand will guide me, your right hand will hold me fast.

Psalm 139:7–10 (NIV)

Set Your Sights:

One of the biggest lies Satan will offer you on a silver platter is you are all alone and no one else on the planet understands what you're going through. He knows if he can isolate you, he has a better shot of keeping you in bondage. Don't accept the dish he's offering.

Jesus was also served this lie at a time He needed His friends and family the most. The soldiers were coming, the time of His sacrifice was drawing near, and the men He loved and poured His life into would betray and abandon Him.

In the natural, it would look as if He was alone, but He knew the truth and declared, "Indeed the hour is coming ... that you will be scattered ... and will leave Me alone. And yet I am not alone, because the Father is with Me" (John 16:32).

Hit Your Mark:

The enemy wants you to believe God is a million miles away, oblivious to what you're going through, but assure your heart He is with you every second of every day. It doesn't matter where you go, He is there to comfort you, to be your friend and confidant. Even if you are alone in the physical sense, you are never alone.

December 9

The Target:

For the word of God is living and powerful, and sharper than any two-edged sword, piercing even to the division of soul and spirit, and of joints and marrow, and is a discerner of the thoughts and intents of the heart.

Hebrews 4:12

Set Your Sights:

On your journey, racing thoughts can sometimes overwhelm you, making it difficult to see things clearly. They create a tangled mess in your mind, leaving you feeling exhausted and panicked. It can be hard to determine where those thoughts are coming from. Are they from you, the enemy, or God? What do you do with that mess?

You take each thought one at a time and use the wisdom from today's verse to sort them out. God's word will take those frenzied thoughts and show you what is truth and what is a lie. Only the extreme sharpness of the Word can separate between soul and spirit, which means it can distinguish between your thoughts (soul) and the thoughts from your born-again spirit that are of God.

Hit Your Mark:

Act on this verse and the Word will do what it says it will do. One thought at a time, get in the Word and find out what it says about what you're thinking. If the thought doesn't line up with the Word, it's not from God and shouldn't be afforded one more second of consideration. That's one less thought in the jumbled mess. One thought at a time. Untangling the mess. Letting the Word do the work.

December 10

The Target:

For we have not an high priest which cannot be touched with the feeling of our infirmities; but was in all points tempted like as we are, yet without sin.

Hebrews 4:15 (KJV)

Set Your Sights:

The unchecked thought that God doesn't understand what you're going through can create a false sense of distance between the two of you. Maybe you're even a little angry because you don't think He gets it, that He's never experienced it Himself, so how can He possibly understand. That is absolutely, without a doubt, not true.

Jesus has physically felt and experienced everything you could possibly feel and experience. When Isaiah 53:4 says He bore your griefs and carried your sorrows, it means He took the load of your mental and physical anguish and pain, all anxiety and tragedies, and He carried them away.

He experienced betrayal, rejection, and loss. He experienced sickness and the consequences of sin in His body to the point He was marred beyond recognition as a human (Isa. 52:14). He was fully man, so He can relate to and understand what you're going through.

Hit Your Mark:

Know today that if you feel it, He has felt it. If you are experiencing it, He has experienced it. He understands and has compassion for you. He's been there, done that, and knows how to walk you through it. Don't push Him away because of a lie of the enemy. Draw Him close and let Him help and heal you.

December 11

The Target:

My son, give attention to my words; incline your ear to my sayings. Do not let them depart from your eyes; keep them in the midst of your heart; for they are life to those who find them, and health to all their flesh.

Proverbs 4:20–22

Set Your Sights:

In this case, to find something means you not only locate it but also take possession of it. For example, imagine you lost the key to your car, so you search purposefully until you find it. Once it's located, you aren't content to simply know where it is, so you pick it up and put it to use in your car.

Locating a verse about healing and reading it over a few times, but nothing more, would be the equivalent of finding your key and not using it. To possess a verse means you let it "sink down into your ears" (Luke 9:44). When the Word sinks in, it goes deeper into your memory and holds it there until you understand it, leading to the life and health for your body He has promised.

Hit Your Mark:

As you take possession of God's word through study and contemplation, it will become alive in you, producing life and health in every area of your life. View the Word as the key to starting the engine of healing, prosperity, and freedom. Search for it as if it is the most valuable treasure on the planet … because it is. It is the key to everything.

December 12

The Target:

Therefore, whether you eat or drink, or whatever you do, do all to the glory of God.

1 Corinthians 10:31

Set Your Sights:

Eating and drinking should be done to the glory of God. The Word doesn't provide a list of food to be consumed or avoided, so what does that look like? An example might be if you have a conviction not to eat meat or dairy, then don't eat meat or dairy. Being obedient to His leading in what you eat is one way you give Him glory.

There is a ditch to be aware of, as food can quickly become an idol. Indicators you've fallen into that ditch might be that you give credit for your health to the food you're eating or the supplements you're taking, or maybe you experience fear if you eat something that's not in "the plan." This suggests your faith is in the food and not in the true source of your good health.

Hit Your Mark:

When it comes to diet, eat what is in your heart to eat, but keep your faith firmly anchored in Him. A helpful ditch avoidance tool is to give thanks for your food and recognize it is blessed by His Word and prayer (1 Tim. 4:5). It's a great daily reminder that your food, life, and health come from Him and that's right where your faith should be.

December 13

The Target:

Yes, again and again they tempted God, and limited the Holy One of Israel.

Psalm 78:41

Set Your Sights:

The purpose of Psalm 78 is to show that despite the disloyalty and disobedience of the Israelites, God loved, watched over, and provided for them. Then it states something almost unbelievable: their rebellious actions limited God. God did mighty things for them during their defiance, so imagine what He could have accomplished with their cooperation.

There are four behaviors identified in this chapter that can limit the ability of God's word to work in your life—disobedience (v. 10), doubt (v. 32), insincerity (vv. 36–37), and forgetfulness (vv. 11–17). Let's focus on forgetfulness. The Israelites didn't experience God's best because they didn't remember His power or what He had already done for them.

When you are struggling with symptoms, a new diagnosis, or a bad medical report, it is easy to forget … everything: the revelation you've had, the improvements and progress that have been made, His goodness and faithfulness. The cure for forgetfulness is simple: remember.

Hit Your Mark:

Take the time today to remember the things God has done for you. Remember the answered prayers and how He has come through in other situations. Remember. Don't allow what you're experiencing at this moment to limit what He can do for you in the next. Remember. Take the limits off of God.

December 14

The Target:

When Jesus saw him lying there, and knew that he already had been in that condition a long time, He said to him, "Do you want to be made well?"

John 5:6

Set Your Sights:

Believe it or not, the answer to this question isn't always a resolute "Yes!" For some people, illness has become a part of their identity, defining what they can do and who they can be. With others, they may want to be healed but have lost the will to fight and are just going through the motions of trying to receive. They can't see themselves any other way but sick.

The phrase Jesus used for "want to" means more than wishing for something. It means to be determined, dead set on, insistent, single-minded, unwavering, deliberate, and tenacious. Jesus is asking if you are unyielding and absolutely committed to being healed, not willing to let any symptom or circumstance stand in your way. He asked this question because He knows that healing for the body starts in the attitude of your mind.

Hit Your Mark:

Ask yourself these questions today: Have you lost the will to keep fighting? Have you been sick so long you can no longer see yourself well? Open your heart to the Holy Spirit and let Him show you the truth, revealing any hindrances blocking you from healing, and then let Him have them. Get determined to receive again. Nothing wavering. Nothing holding you back.

December 15

The Target:

However, when He, the Spirit of truth, has come, He will guide you into all truth; for He will not speak on His own authority, but whatever He hears He will speak; and He will tell you things to come.

John 16:13

Set Your Sights:

When you accepted Christ as Lord and Savior, the Spirit of truth came to you and is now present within you to lead and guide you into all truth. God's word is truth (John 17:17), and the Spirit's job is to teach it and make it understandable to you, connecting the dots between the Word and your reality.

The Spirit will also show you things to come, which means He knows the best route to get you where you're going. He knows what you need to know to receive your healing, and what you need to know may not even be specifically about healing. You may need instruction about your authority over the enemy or the power contained in forgiveness. No matter the subject, the Word holds all the necessary power to heal you (Prov. 4:22).

Hit Your Mark:

Your healing may not come in a box labeled "God's Word About Healing." Don't get so focused on healing scriptures, only listening for the Spirit about healing, that you miss it when He tries to talk to you about something else. That "something else" may be exactly what you need to flip the switch and receive your healing. Let Him lead you. Then trust Him and follow.

December 16

The Target:

"Is not My word like a fire?" says the Lord, "And like a hammer that breaks the rock in pieces?"

Jeremiah 23:29

Set Your Sights:

A fire consumes everything in its path. For example, fire fell at Elijah's request and devoured an entire sacrifice—the wood, stones, and dust of the altar and the water in the trench surrounding it (1 Kings 18:38). The fire of God, His Word, has the power to consume everything it contacts. Cancer, fatigue, and viruses, you name it, are no match for the intensity and heat of the word of God.

This hammer isn't an ordinary carpenter's hammer used for driving nails. It is a fierce weapon capable of leveling mountains. Not a pebble and a stone, but a mountain. No matter how big the mountain is standing in the way of your victory, the word of God can smash it to pieces. There is no mountain the Word can't pulverize into nothingness.

Hit Your Mark:

Get the proper perspective of your problem today. It is nothing compared to the power contained in the Word. See that problem being consumed with fire or crushed to dust by the hammer of the Word. When you speak the Word, fire goes forth. When you speak the Word, the Holy Spirit picks up His hammer. Power to consume. Power to crush. Believe it. See it. Speak it.

December 17

The Target:

For I know that this will turn out for my deliverance through your prayer and the supply of the Spirit of Jesus Christ, according to my earnest expectation and hope that in nothing I shall be ashamed, but with all boldness, as always, so now also Christ will be magnified in my body, whether by life or by death.

Philippians 1:19–20

Set Your Sights:

Paul had an earnest expectation he would be delivered, meaning he had an intense anticipation that something good would happen. What's amazing is he went on to say, "whether by life or by death." Paul's attitude was that he expected positive results no matter the outcome. If he was delivered, great. If he died, great. In his mind, it was a win-win situation. That attitude will keep you walking in joy and confidence regardless of your circumstances.

Expectations can work for or against you. Expecting good will lead to a positive imagination where you see good happening. Expecting bad will lead to a negative imagination where you see every possible terrible outcome. Good or bad, your faith will bring substance to what you imagine (Heb. 11:1). Expecting the goodness of God will cause your imagination to reflect the Word you're believing, and a positive change in your situation will result.

Hit Your Mark:

If you tend to always look at the worst-case scenario, follow Paul's example and purpose to expect the best in every situation. Moving from negative to positive thinking isn't an easy adjustment to make, but the benefits are worth the effort. Change your expectation. Change your life.

December 18

The Target:

And she went up and laid him on the bed of the man of God, shut the door upon him, and went out.

2 Kings 4:21

Set Your Sights:

This is the account of Elisha and the Shunammite woman. Once childless, Elisha spoke over her to conceive a son, and that's precisely what happened. One day, her miracle child suddenly died in her arms. The first thing she did was lay the boy on Elisha's bed and shut the door. Why shut it? She was closing the door on unbelief and choosing not to look at the very thing that could cause her to question God's promise to her.

She also refused to let her emotions control her or speak negatively. Twice she replied to questions about how she was doing with "It is well" (vv. 23, 26) when it was very definitely not well. Her son was dead. Her thoughts were fixed on the promise, not her reality, and this drove her to Elisha. Because of her unwavering faith in God's promise, she saw her son raised from the dead.

Hit Your Mark:

Today is the day to shut the door on whatever is causing you to doubt the promise of healing that has been given to you. Stop looking at the symptoms that are still there. Stop reviewing the medical reports. Stop looking at the prognosis. Shut the door on all of it and set your sights on the promise.

December 19

The Target:

Then Elijah said to Ahab, "Go up, eat and drink; for there is the sound of abundance of rain."

1 Kings 18:41

Set Your Sights:

Three years earlier, Elijah prophesied a three-year drought in Israel. At the end of the three years, God told Elijah the drought was over and the rain was coming, so he went to the top of Mount Carmel with his servant to watch for it. Blue skies. No clouds. Dust from the parched ground blew into his eyes and mouth. Not even a hint of rain.

Seven times Elijah sent his servant to look for signs of rain. Bupkis. But Elijah trusted that if God said it, it was going to happen. So despite what he saw, the rain was coming. Nothing changed, but he kept looking. Expecting. And then … a tiny cloud. Then the skies became black and the clouds rolled in with the wind. And finally, a great rain. Just as God promised.

Hit Your Mark:

A delay in healing is not a denial by God to heal you. He already did that through Christ. Don't stop expecting it. Keep watching for improvement, no matter how small. Keep believing you're free and healed because God said so. Let that settle it. If it's decided for you, it's only a matter of time until the storm blows in and the great rain comes, manifesting what you're believing for.

December 20

The Target:

*For sin shall not have dominion over you, for you are
not under law but under grace.*

Romans 6:14

Set Your Sights:

Before the fall of man in the Garden of Eden, it was a perfect existence. There was no sickness or pain, no anger or unforgiveness. It was paradise. Sin brought the entrance of every evil work of the enemy to mankind. Anything that is in opposition to the promises of God has its origin in sin. When the Word talks about sin, it encompasses all its byproducts: sickness, disease, depression, and poverty. The label of "sin" covers it all.

For that reason, whatever is contrary to the promises can be substituted for the word "sin" in this verse. Since you are under grace, sickness shall not have dominion over you. Cancer shall not have dominion over you. Grief shall not have dominion over you. And no matter where sickness abounds, grace abounds much more (Rom. 5:20). No matter where any byproduct of sin abounds, grace always has the power to overcome it.

Hit Your Mark:

Whatever you face today, plug that word into this verse and Romans 5:20. Make them your own. Meditate on them. Let it sink in that no matter what it is or how strong it appears to be, it will never overshadow the grace of God. You already have the victory because grace has overcome it all.

December 21

The Target:

I have set the Lord always before me; because He is at my right hand I shall not be moved.

Psalm 16:8

Set Your Sights:

This verse reveals how to walk through life with confidence and victory so that even as the world is moved around you, you will not be shaken as it slips and falls. The key is always setting the Lord before you and recognizing He is right by your side.

The word "set" means to level, counterbalance, and adjust. When He is set before you, you are leveling up and adjusting your thinking to line up with His. You consistently counterbalance what you experience with your knowledge of His Word and will.

This, in turn, will result in your thoughts becoming more like His. With Him by your side and on your mind, no sickness, no pain, and no demon in hell will be able to stand against you and remain in your body. With Him, your walk will be unshakable.

Hit Your Mark:

If you are living in fear and doubt, easily shaken by the storms of life, and are ready for a change, do what this verse says. Unbelief and fear will disappear as you adjust what you see and think to reflect what God sees and thinks. Don't allow anything else besides the Word to be set before you. That's how to change. And that's how to be unmoved.

December 22

The Target:

For where envying and strife is, there is confusion and every evil work.

James 3:16 (KJV)

Set Your Sights:

Envy and strife cover a wide range of negative emotions that are very easy to get drawn into, all of which can open the door to every evil work of the enemy, including sickness, and make faith for healing of no effect. Strife is contention, which includes heated disagreements, conflict, friction, and quarreling. It includes picking at each other over little, insignificant things.

Envy includes jealousy but also offense, an effective enemy of healing. In 2 Kings 5:1–14, Naaman almost missed out on healing because of offense. In Matthew 13:53–58, Jesus could not do many mighty works in his hometown because of their offense. Naaman and the people Jesus was ministering to had a choice. One chose to not be offended and was healed. The others chose offense and walked away from Jesus unchanged.

Hit Your Mark:

No one can make you walk in strife or be offended. You may not be able to control how people treat you, but you can control how you respond to their actions. Don't allow offense to stand in the way of being made whole. Examine your heart today and let go of any bitterness or resentment that may have been caused by offense. It's not worth it. Let it go.

December 23

The Target:

Heaven and earth will pass away, but My words will by no means pass away.

Matthew 24:35

Set Your Sights:

There will come a day when heaven and earth will wear out and fade away. That is what is promised, but so is this: God's word will never lose its power or fail to accomplish its purpose. It does not have an expiration date and didn't lose its potency with the death of the original twelve disciples. It will work for anyone at any time. It is eternal.

One sure thing to keep God's word from accomplishing its purpose in your life is to not take the Word and mix it with faith (Heb. 4:2). Hearing the Word and letting it affect you profoundly through meditation and study will lead to a belief capable of overshadowing any doubt. The belief in the promise that results will activate the power of the Word in your life, and you'll see it come to pass in your mind and body.

Hit Your Mark:

Take heart today that God's word will never change or pass away, no matter what you're experiencing. When everything seems uncertain around you—the world, politics, news, weather—the Word is forever certain. What you see and experience don't affect the validity or power contained in the Word. It is unchanging. Unwavering. Truth.

December 24

The Target:

Let us hold fast the confession of our hope without wavering, for He who promised is faithful.

Hebrews 10:23

Set Your Sights:

Holding something fast can mean restraining the course of it. For example, the captain of a ship must hold fast to the ship's wheel to maintain its course. If he doesn't hold it tightly or stops paying attention, especially if there is a fierce wind, the ship will go somewhere he doesn't want it to go. Driven by the wind, going this way and that, he won't reach his destination.

The ship represents your life, and the steering wheel which drives its direction is your confession (James 3:4). You hold your confession tightly and under control by paying attention to what you say. If your confession opposes God's word about your situation, your wheel will turn and you will veer off course. If your confession is filled with truth, you will keep a steady course and reach your destination.

Hit Your Mark:

Whether surrounded by peaceful waters or a violent storm, let your confession be fueled by the hope that God is always faithful to His promises. Set your course for healing and let your confession guide you through the waters until you get there. Most importantly, never forget that Jesus is with you to help you hold the wheel, assuring you will reach your destination.

December 25

The Target:

We are hard-pressed on every side, yet not crushed; we are perplexed, but not in despair; persecuted, but not forsaken; struck down, but not destroyed.

2 Corinthians 4:8–9

Set Your Sights:

This verse, although talking about persecution for your beliefs, can be of great encouragement to you if there is ever a time on your journey you see no way out. A time you feel you're being pursued relentlessly by the enemy from all sides at once. A time you feel knocked down and lack the strength to try again. A time you feel like giving up.

BUT GOD. When you see no way through, God will show you the path (Prov. 3:6). When you are on the run, He has your back and a place to hide with safety, rest, and healing (Ps. 46:1, 139:5). When you get knocked down, He will pick you up (Ps. 37:24, 145:14), dust you off, and give you the strength to look the pursuing enemy in the eye and say, "Enough! My suffering is over!" (Mark 5:34 NLT).

Hit Your Mark:

Maybe you are here (the place where the long battle is wearing you down), but you can be "there" (the place of divine health). "There" is worth the battle. "There" is worth believing God and reaching up your hand for help again and again. "There" is the place Jesus built for you. Trust God only, lean on His strength, and don't ever give up.

December 26

The Target:

You will also declare a thing, and it will be established
for you.

Job 22:28a

Set Your Sights:

The definitions of "declare" and "establish" add a hefty weight to today's verse. Declare means to cut off, destroy, and divide. Establish means to rise up against, stir up, and succeed.

This means as you declare God's word to cut off your enemy, to separate it from yourself and completely crush it, the Word rises up and succeeds in what it said it would do. God is listening for His Word to be spoken from the lips of believers so He can bring it to pass (Jer. 1:12).

When He hears it, the Holy Spirit picks up His sword and begins to slice off your opponent, piece by piece. You'll feel the Spirit stirring within you as you speak it out, rising up on the inside to utterly defeat that thing that shouldn't be there. That's the power of His Word when spoken from your lips.

Hit Your Mark:

Imagine the Holy Spirit with His sword—mighty, powerful, unbeatable—standing between you and the enemy, and every time you speak God's word above the lie, He takes another swing of His sword. Another chunk of your enemy, gone. It is only a matter of time until nothing is left, it is cut off and destroyed, and you are left standing in victory.

December 27

The Target:

For the grace of God that brings salvation has appeared to all men.

Titus 2:11

Set Your Sights:

The word "grace," as used here, refers to God's unconditional favor and goodwill. His grace can't be earned and is a gift given to those who don't deserve it. You become the recipient of His grace through faith in Jesus when you recognize it's available, believe it, and accept it (Eph. 2:8).

God's grace brings salvation, which includes everything you need to experience a whole, abundant life in spirit, soul, and body. It carries the concepts of safety, soundness, health, and well-being.

The great news is that God's grace has been made available to all men, from the least to the greatest. Poorest to richest. Saddest to happiest. Meanest to kindest. Stingiest to most generous. "All men" includes you. You are not excluded. The totality of His grace is for you.

Hit Your Mark:

Nothing in this world can separate you from the grace freely given to you when you accepted Jesus as your Lord and Savior. In the personal gift of grace you received, He didn't forget to provide you with healing, and He didn't forget the joy and peace. Nothing was missing or omitted from the grace He gave you. It's all there. All yours. Believe it. Receive it.

December 28

The Target:

And daily in the temple, and in every house, they did not cease teaching and preaching Jesus as the Christ.

Acts 5:42

Set Your Sights:

The apostles had been proclaiming the message about Jesus, which the high priest didn't like, so he gathered them up and threw them into prison, strictly forbidding them to speak about Jesus any further (Acts 4:18).

Once released, they were strengthened by the Holy Spirit and continued to speak boldly, resulting in the enraged high priest throwing them into prison again (Acts 4:31, 5:17–18). They were tenacious about spreading their message, knowing its power, and wouldn't be daunted by minor obstacles like the high priest and prison.

Their message of redemption and healing by the blood and stripes of Jesus belongs to you today. Be bold to proclaim it. Be tenacious in pursuing it. Don't let any obstacles the devil may put in your way (symptoms, fear, labs) cause you to swerve off course and prevent the power of that message from working in you.

Hit Your Mark:

Decide if you will set your sights on the obstacles or the message today. Focusing on the obstacles will keep you imprisoned and lead to defeat. Focusing on the message will lead to confidence and boldness and enable you to blow past any obstacle like it's nothing. Because that's exactly what it is in light of the message. It. Is. Nothing.

December 29

The Target:

And Jesus said, "Who touched Me?" When all denied it, Peter and those with him said, "Master, the multitudes throng and press You, and You say, 'Who touched Me?'"

Luke 8:45

Set Your Sights:

A common argument of the enemy is: If you mess up, God will withhold healing from you, and since it's your fault, you'll just have to live with it. The healing of this woman with the issue of blood unravels the argument entirely.

She was healed after touching the hem of Jesus's garment. He knew someone touched Him, so He asked them individually, "Was it you? How about you?" Don't miss this. Every single one of them denied it, including the woman.

Despite the fact she lied to His face, He didn't reverse her healing. After she repented of the wrong, He simply called her "Daughter" and said, "Your faith has made you well. Go in peace." What an undeniable demonstration of the power of His love to cover a multitude of sins (1 Peter 4:8).

Hit Your Mark:

God doesn't want or expect you to pay penance for your sins because He has forgiven and forgotten them all—past, present, and future (Heb. 8:12, 10:12). While it is true sin has consequences, it is equally true you don't have to needlessly suffer because of them. Admit your mistake and move on, knowing that no matter how bad you messed up, His love is in ample supply to cover your sin and heal you.

December 30

The Target:

*God, who gives life to the dead and calls those things
which do not exist as though they did.*

Romans 4:17b

Set Your Sights:

Paul was referring to when God changed Abram's name (meaning "high father") to Abraham (meaning "father of a multitude") one year before his son, Isaac, was born (Gen. 17:5), thereby declaring him as the father of many nations before anything had even happened in the natural.

Abraham's 99-year-old body came alive when he put his faith in that declaration. The impossible became possible as he based his faith on what God said He would do, not on the physical proof before him. That is an illustration of God's kind of faith.

That kind of faith raises the dead. It hopes, no matter what. It believes, no matter what. It speaks the truth, not the facts. The solution, not the problem. Operating in God's kind of faith means you call those things that are not as though they were. And then they are.

Hit Your Mark:

It takes concentrated effort to exercise God's kind of faith in the midst of opposition. See what you're believing for in your mind and then give substance to it by speaking it out with your mouth. As with Abraham, the dead will come to life and change will begin. What seems impossible will suddenly become possible. See it. Speak it. Receive it.

December 31

The Target:

Then your light shall break forth like the morning, your healing shall spring forth speedily.

Isaiah 58:8a

Set Your Sights:

This moment describes your "suddenly." It's when you've been believing, speaking, and acting, and nothing seems to be changing. But you don't care. You know God's word is true and that's all that matters. How you look doesn't matter; what you feel doesn't matter. Nothing matters except His promises to you and the health and healing you know that you know that you know are yours.

Then, suddenly. That moment when what you're believing for happens. One minute it's there; the next minute it isn't. Suddenly. Every time you speak the truth over the lie, every time you step out and act in faith, His Word is working in your body. Every second of every day, whether you see it or not, it is working, bringing you one step closer to your suddenly.

Think of the caterpillar. You don't see it change into a butterfly, but you know that change is taking place inside the cocoon. And one day, it emerges. Changed. Beautiful. Suddenly.

Hit Your Mark:

The beauty of the suddenly is that you don't know when it's coming. It could be in the next second, the next minute, the next hour, or the next week. Keep believing, keep speaking, and keep acting on what you believe. Your suddenly is coming.

About the Author

Teresa Houghteling is the founder of Fully Known Ministries, an established teaching ministry and international missions ministry to the more difficult-to-access regions of the world, which operates under the name Project 142. A gifted communicator, she offers a transparent, first-hand-experience perspective through her social media and live stream ministry. Breaking complicated spiritual truths into easily understood turnkey application bites, she equips believers to live fully and tangibly in God's truth. Teresa has devoted herself to full-time ministry since graduating from Bible college in 2016. She is the author of *The "Unhealed" Believer: What to Do When You've Done It All*, which provides practical takeaways essential to getting and staying healed. After spending several years on the mission field in the Middle East, she now lives in the Mid-Michigan area and enjoys spending time writing and camping with her husband Patrick.

Find out more about Teresa at https://www.amazon.com/author/teresahoughteling.

Printed in Great Britain
by Amazon